MOVIEMAKERS AT WORK

MOVIEMAKERS AT WORK

MICROSOFT PRESS

Interviews
by David Chell

PUBLISHED BY
Microsoft Press
A Division of Microsoft Corporation
16011 N.E. 36th, Box 97017 Redmond, Washington 98073-9717

Library of Congress Cataloging in Publication Data
Chell, David, 1947-
Moviemakers at work.
1. Moving-pictures—Production and direction.
I. Title.
PN 1995.9.P7C438   1987   791.43'023   86-33114
ISBN 1-55615-037-7 (cloth)
ISBN 1-55615-003-2 (paper)

Printed and bound in the United States of America.

1 2 3 4 5 6 7 8 9 FGFG 8 9 0 9 8 7

Distributed to the book trade in the
United States by Harper & Row.

Distributed to the book trade in Canada by General Publishing Company, Ltd.

Distributed to the book trade outside the United States and Canada
by Penguin Books Ltd.

Penguin Books Ltd., Harmondsworth, Middlesex, England
Penguin Books Australia Ltd., Ringwood, Victoria, Australia
Penguin Books N. Z. Ltd., 182-190 Wairau Road, Auckland 10, New Zealand

British Cataloging in Publication Data available

CONTENTS

CINEMATOGRAPHY

EDITING

SOUND

ACKNOWLEDGMENTS

In a very real sense, a book is as much a collaboration as the films discussed in the following pages; it is a product of many creative contributions. I would first like to thank the nineteen moviemakers for their cooperation and patience in the long process of creating their interviews.

At Microsoft Press there are many who work not behind the camera, but behind the printing press. I am, of course, indebted to Min Yee and Susan Lammers for their having asked me to contribute this book to Microsoft Press's *At Work* series. Special thanks go to project editor, Marie Doyle, without whose organization and creative contributions you would be holding a disaster in your hands instead of a book. Thanks also to Rebecca Pepper for her insights and painstaking attention to detail with copyediting the manuscript, and to Lee Thomas for her steadfast refusal to succumb to "proofreader's delusion."

Kudos to Darcie Furlan, the book's designer, who also masterminded its production. Thanks also to Becky Johnson for her cover design and to Russell Steele for his meticulous typography. The work of the marketing staff, Theresa Mannix, James Brown, and Karen Meredith, is much appreciated (especially when we hit the bestseller list). And a debt of gratitude to Linda Pennington, who gave her thoughtful attention to clearing up many obstacles along the way. I am grateful to many others as well, both inside and outside the Press, who helped make this book a reality. Perhaps one day we'll get a glimpse behind these scenes with a book entitled *Publishers at Work*.

INTRODUCTION

At the Grande Café on the Boulevard des Capucines in Paris, on a December evening in 1895, the first paying audience was treated to the *cinématographe*, a series of brief film clips shown by the Lumière brothers on an apparatus of their own design. They were primitive documentary bits of Parisian life, the most exciting of which was a train rushing toward the camera.

In the audience was a sideshow conjurer and cartoonist named Georges Méliès. Dazzled by this new medium, he bought a projector and began showing films as a part of his theatrical magic show. Soon he began making his own films, and during the next ten years he would explore this new medium and lay the foundation for the film industry's accomplishments in the nearly one hundred years to follow. Movies like *A Trip to the Moon* and *The Conquest of the Pole* gave the world not only a fleeting hint of the potential of this most powerful medium of communication, but also an idea of film's limitless possibilities for creating other worlds and for creating that entertaining and meaningful cultural artifact called art.

Since the first crude scratchings of early humans, art has been a synthesis of creativity and technology. An exploration of this synthesis is this volume's most important common ground with its progenitor, Susan Lammers's *Programmers at Work*. Whether we are talking with filmmakers, computer programmers, scientists, musicians, or artists, their work hinges on the mysterious and fascinating process of creativity. It's often responsible for their heartbreaks as well as their achievements.

This book is not an exposé of Hollywood's privileged inner sanctums with titillating scenes of glamour and decadence. This is not a book about movie stars. Neither is it about directors, producers, nor, regrettably, screenwriters. Although thoughtful interviews with those people would be fascinating, this book turns its attention to stars of a different magnitude—stars that are largely uncharted and whose achievements are unacknowledged outside the motion picture industry. Yet their work is what brings the writer's creation, the producer's dream, the director's vision, and the actor's performance to life. Their work is what makes a movie a reality for the millions of people in the audience.

Who exactly are these moviemakers? They are a diverse, talented, and dedicated group whose creative contributions place them between the conceptual world of the writer, director, producer, and performer, on one hand, and the motion picture proletariat of equipment technicians, wardrobe attendants, truck drivers, script supervisors, set decorators, hair stylists, gaffers, grips, and gofers on the other. The gifted and accomplished people who speak to you from these interviews light the set, compose the image, and expose the film. They cut the film into thousands of pieces and put it back together in the editing room. They record and mix the myriad sounds we hear in the darkness of the theater. They design the sets, the props, the locations—in short, everything we see. They create faces and clothes. They painstakingly draw and paint the film one frame at a time, or they hurdle enormous technical obstacles to create what no one has ever seen before through that catchall of devious trickery, special effects.

The major problem with a book like this is one of scope. The approaches to films are as varied as the filmmakers. With as broad a representation as possible, I wanted to sample the best in the business. I strove to assemble a group with international perspective, including film veterans and upstarts, men and women, Hollywood professionals and independents, young and old, and entertainers as well as those with different messages.

Tracking down these globe-trotters was another puzzle. The interviews reveal that working in film often means living in distant locations for months at a time. Sometimes these locations are exotic and exciting; many times they are just plain miserable. The interviews were conducted in San Francisco, New Jersey, Chicago, and Seattle, as well as in the production centers of Los Angeles and New York. In some cases, the reason I interviewed one person and not another was simply a matter of availability.

As an exploration of the art and craft of making movies, my questions, both open-ended and specific, were designed to illuminate the particular profession and the person's work habits as well as to let the filmmakers express themselves on what mattered to them most. I wasn't interested in battering them into confessions or getting them to expose secret film projects or gossip. I was looking for their passions and concerns, their personalities, and their interests outside the world of film, in addition to their insights into the remarkable collective creative process of making movies. I went in search of what it means to be a filmmaker. What sorts of lives do they live and want to live?

What do movies mean to those who make them? What should they mean to all of us? The fascinating answers speak for themselves.

In arranging the order of these interviews into areas of film production, I began with cinematography—what is for many the heart and soul of film-making. We then proceed away from the camera to editing, sound, production design, and so on. For balance, we return to the image-making process in the latter part of the book with computer graphics, animation, and special effects. In special visual effects, we find we've come full circle, as it is a field that shares much with cinematography, our starting point.

Allen Daviau gives an enthusiastic account of the struggles and satisfactions of the cinematographer, while British cameraman Chris Menges reflects on the frequently overlooked social and political aspects of film.

In the cutting room, we encounter the polar personalities of editors Carol Littleton and Thom Noble, whose wild divergence manages to confirm as many aspects of editing as it throws into question.

Postproduction sound technician Bill Varney provides a venerable realist's look at this crucial and largely anonymous studio realm. Then, from his vantage point on the East Coast, Chris Newman illuminates the challenging work of production sound—the recording of live sound on the studio set or on location, whether it's the streets of Manhattan, a Central American jungle, or suburban New Delhi.

Patrizia Von Brandenstein explores the very interesting, wide-ranging responsibilities and creative endeavors of the production designer, while another perspective on this movie profession is provided by the multitalented Eiko Ishioka.

Costume designers, like production designers, have the opportunity to immerse themselves in other worlds and other times. Kristi Zea allows us a glimpse of this creative process. The creation of other realities is further explored by makeup artist Michael Westmore, who reveals the art of makeup as well as the business of creating convincing characters for the camera.

Animation is an unusual domain peopled by artists whose techniques range from the painstaking methods used since *Gertie the Dinosaur* to those afforded by the most advanced electronic media. Sally Cruikshank and Jimmy Picker are animators of the old school, creating lovable, distinctly human characters—Cruikshank in two-dimensional, hand-drawn animation and Picker in three-dimensional clay figures that he manipulates in front of the camera. Despite its veneer of technological sorcery, the computer graphics seen in motion pictures and television is also a form of animation, and Robert Abel gives us a guided tour of the achievements and seemingly limitless potential of this dazzling medium. Gary Demos, a software and technical expert, provides insights into the actual creation of computer-generated graphic images.

Special effects is a field of bald-faced deception, thrilling visions, arcane techniques, and diverse talents. The products of this profession fall into two categories: mechanical effects and visual effects. Roy Arbogast creates fire, smoke, rain, snow, explosions, car crashes, full-size sharks and dinosaurs, and whatever else the script may call for in the way of mechanical effects to be used in the studio or on location. Matte painter Chris Evans illuminates his *trompe l'oeil* art and craft, while the intricate, misunderstood specialty of film miniatures is explored by Mike Fulmer. Dennis Muren provides a survey of visual effects, those convincing glimpses of life created in the hermetically sealed world of the visual-effects studio.

Sophisticated visual effects are tremendously technology-dependent, and the scientific and technical aspects of these effects are Jonathan Erland's domain. He allows us to understand some of the complex techniques that make modern film imagery possible, while hinting at intriguing developments to come.

Each interview is rich with individual personality, with anecdotes of personal history and life on the set, and with details of craft and technique. Allen Daviau tells about shooting the only television commercial directed by Billy Wilder, and Thom Noble describes learning new editing techniques from the late French director François Truffaut. We learn from Jonathan Erland how to make realistic snowballs that don't melt. Eiko Ishioka talks about the role of working women in modern Japan. The moviemakers bring us unexpected gifts—delightful gems of personal philosophy and observations about life and movies. Among them are Evans's insight into the place of film in the history of art, Abel's and Erland's visions of the future, and Littleton's reflections on the power of the motion picture.

The *auteur* theory of the director as the sole creator of a film may have done wonders for the egos and bank accounts of those who have fallen for its sophistic charms. It may even help sell movies. But, as these interviews illustrate, the fact remains that film is a truly collaborative medium. A movie is conceived in the mind of the writer, the producer, or the director, but it is brought into the world by diverse creative contributions. What ends up on the screen is the product of many talents.

Taken together, the interviews provide a generic biography or natural history of the birth of a typical movie—not its conception in the mind of the writer or producer, nor its life span in the theater, but a film's creation from the screenplay's plan in a gargantuan collective effort. A side effect of reading about these individuals is a better understanding of how movies are made.

At times, a portrait of a particular film project begins to emerge from the shared experiences of those interviewed. By chance, I interviewed several people who worked together: Noble and Newman worked on *The Mosquito Coast;* Zea, Littleton, and Arbogast worked on *Silverado;* and Newman and Littleton worked on *Brighton Beach Memoirs.*

Certain expected patterns emerged from the interviews—patterns of professional commitment and sacrifice, of perseverance, caring, vision, obsession, and love of The Movies. Above the individual's particular work, a portrait coalesces of a common experience, a certain kind of life led while working on a film. There are long hours; separation from family, home, and friends; conflicts and squabbles; collaboration and creation; and immersion in another life for months on end, as if the filmmaker were actually two people, not one. Several of those I talked with told of taking days or weeks to decompress from the experience of making a film. I thought of explorers coming back from the depths of the ocean or space and readjusting to life here on Earth. It's easy to get the impression that the challenging and trying nature of the work is as much of an attraction for some as the deep satisfaction and the financial reward. Indeed, many in the film business exist for it alone; their families and friends are merely supporting mechanisms, like the grocery store or car. But for the most part, those interviewed here have integrated the demands of film with full and diverse personal lives.

Beyond the common concerns of work and family, what ties most of the interviews together is a strong sense of the important role film plays in our society. Many of those interviewed are troubled by films that glorify violence and aggression. They talk about the types of films they like to do and those they prefer to stay away from, and they raise questions of ethics and quality that we all should be asking before we buy our tickets.

Another consensus of these interviews is a certain apprehension about the state of the motion picture business today. Those interviewed express their frustrations with shortened production schedules imposed by producers whose attitudes are increasingly that of factory managers, as if they were in the business of manufacturing doorknobs. There is anxiety over the problem of exhibition standards. Why develop digital sound, sophisticated visual effects, or sensitive 70-mm film stocks if the movie will end up being shown in that wretched marvel of modern merchandising—the multiplex theater?

In addition, there is the perennial vicious circle of insipid scripts, un-discerning critics, and audiences afflicted with lowered expectations.

Yet entertaining, memorable, and important films do manage to get made. Without exception, the moviemakers interviewed here were optimistic and enthusiastic about the future. As readers, we can share a bit of the exhila-ration they feel when involved in imaginative, meaningful projects. Their words evidence a tenacious faith in film's capacity to enrich our culture and inspire us personally. It's difficult to avoid the realization that meaningful films continue to be made in large part due to the efforts and vision of moviemakers like the ones you will meet in these pages.

These moviemakers open a window to the complex process of filmmak-ing: the great numbers of people, the enormous amounts of time, and the painstaking attention to detail that are daily demands of the business.

Impressive as these moviemakers' efforts are, they remain meaningless until the projector rolls and the film's story begins to live in the minds of its audience. Most of these moviemakers delighted in contributing to good sto-ries. In these pages there is a love of all kinds of stories, from those told with slapstick humor to those woven into important social issues, from comedy and action to tragedy and introspection.

As a disseminator of our society's myths and ideas, the movie theater has replaced the balladeer, the cathedral and, for many, even the novel. Most of these moviemakers you will meet here clearly find enormous satisfaction in contributing to this storytelling and in the awareness of its powerful role in our culture. These moviemakers, through their commitment, their enthusi-asm, and their insight, allow us a glimpse of the truly wondrous experience of making movies.

INTERVIEWS

Allen Daviau

CINEMATOGRAPHY

*A*lthough he was born in New Orleans in the early forties, Allen Daviau has spent almost all of his life in Los Angeles. His early interest in cinematography was frustrated by the nearly impenetrable Hollywood studio/union system of that time, so he began using his own 16-mm camera to shoot film free-lance. Doing television commercials and human-interest spots for a local radio station led to rock music promotional films, the beginnings of the music video phenomenon. Daviau then did national television commercials, documentaries, educational films such as David Wolper's Say Goodbye, and several Movie of the Week features. He photographed Steven Spielberg's Amblin', the short that began Spielberg's career. He went on to shoot a new sequence for the revised edition of Close Encounters of the Third Kind and served as cinematographer on E.T., The Falcon and the Snowman, and The Color Purple, receiving Oscar nominations for the last two films.

Daviau is now preparing to photograph a feature film entirely on 65-mm negative, the first such film to be made in *the West since David Lean's* Ryan's Daughter *in 1970.*

I talked with Daviau at his hotel in Seattle where he was at work on a project, the tempting details of which must regrettably remain secret. He is friendly, warm, and straightforward—the type of person who makes you feel immediately at home and at ease. A lively speaker, Daviau filled the room with a contagious exhilaration as he roamed over various topics. He followed a circuitous logic from one fascinating subject to another and then yet another until we had both been drawn far from the original question to other distant realms of cinematography, technology, or personal anecdote.

During the interview, people from a local store delivered a new television. Under Daviau's direction, they proceeded to connect the necessary cables and wires for the cable television, VCR, and videodisc that Daviau uses in discussing concepts and ideas with the director and other members of the crew. Not only is Daviau extremely knowledgeable about the technology of cinematography and film, but he is also a genuine devotee of cinema and technology; his interests range from the history of cinematography to cinema and its aesthetics to the latest developments, such as optical discs and digital, high-definition television. I began the interview by asking Daviau about his background in shooting television commercials.

DAVIAU: I have the distinction of having photographed the only television commercial ever directed by Billy Wilder. It was a special commercial—a two-minute one for the Norton Simon Museum.

INTERVIEWER: When was that?

DAVIAU: It was '74 or '75 when we did this. Wilder had volunteered his services. I got the job through the commercial production company because they knew I was gung ho about art and painting and that I would really enjoy doing the thing with Wilder. So we went on a tour of the museum—Billy Wilder, Frank McCarthy, myself, and some people from the production company. I had a small tape recorder just to take notes of what was said. Well, I have ninety minutes of Billy Wilder doing a monologue that is just the most wonderful thing. The only problem is I wish I had better references as to which paintings he was pointing at and which rooms we were in. But I didn't want to inhibit him by doing that.

INTERVIEWER: And he was very knowledgeable about all the art?

DAVIAU: Oh, Wilder is one of the foremost art collectors in this country. His collection of paintings is just stunning. He is very, very knowledgeable and very, very funny at the same time. The guy just goes on and on and on. It was great, and he was great to talk to.

INTERVIEWER: *How was it to work with him?*

DAVIAU: It was an experience. His way of working is completely opposite from the way that commercials are usually made. In commercials, we shoot take after take after take. We cover every which way so that there is every option possible in the editing room. Well, Wilder loves to do one take on a scene and walk away from it. He wasn't there when I shot a lot of stuff of families in the museum. I shot a mere 9,000 feet of film, which was nothing, it was an hour and a half of dailies, of which I was very proud. So the first time he came to see the dailies, well, after three minutes he was bored to tears.

He had said one thing that is absolutely true: "There is no way you can direct an actor to look at a painting." It's really true. You have to photograph the process of someone discovering a work of art. That's what I was doing inside the museum with long lenses. It was a great experience to get to work with him. I was thinking about that tape again after the recent AFI [American Film Institute] tribute to him, and he seems as feisty as ever eleven years later. He is a true original.

INTERVIEWER: *Do you ever do commercials anymore?*

DAVIAU: Oh yes. Cinematographers today, particularly those of us that started through commercials, work in commercials between pictures. It is a wonderful way to keep your independence. It's a tremendous income. It gives you a great variety of subject matter to deal with—different photographic challenges. Advertisers are always looking for somebody who can photograph something in a different way. Certain types of accounts and certain agency people—the creative ones—really want you to try new and different things. So commercials are a wonderful way for you to keep your skills up and to try the latest techniques. If there is something I've been wondering about, in three days' time I'll have had a chance to see how it turns out in an actual working situation.

Commercials can be to cinematography what NASA has been to so many sciences. You have somebody who is financing research on the edge. And that's one of the things I really love about working on commercials. I have a separate agent whose job is just to keep me working on commercials. I call her when I am finishing a picture and say, "OK, early August I'll be available."

INTERVIEWER: *You did commercials for many years, didn't you?*

DAVIAU: Yes. I didn't come through the standard structure. I didn't have a show business family and so on. I didn't get to start in the union system.

The traditional union system started you in the loading room in the studio. It was all very studio-based because that was the reality when it was created. If you were interested in the photographic end of the movies, either your father or your uncle or a close friend of the family got you into the loading room. That was the apprentice program. You started loading magazines, then you unloaded magazines and marked them and sent the film to the lab. Then you moved out of the loading room and became a second assistant responsible for the slate and the camera report. You did that for a number of years and then you were able to make the move to first assistant. As first assistant, you actually threaded the camera. You were responsible for all the machinery, for changing the lenses and, most importantly, for measuring the focus and focusing during the shot. This is still one of the great, great unappreciated arts in cinematography today—what a first assistant does. And from first assistant you moved to camera operator and actually got to sit at the panning and tilting wheels and move the camera during the shot according to the way the director of photography and the director wanted the shot to be framed or composed. You coordinated the camera movement with the dolly grip or the person who moved the crane.

> *"I'm in motion pictures because I love making art with technology."*

And all along the way, there's a tremendous amount of responsibility. As a camera operator, when the cameraman or the director turns to you at the end of a take and says, "How was it?" you must say either, "Got it," or "Gotta do it again." You had better be sure of what you are saying, because after they strike the set and the cast of thousands leaves, if you didn't get it when you said you got it, you're not going to be very popular. And even in the loading room, a kid can open the film can with the light on and ruin a scene that cost a million dollars to shoot. So the responsibility is there from day one. It just becomes more and more complex in how it's executed. And then, when you finally became director of photography, you would have mastered all these other crafts and you were supposed to know how to direct everybody in whatever you wanted done. You were then responsible for the overall picture.

I didn't get to grow up in that system, because I didn't have any connections to get into the loading room in the first place. And I dearly would have loved to have gotten into the loading room. In fact, when I was eighteen years old I went down to the union office to ask if they had an apprenticeship program, and they sort of sneered at me, to put it mildly. "Yeah kid, why don't you go peddle your papers someplace else." They denied the existence of it. But I was very lucky because I was doing this at the start of the sixties, and things changed a lot in the sixties. There were more opportunities. Back in the forties and fifties, people with the same inclinations as I had nowhere to go. You might be lucky and get involved in industrial work or educational films, but that never got you any closer to real motion pictures.

INTERVIEWER: *How did you finally get started in film?*

DAVIAU: When I finally got into the business, it was through what would be called rock videos today. We called them rock and roll promotional films then. Commercials were breaking loose. There had been a tremendous revolution in photography. All these wonderful young still photographers had come exploding through advertising in New York in the fifties—people like Howard Zeiff and Melvin Sokolsky. They were using wonderful lighting techniques that they developed in still photography, doing great single-source lighting through large, diffused, windowlike things and producing a certain beautiful, natural rounded look. They carried that technique right into television commercials because they could see that as the print medium declined, television advertising became the thing. Innovative motion picture directors would sit at home, see television commercials and say, "Why can't my movie look like that? How come my movie looks like ten years ago's lighting or twenty years ago's lighting?" So in the sixties, a tremendous motion picture industry started up outside of the traditional Hollywood studio structure.

INTERVIEWER: *This sort of thing was happening all over the world in the sixties, wasn't it?*

DAVIAU: The existence of the independent or nonunion motion picture was becoming more and more a fact. Younger cameramen from different disciplines were coming into the film business. We had people coming in from Hungary, like Vilmos Zsigmond and Laszlo Kovacs, doing fantastic work on very low-budget pictures. They were also working in commercials, blending those two together. The look of film began to change.

Plus the equipment had changed. In France in the fifties they developed a camera at a company called Eclair, which made a 35-mm camera—the CM-3, or the Camaflex as it sometimes was called. It was a hand-held 35-mm camera, and people were making movies with it. That's when the French new wave exploded. Godard and Truffaut and Chabrol were running around with cameramen like Henri Decaë and Willy Kurant and Raoul Coutard, shooting with the new cameras. They were doing very simple bounce lighting in interiors; they were using high-speed film stocks and high-speed lenses and hand-holding these cameras.

Even earlier, Stanley Kubrick in New York was shooting a film called *The Killing* and he was doing it with Tri-X film. A lot of people don't realize that Stanley Kubrick came to film after being a photojournalist for *Look* magazine. He did photo essays. He wanted his films to look like his still photography, and he succeeded in doing it.

Simultaneously, an old-timer, James Wong Howe, was back in New York doing a picture called *The Sweet Smell of Success*. He shot that film in Tri-X. And now there was a Hollywood studio film that looked just as avant-garde as anything and had more guts to it, because Jimmy Wong Howe knew how to do any kind of lighting in any circumstance. He was taking the new tools and showing the new dog some old and new tricks. It was inspirational!

INTERVIEWER: *All this was going on before you had the chance to get behind a camera?*

DAVIAU: Yes. I was watching movies and saying, "Wow, why does this look like that?" And I was doing still photography. I was working in camera stores, I was working in labs, I was doing stage lighting. I was doing anything I could because nobody was letting me shoot movies at the time.

INTERVIEWER: *When did you get your first movie camera?*

DAVIAU: I was working in a camera store in Studio City, California. For a very long time, there had been no competition for the Bolex, the Swiss 16-mm amateur/professional camera. Suddenly, a French company called Beaulieu came out with the 16E, which is an electric-motor-drive thing with a gorgeous reflex viewing system, very lightweight, and it would shoot from two to sixty-four frames per second. Well, I had to have one of those! The people who owned our store had a Bolex franchise. They, of course, weren't interested in handling the Beaulieu. So I told the Beaulieu people, "You sell me one of these at half price and I'll use it as a display model in the store and I'll sell them from there." They got a good deal. I sold both their 16-mm and super-8 cameras, and eventually the line got into the store. I was able to horse-trade for some used Angenieux lenses, and I was set up to do some basic cinematography.

But I could only do so much on my own, on my camera-store salary, because the 16-mm film and processing was hideously expensive compared to super-8. There was no home videotape at the time. But I found that if I got people to pay for the film and the processing, I could do a few things. I always love to say my first job was shooting movies for a radio station, which was actually true. This was in '65. A friend of mine, Ron Jacobs, along with a guy named Bill Drake, had taken over a radio station in Los Angeles. It had been running a middle-of-the-road format, and they took it into rock and roll. It was the start of the whole RKO chain of rock and roll radio stations that transformed pop music radio in this country. So I would go out and shoot these little pieces on "The Boss Jocks at the Funny Car Raceway" or "The Summer of the Big Kahuna" promotion and different things that the radio station was

"I describe the job of the cinematographer as helping put the director's dreams on the screen."

doing. I'd shoot a hundred or two hundred feet of Kodachrome, stay in the camera store after work, and use their editing stuff and splice it together. Then I'd deliver it to the station and they'd run it on the afternoon dance party show on television channel 9 that one of their DJs hosted.

Out of that grew a TV show on Saturday nights called *Boss City* that was produced by the radio station, at least in its initial stages. A friend of Ron's named Peter Gardiner came out from New York to produce it, and Peter wanted to use a lot of film. Ron introduced me to Peter. I was able to show Peter a student film that I had done for a friend of mine at UCLA.

INTERVIEWER: Did you go to film school?

DAVIAU: No, I never went to film school. I didn't have the grades for UCLA or the money for USC. But I had a friend who went to UCLA, and I actually shot a student film for him. That film got me my job as the cinematographer on *Boss City*. And on that show we did interpretive pieces, either with or without the performers of a current hit record. Today, they would be called music videos. We called them promo films. The record companies saw them. Dick Clark saw them and said, "Why don't you guys make these films for our acts?"

So Peter founded a little company called Charlatan Productions and we were in the rock and roll film business, and that's how it started. We were making three-minute films for $3,000, including prints. There were only two of us. I was the cinematographer and the editor and Peter was the writer, director, and super salesman who got these films on the road. And gradually, as we grew bigger, we were able to hire additional people. I mean, we hired folks who were just out of film school or who were film enthusiasts, not necessarily professionals in the business. We couldn't afford to pay anything near professional rates. We actually wound up with a real office, with a secretary answering the phone and handling the accounts. A guy named Tom Rounds, who later became a megastar of radio syndication, handled our management and sales work.

During that time—it was 1967—I was introduced to a guy who was looking around for a cameraman because he wanted to make a film in 35 mm and he needed somebody to shoot it. That's how I met nineteen-year-old Steven Spielberg. And Steven had been making his own films in 8 mm since he was about twelve years old. He made an 8-mm feature back in Scottsdale, Arizona, that ran seventy minutes or so. He had gone on from there to make some 16-mm films in Los Angeles, and people at Universal would look at them and say, "That's terrific, Stevie. Someday you'll make a real movie." But nobody would give him a job. He was growing old—he was all of nineteen—and he was feeling that time was weighing down on him and he had to get something made. But he knew that to impress the people at Universal, he had to show them something in 35 mm. One of the toughest jumps is to make your first 35-mm film. He knew that as a director he had to show 35-mm work, and as a cinematographer I knew the same thing. It was our dream. So we made a twenty-four-minute short entitled *Amblin'* in beautiful 35-mm Eastman color.

INTERVIEWER: *Do you find the collaborative nature of film exciting or frustrating?*

DAVIAU: I think that film is by its nature a collaborative art, and if you don't enjoy collaborative art you shouldn't be in film. Even when you work for somebody who has a singular personality, a strong personality, who leaves his mark in every area of his film, as does Steven Spielberg, you can enjoy what your creative contribution is in terms of working with him. I describe the job of the cinematographer as helping to put the director's dreams on the screen. In other words, the images that are moving through the director's mind have to be captured, fixed, put on film, and put up on a screen for people to see.

And it's how you work with somebody, or a number of people, to get this image that may be floating around in one mind or in a group of minds, that's important—to get them all to come together. Because every person and every element that happens in a film comes together at that one point where the emulsion's exposed. Through that lens right there—that's where it all focuses; the energy and the feelings of all those people contributing to the process is, to me, the excitement of working in film. If you stand on a film set, you can watch all the confusion: all these people moving around and around in circles. But in the middle, in the center, it all gets down to the point where it's going to move through the camera lens. It's a very, very exciting place to be.

INTERVIEWER: *And everyone involved leaves their mark in some way.*

DAVIAU: Yes. One of the things I advise people to do—people who may have nothing to do with the film business—is to sit when a film ends and watch that list of names roll by and try and guess what they all do. They all do something. And some of these jobs are so esoteric that people in the film business don't know what they are doing. What's a Foley editor? How did that term come about? Some of the jargon that was formed fifty or sixty years ago is still around. Film people love the mixing of old tradition with the new technology. At least, that's an aspect I enjoy.

INTERVIEWER: *What do you like best about filmmaking?*

DAVIAU: I'm in motion pictures because I love making art with technology. I think it's the most exciting place to be. Our art form is now almost a whole century old, which is so very, very young. I mean, we haven't yet reached the hundredth anniversary of the first cranked-out Edison or Friese-Greene image. It hasn't been a hundred years yet, and look what's happened in that length of time! And yet the art of film draws from art forms that go back many, many centuries. I'm continually influenced by things I see that existed for many centuries, and at the same time, I'll be influenced by something that was just created yesterday—by so many different elements, old and new. Making art with technology is a collaboration with many people and many different media besides the film medium.

Another reason why I love this business, and you might describe it as the cinematographer's unique perversity, is that in this absolutely chaotic, screwed up, very imperfect world, within the frame everything's perfect for an instant. I mean, in our madness, everybody that works in this business always says, "Now we're going to get it right for once." You are shooting a picture, a period piece set in 1906, and two feet out of frame is a 1983 GM truck. But you are so selective in what you see and what you choose to put in a frame to make something perfect.

INTERVIEWER: *Do you ever feel bogged down by the incredible complexity of the filmmaking process?*

> ## *"Do we steal? You bet, but we only steal from the very best!"*

DAVIAU: If you are going to be in film, you have to enjoy the idea that you have all this apparatus around you. There are times when it gets in the way and you say, "Oh my gosh, if only I could be out, just me and my Nikon, framing this on Kodachrome, going click and going home." And you turn around and there are literally about 300 people, all standing there waiting for you to tell them to do something or waiting for something to happen. You have a tremendous amount of responsibility because the meter is running—you are spending a lot of money! These people are all well paid. They have all brought their years of expertise. They have alternate answers if you have a problem. You're responsible for saying, "Hold on, not yet, not yet." And all the forces of finance and so on are trying to get you to do it a little sooner than you want to do it. Very complex.

INTERVIEWER: *Have you developed a particular style?*

DAVIAU: What I like is not so much any one certain style. I'd say that if anything is consistent about my images it is that I love clarity, I love directness. In all the visual arts, but particularly in motion pictures, where every frame is different and there are twenty-four of them every second, what we really do with all the combinations of framing and lighting and so on is direct the eye somewhere. In each frame we direct the eye to where we want it to be—where it makes a dramatic impact at a given moment. A second later it may all be rearranged, and the eye has to go someplace else in that frame. I think if I take pride in anything, it is that my images read quickly; the impact is there without the audience having to search for it.

I love being involved in the storytelling process. I want an image that is composed and lit, that gives the audience the information, the feeling, and the emotion that we want it to feel exactly at the right moment. I'm more chameleonlike than a lot of others, rather than going with one style. I'd hate to rule out any solution to the problem of telling a story.

Sometimes the look of a film is something that is designed from the very beginning. But I don't think that ever happens totally. With every film, you find the look of the film as you go along. I love to have all my options open, whether I want to do something in the most modern way with the newest light that nobody even thought of having some years ago or whether I reach back to some idea from a film shot fifty years ago.

INTERVIEWER: At what point in a film's life do you get involved?

DAVIAU: I get involved as early as possible. One of the key things that's kept cinematographers from being properly involved with a film in the past was the way their contracts were written. Once you were assigned to a film, you went on salary on a given date and you stayed on salary through the completion of the photography. The problem is that, because of the continuous expense, cinematographers are sometimes not brought on early enough. I have arranged with my agent a contract clause that I call noncontinuous prep. It means that the second I agree to do a film, I want to be in on the very first discussions with the production designer and the director. Then I may go out and work in commercials, but stay in touch, see the rewrites of the script, and so on. Then I'll get a call, "Okay, we're going up to Seattle and look around." And boom, I'll just go on the clock for those days that we go up there.

The most important thing is that you meet with the people you are going to be involved with creatively from the beginning, when the things that affect the look of the film are being discussed. What are the sets going to be like? What locations are we going to shoot on? You are developing ideas about certain special effects and how they are going to be accomplished and what you want them to do. And you have to be involved at an early stage on the budgeting. You have to be able to say, "Guys, I don't think this is going to work. I think we are not allowing enough time for that. We should definitely add that shot." And as things move along, one of you gets an idea and calls up the other people. I had a phone call earlier. The guy said, "I can't shoot that scene of the house on stage. I am sure he's going to want the front yard." And he was right. He said, "Is that going to put us into another night?" I don't think it does. I think we can add this shot to our one night's work in front of the house and not have to rerig the whole thing for a second night.

The earlier you start thinking about these things, the earlier they'll come together. That's why these videotapes are all over the hotel room here. Tomorrow evening when the director gets back from L.A., we are going to sit here and just zap images at each other and say, "I thought this might be useful in such and such a scene." I'm going to show him a segment from *Beauty and the Beast* and say, "I think this is highly applicable. It's a 1945 black-and-white film, a very esoteric fable, but it could have great relevance to one or two things that we are doing here." That's how we talk our way toward how a film eventually looks.

INTERVIEWER: *Old films are a good place to lift ideas from, then?*

DAVIAU: Do we steal? You bet, but we only steal from the very best! We have a wonderful heritage in cinematography of the people that created an incredible, incredible art medium from the ground up in such a short time. It's all been within a century.

I enjoy seeing things in the history of our own medium that are still as valid now as when they were first created. I'll look at a film like *Beauty and the Beast* and say, "What a perfect person to steal from"—Henri Alékan, a great French cameraman! A cameraman of such elegance that you can't believe what you are seeing.

There is a book that Jean Cocteau wrote, *Diary of a Film*, about the making of *Beauty and the Beast*. He described, on a day-to-day basis, what it was like to be shooting that picture in the French countryside in the last days of World War II. He talks about all the problems: "The power went out because there was an air raid here, and my negative went down in the tank so that we have to reshoot the scene." When you see this wonderful film, it's hard to imagine there were all those problems!

I have a picture on laser disc, George Stevens's *A Place in the Sun*. There is a film that was made totally in the studio system at its height. It was really filmed in '49, although it was released in '51. It is a really amazing, daring, pioneering, avant-garde film that was made with all the accoutrements of studio production by absolute professionals, using some very exciting new talents. The young Montgomery Clift, the young Elizabeth Taylor, and the young Shelley Winters acted in it. And there was the director George Stevens, who worked in a manner of covering everything and shooting every possible angle, to the point that when he sat down in the editing room, he had it every way you could think of. You look at that picture today and it holds up so beautifully. It is a very, very romantic, very dramatic film, and yet at the same time it is right up to the state of the art of the cinema at the time. It had to be one of those rare instances where everything worked perfectly for the filmmaker. I'll look at a film like that and I'll look at all kinds of films for ideas.

INTERVIEWER: *So you are involved not only with the film itself—its emulsion, lighting, and so forth—but also with atmosphere and characterization?*

DAVIAU: Yes. All the things that add up to making the film. When you first sit down and read a script, you get images immediately in your head—you start seeing things in a certain way. Then you'll sit down with the director and the production designer and compare images, so to speak.

"...commercials are a wonderful way for you to keep your skills up and try the latest techniques."

We are the people that a director sits and dreams with. You try and share that dream. And everybody influences everybody else. You walk around and look at locations, or a production designer shows you a rendering, and you say to each other, "Oh, I hadn't thought about it quite that way. But you know, that's nice." Or, "Well maybe it shouldn't be afternoon then," and "If there was a skylight there, or if there was a little stained glass window. ..." That can be very productive. Ideas tend to flow when you are sharing them.

INTERVIEWER: *So the production designer is very important to your work.*

DAVIAU: After the director, the most important person the cinematographer communicates with is the production designer. It is truly a title of honor—production designer. In the beginning, there weren't any production designers; there were set-construction people. They built the sets. A guy named Huck Wortman built D. W. Griffith's sets. He also happened to be a magnificent production designer who could do anything. But his title was set-construction man. The terminology evolved through set designer, art director, and now an art director that has arrived and is recognized as making a real contribution is called a production designer. It's a heck of a credit.

The production designer plays a very important role. For example, we have a real house in Seattle that we are going to use in shooting exteriors, but we will shoot the interiors on stage in Los Angeles, because the production designer will cheat certain things in the interior of that house. In the film, when you cut from an exterior of the house in Seattle to the interior of the house on stage at Universal Studios, nothing will jar you. The windows won't change places or anything. But maybe we'll cheat the height of them a little bit. Maybe we'll move a few things around that will allow me to get a better slant for light to come in a certain way. Or I think there's a bathroom under the staircase, which is absolutely insane, for one particular gag. Because of that kind of thing, better that I get involved in the beginning than if I show up on the set and say, "Oh, you really screwed me putting that there. I don't know what I'm going to do with that."

I think that a lot of this stuff is a matter of communication. When you have people that you communicate well with, that you really like working with, that's a big part of why things turn out well.

INTERVIEWER: *What do you do after your brainstorming sessions with the director and production designer?*

DAVIAU: On this picture, for example, I will start going to see some rehearsals with the actors this week. I will usually stand by the director, or maybe I'll stand at the other end of the room and see the action in reverse. We have to think that way a lot. If I have two people talking to each other, we think in terms of where the camera is going to be placed to catch the gist of the conversation. The normal procedure is to show both people and then get coverage of one or the other in close-ups, extreme close-ups, or whatever. Sometimes I don't have to do that at all. Sometimes it's all delivered simply on the face of the person reacting and not the person talking. Usually the covering shots will be done anyway, just to see, but sometimes the director will have such a strong feeling that he'll say, "No, we don't need to see him," no offense to the actor. Oftentimes I'll look for the indirect way of expressing something.

INTERVIEWER: *Who else do you work closely with?*

DAVIAU: I like to enjoy a good rapport with the editor. Cinematographers don't have that much to say about editing per se, but with certain things, you want to get your oar in—certain takes that you think are particularly good.

I also work with the effects people. You're also interviewing a guy I have the greatest affection for: Dennis Muren at ILM [Industrial Light & Magic]. He is just magnificent. Unlike many of the special-effects people who give you all the "thou shalt nots," Dennis will just say, "Go ahead and shoot it how you want it to look and we'll work around that look." Dennis has such confidence in his ability to use his color separations, to make the contrast of a scene make sense with the footage of his miniatures or his Go-Motion figures. When we shot Elliott and E.T. on the bicycle flying through the skies at night, we shot that right out in the backyard set on stage. Dennis came in and set up his blue-screen. I remember we started lighting the set for nighttime. I took the fill light way down to what I'd shoot with if I were shooting a normal shot. I said, "Is that too far?" And he said, "That the way you like it?"

"Uh huh."

He said, "Fine." We shot it and he put it exactly where we wanted it! The other stuff—the daytime bike-flying stuff—Dennis did up at ILM. That is really his baby up there. The compositing of the spaceship landing and that kind of thing is really remarkable. I normally do not have the patience required for special-effects work, the kind that Dennis does. I have the utmost respect for his work. It is a joy working with him.

INTERVIEWER: *Do you see a lot of contemporary film?*

DAVIAU: Oh yes. We're going to go next door here and see *Top Gun*. I hear that's a marvelous film visually. It's a summer "boom-boom" film, but I know of the people involved. So, we're just going to go in and see their work.

INTERVIEWER: *In today's film, do you have many technological advances that affect the way you work?*

DAVIAU: Well, film technology was very complacent for a number of years. The studio assembly line became so smooth that nobody questioned the tools—the cameras and the lights and so on. The film stock was progressing, but not much else. And then these bandits came from the outside—people from commercials and people from other countries—and we started seeing that films could be made in other ways. We didn't need the sound stages; we went outdoors, we used fast lenses, we pushed the film to its limits, and we found ways to make movies that the studios hadn't. The studios had given us a marvelous heritage, but they needed to be awakened. And a lot of the people that started in the late fifties and into the early sixties really did it.

I was lucky to come along when that revolution had already started. We got used to going into real locations and shooting without having a ceiling that came off, without a whole grid to hang lights from. We could come in, set up, and shoot a scene in this room exactly as we are seeing it now, using only available light for the day scene, and turn around and shoot a night scene in it in a few hours, too. We'd clamp grip arms out on the balcony and hang some lights out there and use the real fixtures and hide lights just out of frame in the corner.

All those things were part of our educational process. So when we finally got into the union, into the major studios, and into mainstream films, we were able to use the resources that they offered plus all the experiences that we'd had on the outside. We've been able to see, starting in the seventies, the two schools of thought coming together. And now there is a whole other one starting—there's a whole group of kids out there. Now we are going to be the complacent ones. I try and stay aware, and I do watch my MTV, and I do try and see the new films.

> *"When I finally got into the business, it was through what would today be called rock videos...."*

INTERVIEWER: *So it's important to you to continue the learning process.*

DAVIAU: It's a tremendous learning thing. I think that, because of the way people in our age group came into the medium, we are very committed to sharing information. I don't know of a cinematographer that isn't happy to tell you how he or she did something. You can call them up and say, "In the scene in such and such, what exactly were you doing there?" and they will tell you. Years ago, I called up Haskell Wexler and asked, "How did you do the thing with the liquid light show in *Medium Cool?*" And he told me, "Well, this is the way I did it, but I wasn't happy with it and it didn't work. If I had it to do over ..." and he told me what he would have done. So I went out and I did a test using some of his suggestions and, gee, it worked great. I've never forgotten that kind of thing. I think we all are very aware of what we owe to the next generation coming up. I make it a point to accept every single film school invitation to come out and talk and show film and answer questions.

INTERVIEWER: *What are the kids like that you talk to?*

DAVIAU: I think it's the same in any endeavor. In a typical film school or film-enthusiast audience, you'll see a couple of pairs of bright eyes that ask all the good questions. Then somewhere near the end there will be one real quiet person in the back that hasn't said much, who will come up with the best question of the whole day. Then there's the person who was too shy to ask any questions at all. They'll come up to you afterwards and talk with you. Out of a group of thirty or forty, there are always three or four that you can tell are going to do real, real well with it. Each of them will find their own way of doing it.

INTERVIEWER: *If they can get into the union.*

DAVIAU: Cinematography has been, because of the union situation, such a closed-off thing. I think we're going to see cinematography and the other art forms become more available to people simply because the means are being spread around the country. I mean, look, whether Hollywood or my union or any of us likes it or not, North Carolina is becoming a major filmmaking state. With *The Color Purple* last year, we went to North Carolina, in the southern part of the state, and shot a completely union, absolutely straight-arrow Hollywood-crew motion picture. Whereas in the northern part of the state, Dino De Laurentiis and a guy named Earl Owensby were shooting completely nonunion pictures or they were shooting mixed-crew pictures. But suddenly, North Carolina! Kids in North Carolina can go get work in the film business. That would have been unheard-of ten years ago.

And here in Seattle I did a seminar for the Washington Film and Video Association back in the fall of '82, and boy, the people that showed up were just terrific! We had a wonderful time. We did a hands-on seminar—lighting different kinds of situations. I ran *E.T.,* turned the sound down low, and then I talked through the film: "If you think this is a good shot, you should have seen what we really wanted to do." Or, "You should see what's just outside of the frame over there." Or, "I had to do this and this and this." And people really wanted to know.

INTERVIEWER: *What do you like better, videotape or videodisc?*

DAVIAU: Well, the thing is, they are both victims or beneficiaries of where they came from. The original source of the material declares a lot. *Beauty and the Beast* was transferred off a print from a dupe negative, as a subtitled dupe negative print. It's kind of murky. It's obvious the print had been badly waxed or had oil damage on it. I think I have seen the very print from which this thing was mastered. It's a shame they didn't go to France and get an original negative print. This film was made in 1945. They could have been able to go to the original neg, or fine grain, to get the best materials possible, then transfer it and do the subtitles electronically. See, it's old-fashioned to think, "Oh well, we'll use a subtitled print." Yeah, it's cheaper, but you have a film that's a classic! It's a marvelous study film.

When the laser-disc system was announced all those years ago, I said, "This will be the greatest boon for teaching film that has ever occurred." They made this great medium, CAV [constant angular velocity] videodisc: you can slow-mo, you can stop, you can still-frame, you can triple-speed, you can go backwards, you can chapter-head—all these wonderful teaching tools. And then the vast majority of the discs released are extended-play, an hour per side, and no special effects other than scan fast forward and back. Do you know about the outfit called Criterion? They do custom-made videodiscs; they did *Citizen Kane,* they did *King Kong.* And most of theirs are CAV format. I just got a beautiful new videodisc of *Swing Time,* the Astaire-Rogers thing from 1936. With CAV discs like that, you can really study films. A film teacher can sit there and say, "Now take a look at this section again. Why do you think he cut on that frame?"

But then, movies are released on videodisc in the extended-play format—all because some jerk writes letters to complain that he's got to change the disc every half hour! Well, then he should buy a videotape and not bother with this medium! The distributors are still thinking the videodisc is a mass-market medium. MCA tried to market the laser disc as a mass-market medium. It wasn't. It isn't. It failed as such.

INTERVIEWER: *What do you think about the relationship of film and video in the near future?*

DAVIAU: Personally, I feel that film will continue to be the front-end medium for a longer time than most people think. And as you can see, I am a video freak. I love video. I keep track of what's going on with video. But video is not film, and for the front end of the imaging process, you are going to see film hang in there for a lot longer. To the video people who are saying, "Pretty soon we are going to put film out of business," I say, "Don't forget, film is not a stationary target." It's going to continue moving on. Kodak is doing research and development. In just the last five years, we've gotten a high-speed color negative that's changed the way a lot of things are done. And now there are three: the 5294 by Kodak, and Fuji and Agfa both have high-speed color negative films in the 250 to 400 ASA range. These films allow us to shoot with less light without giving up significant image quality.

I love to test films as they come out. I shot a film, a TV movie, in Radio City Music Hall in 1983 where I utilized the lighting of the stage show—the actual lighting done by the music hall technicians. I supplemented it with back light and some additional dramatic cross light for certain scenes. I had Garrett Brown with the Steadicam running up and down the row of Rockettes kicking their legs in unison. We had a wonderful, fun time doing it. And because of this high-speed film, I was able to shoot five musical numbers in three days without overburdening. And yet, just a year before that, to try and shoot available light with only the slow-speed stock would have been a disaster! Forget it! I like to take advantage of the state of the art.

INTERVIEWER: Do the faster films help you in the studio as well?

DAVIAU: I did a segment of *Twilight Zone: The Movie*, with a director named George Miller. He's known as the man who brought you *Road Warrior* and *Mad Max Beyond Thunderdome*. We did a little segment with John Lithgow, whom I am about to work with on a comedy now. John starred in a film called *Terror at Twenty Thousand Feet*, about a guy in an airplane in a storm and a menacing creature out on the wing. Well, there was a classic example. The way that film was done was entirely due to several new developments. We had the high-speed film stock, and we used new developments to do some great new lighting.

> *"In this absolutely chaotic, screwed up, very imperfect world, within the frame everything's perfect for an instant."*

George Miller, who is well known for filming only in the outback of Australia—roads, deserts, and real locations—comes to Hollywood, and the first thing he wanted to do was to make a totally studio film, with studio special effects—an airplane mock-up and lightning machines and creating an artificial storm with rain and wind and all the rest of this. This man took advantage of his surroundings: "Well, if I am going to go to Hollywood, I might as well use what Hollywood has to offer."

George wanted to be able to move the camera anywhere in that plane, at any time, without having to yank walls out to allow room for a camera to look through. And our inspiration for this was really a film called *Das Boot*, the German submarine film. In fact, we made up some gag T-shirts for the film that said "Das Plane" on them. The production designer, Jim Bissell, told

Warner Brothers that none of the existing airplane mock-up sets would work for what we wanted to do, because they had ceilings you just lifted off for the old-fashioned lights to blast in. George knew about the Steadicam. So I told Garrett about the project and he got very excited, because everbody had always used the Steadicam to chase people up six flights of stairs and step out the window onto the crane and the crane pulls back and the house blows up—that kind of shot. We talked about how the Steadicam can be really good for subtle little scenes, delicate camera movements around and through crowds of people and tight spaces. You can't really do them with a conventional dolly and track unless you've got sixteen grips moving furniture out of the way and then putting it back into place.

And the Steadicam turned out to be a wonderful way to create the atmosphere and the feeling of the movement in the plane. I said to Garrett, "Can you adjust your gyros around to make it an unsteady cam?" And the feeling of being in the plane in the storm was achieved because he figured out how to make the camera lurch around and give you that wonderful seasick feeling. And I said to John Toll, hand-holding his camera, "Take the darn thing and shake it." Sometimes it was the most effective thing.

So I had Garrett Brown using a Steadicam. I had John Toll, who has, I would say, the finest hand-held camera technique that I've ever seen. I really feel that for some circumstances nothing can beat the Steadicam, and in other circumstances nothing can beat John Toll hand-holding the camera. But I had both; I had the two best in the world for this.

INTERVIEWER: *How did you light the interior of the plane?*

DAVIAU: Well, it's easy to use an airplane mock-up, a set, and film a day scene in it. But it's difficult to do a night scene because of how planes are lit at night. The only lights on planes at night are the little reading lights in the compartments overhead and maybe some very slight fluorescent that's in the aisles; that's really about all there is.

So how do we light it so they can work freely and see everything and yet keep it realistic in having the feeling of being inside an airplane? I thought about this and talked it over with my lighting gaffer, Pat Kirkwood. Pat knew a company that built low-voltage lamps, not for motion pictures, but for industrial purposes, where you need to have a lamp that fits in a very small space and that puts out a great amount of light with very little heat. This was exactly our problem. We wanted to build the lights into the set, to shoot off the reading lights. And yet they had to be locked into a very small area to keep the plane size proper, and they also had to be truly adjustable. Well, we went out and enlisted the guy who owned the lamp company and he was really helpful. Pat worked on designing some little diffusion screens that he could throw in front of the lights. We could turn the lights and aim them at different places, and all of this would fit inside something that would look approximately like the overhead compartment of a plane.

Then we had other light sources that were new. On the back of the overhead compartments, we had things that looked like small fluorescent tubes that were really incandescent. You never see them in the film; they were set up so that they would always be on the side opposite the camera. But we could build this kind of stuff into the plane. The lights could stay on for a long time without burning up; we didn't have smoke billowing out and we could get past the fire inspector. And yet it gave us just enough light to be able to shoot at a decent f-stop and give George all the freedom of movement that he wanted.

INTERVIEWER: *How did George Miller like his first Hollywood experience?*

DAVIAU: George had video monitor assists from the Steadicam and from the hand-held camera. Here was a guy who had been used to hanging off the back of a camera car careening around corners in the desert. And there he was sitting properly at a desk with a television monitor, with his storyboards, with his script, and wearing his glasses, saying, "Yes, yes, yes, John. That's very good." He thought that was really making movies! I will say, when we did the stuff out on the wing in the storm, he stood right out there in his raincoat with us, getting all the water in his face and encouraging us all to "Be bold! Be bold!" It was just wonderful fun.

INTERVIEWER: *What kinds of things did you do outside the plane for the weather and so on?*

DAVIAU: Well, it was the height of sophisticated technology inside the plane, but outside we had old-fashioned lightning arc scissors. They were probably used on God-knows-what horror films back in the thirties. I mean, the poor guys had to stand there and hit the arcs so that the elements would come together and POW! I talked to Bran Ferren, a special-effects wizard in New York, who has this marvelous computerized strobe-light lightning setup that was used for a film called *Tempest*. But it would have cost us fifteen grand just to fly the thing out there, so it was not cost-effective. We went the old route with the lightning, the new route for inside.

INTERVIEWER: *It sounds like you guys had a great time.*

DAVIAU: That was one of the most fun filmmaking experiences I've ever had because we were mixing the old and the new and flying absolutely on the hairy edge of that negative. We used the new high-speed negative. And any little misguess with it and there was nothing on the film. We were working very close to the edge in much of what we shot, because what you see through the window of the plane when the creature is out there has to be barely there. If it is anything more than barely there it is phony as all get-out. And if it is any less than barely there, people would say, "Hey, I don't see anything either. Do you see something out there?" "No, I don't see a thing!" We only had a chance to do one test on that.

"...if anything is consistent about my images it is that I love clarity, I love directness."

INTERVIEWER: *Did George Miller encourage you to take risks as you filmed?*

DAVIAU: I was very fortunate in that George Miller, like Steven Speilberg, just says, "Try something new. Go for it. Be bold." But George would have forgiven me if it didn't turn out! Steven said to me before *E.T.*—and really, this is something every cinematographer dreams of hearing—"I'll only be half as mad at you if you blow something for going too far than if you blow something for playing too safe." Note the *half* as mad. But that's a great mandate to have. As in any other art form, you've got to take chances to get something exceptional. You're going to have to be willing to be daring, to really get out on the edge.

In that regard, *E.T.* couldn't have been a greater dream/nightmare for a cinematographer. The whole idea from the very beginning was that we just barely see him, but we don't want to see too much of him. What's too much? Well, tune in tomorrow and we'll look at the film and we'll see whether we see too much or whether we don't see him. And again, it was that fine, fine line.

INTERVIEWER: *Is that a function of how good your equipment is, or your skill and judgement, or what?*

DAVIAU: You have to understand the film. You have to understand the emulsion. You have to know what it is capable of recording. You have to have a feel for the bottom line, a real feeling for it. We have marvelous meters—light meters and color meters—you name it. The light meters tell us tenths of stops, but at a certain point, the meter can't do that for you. You can't trust it. I mean, certain things you can establish. You can lay a technological base down, but other things are strictly by your eye. And that comes from the experience of exposing a particular film—knowing where it prints is the way we put it. Still-photography darkroom experience is helpful for understanding what the characteristic curve of a film is, but quite frankly, the way we use color negative films today does not really relate to most people's darkroom experience. And it's not so much the fine points of the technology that really mean anything to a cinematographer as much as it is your experience working with film. You have to be able to say, "Yeah, that'll read. It won't read very well but it will be there."

INTERVIEWER: *How involved do you get with lab work or opticals?*

DAVIAU: With opticals, generally just to check to see how they are coming down the line. If there are optical effects involved, I want to be around when they are being composited and put together.

I feel one of my major, major contributions to a film is the final color timing or grading of the picture in the lab. I look forward to it. So far, I have been very lucky in that I have never been out of the country or far away from the laboratory when that is happening to a film I have photographed. If you care about your film, either you fly back to the lab or they will fly the person from the lab to you with a print. You're the only one who knows where you exposed the negative, where you laid it down.

Now, your daily print reflects closely what you want in that regard. If I get a daily print back during shooting that is way off, obviously I am going to reprint it at that time. But if it is relatively close, I accept it, because it's the cost-effective way of doing it. I know what I am going to do later in the laboratory to position it exactly where it should be on the printing scale. But no one can really lay that in for you in exactly the way you want.

There's one person in the lab that you work closely with: the timer, or in England they're called graders. Jim Schurmann at Deluxe Laboratories is probably the person I have worked with more that any other. And I am sure that Jim Schurmann could take any picture that I have shot, look at the work print, and hit the darn thing on the mark 90 or 95 percent of the time without me there. But that 5 to 10 percent could make a difference to me. And if it's somebody that hasn't worked with you, who doesn't know your work, they can make an atrocity out of your movie. Particularly if they're not sympathetic. It has happened that cinematographers have shot films and wound up on not very good terms with the producer.

INTERVIEWER: *A breakout of interpersonal hostilities?*

DAVIAU: Yes, and then the producer has gone in and printed it up sky high and destroyed the photography. This happened to a very, very well-known cinematographer just a little over a year ago. The guy was absolutely ready to commit murder! As it happened, he had done the work beforehand with the timer, and while he was working on a film in Europe, the producers went in and just cut him off at the kneecaps in the lab. And somebody saw that work and asked, "Hmm, what's he up to?" You take it on the chin.

So to be very specific, I have a phrase in my contract; it is always in my deal memos: "The right to be informed of and present at all answer-print screenings and video transfer sessions." Wake me up in the middle of the night, I will give it to you word for word. Now, I am not demanding control; I just want to be present, I want to be there giving my opinion. And I've found that the majority of producers and directors are delighted that you are interested enough to come back, because we are not paid to do this. We do it of our own volition, showing up at the lab and making sure that the prints that go out reflect our work.

I also like to be there for the timing of the original answer print and to see the result from the dupe negative. Original negative prints are usually seen only in the major cities—L.A., New York, London. Sometimes you'll have one in Chicago, one in San Francisco, but the majority of the country sees the film from prints off the dupe negative. This used to be a very unhappy situation. It's gotten so much better now that in the case of *The Color Purple*, we had a dupe that I felt reflected the original neg prints so well that I was extremely proud of the prints that went out to the rest of the country. But that's from being there and seeing that it was done right.

INTERVIEWER: *You spend so much time on location, in hotels. Is it something you put up with or do you enjoy it?*

DAVIAU: It's a life experience. I'd rather be here than Monroe, North Carolina. Excuse me, Monroe! I'm not married, I don't have kids, so I don't have those family obligations. I find that the guys that do usually have visits back and forth. My girlfriend comes to visit. She loves the idea. She has a business to run back in L.A., but she's going to come up this weekend and probably a couple more weekends. This is a short location. We are only going to be here through June. I was in Mexico City on *Falcon and the Snowman* for four months. Four months in Mexico City! That city will get to you.

You have to be able to escape to your own environment—whatever is needed to keep your head on straight. Because basically, when a film starts, the cinematographer, like everybody else, is making decisions. You are making decisions—boom, boom, boom, boom—and trying to balance art and mammon. You've made a contract with yourself and with the producers that you are going to give them the very best film that you can. But at the same time, and no fooling around, you are on a schedule. You've got to keep to that schedule.

INTERVIEWER: What's it like shooting in Seattle?

DAVIAU: Well, the big sweat here on shooting nights is that they are just too short. I mean, we are going to be hitting solstice and it's going to be getting on to 10:00 before it's usable night. And then, boom! 5:00, day again. I've been leaving my curtains open to check when my light alarm goes off. We have a very big nighttime sequence to do here in Seattle. We are out scouting locations, and my key people—my gaffer, my key grip, and so on—and I are talking about what we are going to have to rig up, lighting-wise, on

> *"As in any other art form, you've got to take chances to get something exceptional."*

these buildings to light an intersection and to light the buildings themselves. They are saying, "You'll be lucky if you can get the one shot that night," because it involves so much stunt work—car stunts and stuff that is beyond our control. But I'm betting that we can light it, get the shot, jump back to this alley behind us, and with a very few rapid changes—panning lights around, not even moving them—I can get another, wider shot of different action. And then I can move the camera down the alley another 20 feet, block off some buildings, see some buildings to the left that weren't seen before, and make it a whole other shot. Simply pan two lights over, pick up the front of the buildings, and I can get three setups out of the time for one.

The other thing about Seattle is that it's like England in that the light is constantly changing. The important thing to remember is, don't shoot the master scene while the sun is out. If we rehearse a scene and I've got nice clear, sparkling sun coming down, I've got to look around and ask, "How long is it going to last?" If I shoot that scene in full, sparkling sun and then an hour later, whoom, there it goes, I've got troubles. I can't light up overcast exteriors to look like the sun shots. So what I'll try to do is shoot one in the sun and then, dear Lord, give me one cloud floating over and I'll shoot another one under the cloud. Then I'll be set. If the sun goes in, I can go ahead and shoot my closeups under silk. I can make overcast a lot easier than I can make sun. We brought up a big 20- by 30-foot sailcloth. It's nice, but you have to be careful because if the wind catches it, you can uproot trees and so on. The major thing in working exteriors is, you have to go with what Mother Nature gives you. If you start being cute and trying to fight it, she'll get you every time.

INTERVIEWER: *Did she ever get you?*

DAVIAU: Well, one of the best sequences I ever shot was in a little film called *Harry Tracy*, which nobody's seen. It was a western we did up in Canada in 1980. The ending of the film was a shoot-out, and we shot it in pouring rain—three days in pouring rain. At the end of the third day, we still weren't finished with it, and the radio said, "Brilliant sunshine tomorrow! Storm's blowing out." We were cooked! Finished! Dead! Because we had to be out of the location. We were making a major move to Alberta, and we were in British Columbia at the time. I don't know whose karma it was, but we all prayed, and we got a fourth morning of pouring rain. The storm just rolled around and came back over! I wish I had recorded the radio guy: "Well, we don't know what happened to our sun. The storm just did the strangest thing." That fourth day we shot and we shot and we shot and we got it all done on take one. Then in the afternoon, whammo, that sun came out and there was not a cloud at all. We pushed it! Filmmakers used to try and wait out the weather. They would peek out and say, "No, not today." Then everybody went back and drank all afternoon. Well, we don't get to do that any more. It's too expensive. It's probably good for us as well.

INTERVIEWER: *Do you ever operate the camera?*

DAVIAU: Actually, by union rules, I am not allowed to operate the camera during the actual photography of a shot. The camera operator does that. It's rather a good system. There are some films where I would rather operate the camera, but I'd say in the majority of the cases, I'm better off standing beside the camera, looking at the faces. I'm a very good camera operator; I'm very proud of how good I am. A good operator is literally looking at the corners of the frame and only feeling the action in the center, very conscious of what's happening in the corners of the frame, keeping the balance in the shot.

But what the director of photography is being paid to do is look at the faces—How is the light on the faces? What's happening? How do they look? Did I catch that expression? Did the glint in the eye when he looked over happen just exactly when I wanted it to? Did the actor fail to turn around all the way? Did he hit the mark; did he miss the mark? Do I need to shoot it again, or was it good enough? And I should be concerned with what's happening with the light. If I'm outside, I should be watching the changing of the weather.

Plus—and this is really important—if I see something that needs fixing on the set, I can work quickly with hand signals in between takes without making a disturbance, without disturbing the actors. You can go for photographic perfection; that is one of the things you are there to do. But the other thing is that you are there to help tell the story, and part of that is giving the actors their space to perform. If you are trying to pin an actor tightly into a certain move, you've got to know when you have to change your lighting to

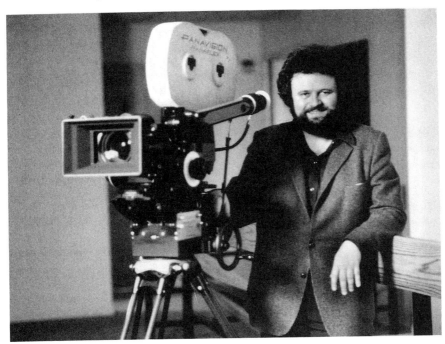

Allen Daviau: The Man With a Movie Camera.

accommodate that actor. There are some scenes when an actor has to express a tremendous range of emotions and really cut loose. You'd better give that actor a lot of leeway to be able to be an emotional person at that point and not be the servant of your light.

One of the people I really enjoy working with is John Lithgow, because he is a complete film actor. The man, in addition to being a marvelous actor and very, very expressive, always hits his marks. He feels the light. He brings to a film all of the things that I feel people who understand the craft of being a film actor can bring. But there are emotional situations when you can't ask John Lithgow to observe those niceties, in which case your job is to get it as close as you can and give them the range to emote. That is everybody's job— the person on the focus, the operator, we're all in the same boat at that point.

One of the most moving experiences is when you are there on a set and something special and emotional is happening in a film and you know you are capturing it and you are capturing it beautifully, and everyone is in sync. This is the wonderful thing about film. Stand back on a film set—stand way, way back—and look at all the people around the camera. Look at that person pushing the dolly, the person operating the camera, the person on the focus. Somebody's walking along with a light, and somebody else has got a flag in front of the light; they're flagging a flare out of the lens just by an inch, because if they go in an inch too far, the flag will get into the shot. And the actors are talking, the camera is moving and the guy's got the microphone and he's dipping that microphone in as close as he dares get it, and the camera operator has to be aware of just where it's happening and everybody's moving toward the same goal and they are all breathing in the same breath. That's a moment of magic. You stand back and you look at that and you say, "How marvelous! How marvelous!"

Chris Menges

CINEMATOGRAPHY

Chris Menges was born in 1940 in Hertfordshire, England. His father—a musician, musical director, and composer who worked for the Old Vic Theatre in London for over twenty-five years—moved to England from Germany before World War I. After his schooling, Menges began work with a documentary production company as a gofer. He worked through several production positions on the film crew before becoming director of photography.

In addition to his photography on many documentaries and feature films, Menges has produced, directed, and shot six documentaries of his own, which have all been aired on British television. Menges himself was the subject of a documentary film produced by Allistair Moffat of Scottish television called Shooting From the Heart. *In 1985 he received an Oscar, a British Academy Award, and the New York, Boston, and Los Angeles Critics' Awards for best cinematography for his work on* The Killing Fields. *Menges lives on a small farm in Wales with his wife, Judy, and their children.*

INTERVIEWER: *What brings you to Los Angeles?*

MENGES: A film by Andrei Konchalovsky called *Shy People.* It's an American film being shot in Louisiana and Los Angeles. It's about discovering a family that's living in the swamps—modern people meet people who are living in the past. It's a terrific story, an original story that he has been working on with some other people. Do you know Andrei Konchalovsky? He did *Runaway Train* among other things. Did you ever read a book called *Let Us Now Praise Famous Men*—I think it's by James Agee and Walker Evans? Well, *Shy People* feels a bit like that. A journalist from New York—a woman—and her daughter go down to the Louisiana swamps to look for a distant relative who's supposedly still living in the swamp area. It's quite an interesting project. It will come out in about a year, if we don't get eaten by alligators.

INTERVIEWER: *What was the last project you worked on before this one?*

MENGES: The last project I finished was *Fatherland,* directed by Ken Loach. The film was made in Berlin and it was a coproduction of French and German television. You could consider it a very small-budget film. I've worked with Ken Loach since 1968, when I was a camera operator on his first feature film, called *Poor Cow.* I've shot several films for Ken Loach, among them *Kes* in 1970.

INTERVIEWER: *How would you define the role of the cinematographer?*

MENGES: It is entirely about enabling the director to realize his or her vision of the story they are trying to tell. It's about photographing a story so that it's believable. It's about giving the actors as much freedom as possible, about giving the director as much freedom as possible. It's about making an attempt to transport the audience to the time and place of the film. It's certainly not about imposing a style. It's certainly not about having preconceived ideas. It's a question of remaining open—perhaps even of remaining vulnerable—to the needs of that day, and being adaptable enough to what is needed from you as a cinematographer in terms of the photography, in terms of the framing, in terms of the camera moves, and in terms of the light.

INTERVIEWER: *When does your involvement with a film usually begin?*

MENGES: I usually get involved with a production several months before shooting starts. It's a great help to be able to work with a director early on, to discover what his vision is and what his requirements are. It's also important to be able to work closely with the art director from an early stage so that we can complement each other's work. The same thing applies to the costume design and the whole early preparations of the film. I think that films are very dependent on successful preproduction work and that the success of a film often depends on the closeness that you have with the director in the early stages of production.

INTERVIEWER: *And when does your involvement end?*

MENGES: My job on a film finishes with the timing of the final answer print. That takes place several months after I've shot the film, after the film's been edited. It's a question of working with the director and working with the laboratory to try and get, as exactly as possible, the most perfect final print of the film.

INTERVIEWER: *What criteria do you use to decide whether or not to become involved with a particular project?*

MENGES: I like getting involved in projects that I will learn from—projects with directors and with scripts that are inspiring, from stories that will somehow enrich the lives of the people who see the film.

INTERVIEWER: *What kind of crew do you usually work with?*

MENGES: The most important thing is to work with a crew that is interested in the film, that has a commitment

> *"To just go quietly out with a tiny crew, with a hand-held camera, is very satisfying."*

to the film and the script, and that is composed, of course, of fine craftsmen. For instance, the sensitivity of the dolly grip—the person who pushes the camera—is absolutely vital to the successful completion of difficult, complicated tracking shots. And, for instance, if you work at low apertures, with the lens wide open, which I often do, you need a fine, sensitive focus puller. The kind of lighting I do would be impossible without a first-class focus puller. It's very much a question of choosing people who can be involved and who also have the temperament to work under extremely difficult situations and do their jobs brilliantly. Those people are worth their weight in gold.

On some films, on big films, I work with a camera operator or operators. In *The Killing Fields* and *The Mission*, Mike Roberts and the rest of the crew were superb and made those films possible. On other films, such as when I work with Ken Loach, I really like operating the camera myself because I feel that the involvement of actually looking through the viewfinder, through the ground glass, enables you to concentrate on the essence of what the shot's about, what the needs of the director are. It lets you concentrate on the lighting; it lets you concentrate on the strengths of the performances of the actors. Let me put it this way: I think the most important thing in photographing a shot is to balance the light in the frame. And it can only be evaluated when the director of photography is constantly looking through the viewfinder. It's a sense of the imagination, the total view of a sequence. When you are looking through the viewfinder, you are more able to contribute to the needs of the director. In a sense, you are inspired both by the needs of the director and by actually looking through that ground glass.

Some cameramen who don't operate, I think, get removed very much from the actual involvement of what's happening in the storytelling. They get more involved purely in the lighting. And that's not the most important part of filmmaking. I think the most important part of filmmaking is the dictionary, the alphabet of how shots are constructed and how the story's being told. It's also a question of spontaneity and reaction and gut feeling to what is happening with the actors—the freedom you can give the director. And I think it's very much easier to do that job if you're operating.

INTERVIEWER: *Is there a certain style or look to your films?*

MENGES: I don't seek to impose a style on a film. For instance, before we went to Colombia and Argentina to shoot *The Mission*, which Roland Joffe directed for David Puttnam and Warner Brothers, Roland and I went to the National Gallery in London to look at paintings. I always try to find out what dreams are in the director's mind, what vision the director might have, and I try very much to remain open to what the director wants. I hope that each film I do is fresh and responds to the script, to the story, to the actors, and that there isn't a definite style, especially the style of a previous film. I hope that I can give to the director and the actors and the writer the freedom to experiment. I hope I can give something original, so that the work doesn't become stylistically dogmatic, so that the work is fresh.

INTERVIEWER: *Do you tend to shoot available light exclusively?*

MENGES: It's quite a difficult question to answer—there's no straight answer to that. I don't work with available light exclusively. If I'm doing a documentary—I love doing documentaries, and I always shoot them with a hand-held camera—I would never use lights, because I think lights force an artificiality on a documentary situation. But, of course, on a cinema film, you need to do the work and you need to have the proper exposure, so of course you will use lights, and sometimes you'll want to use lights to make the light very startling or perhaps very strong.

My lighting depends entirely on the script and the story and, as I said before, the needs of the director. I make an effort to use everything—all the equipment, all the lights, all the developments in cinema technology—to put all of the techniques that are available at the disposal of the particular film I'm working on.

So it depends entirely on the needs of the film. It also depends on the feeling you get when you're on the floor, on the set, and you're with the actors and the director. Perhaps you respond sometimes to what is unspoken. It's a question of reaction. I love very stylistic lighting, and I love working with very natural lighting. I can't say that there is any one particular technique I prefer.

INTERVIEWER: *What kind of factors do you consider when you are setting up a shot?*

MENGES: I love the camera that moves. I love the camera that tells the story in one shot. I like going for the shot that gives the actors the most freedom but also gives a sense of pace and a sense of time and a sense of place. I like shots that develop. You also have to shoot cover so that you can edit. When I'm considering how to set up a shot, I'm looking to the words, the inspiration of the actors, the director, and the writer. I'm looking for the shot that will tell the story in the simplest way. I think that, sometimes, those shots with the camera moving and tracking give the actors the most freedom.

INTERVIEWER: *Do you ever shoot black and white?*

MENGES: I have shot in black and white, and I really enjoy it. I've taken a lot of stills. Still photography is very important to me. It's much more important to me than just a hobby; it's a part of my life. And my best still pictures have all been in black and white.

INTERVIEWER: *How is black and white different from color?*

MENGES: The tones in black and white are somehow more abstract, more simple. With color, you always have to be aware of the clash of color—how color can distract from the story you're trying to tell, from the graphic image you're trying to show.

I don't believe that lighting for black and white is easier. In a way, lighting for black and white is harder; it's much more complicated. In color, you can use just very soft light, and the tones are separated by their colors. But in black and white, they have to be separated by the lighting, by the contrast.

It's obvious that color is a richer palette, and color makes it possible to play with more visual elements. In many ways black and white is more discreet, particularly if you are doing a film with a director like Ken Loach. There, the faces in the story become more important than the background or the costume or the sets. The faces in black and white will stand out in a more simple and realistic sense than if you were shooting in color. But by the same token, I can't imagine *The Mission* being shot in black and white. So much of the strange beauty of that film would have been lost if it had been in black and white. For instance, the film I shot with Ken Loach called *Kes*—one of the films I'm most proud of—was shot in color; but I think in black and white the film would have had a more austere quality and would have been, in fact, a stronger film. But of course the commercial needs of the cinema always demand that a film be shot in color so that it can be released later on television, and the producer can guarantee that he'll recoup production costs.

> *"I think the cinema is very important because it can enrich people's lives, not denigrate them."*

INTERVIEWER: *How have new, faster film stocks affected the way you work?*

MENGES: I think the new stocks—such as the new Kodak 94 stock—have, like fast lenses, opened up the possibility of technicians being able to shoot films in a much freer way. For instance, night scenes in a film I shot for Steven Frers called *Bloody Kids* wouldn't have been possible without the fast stocks. So in that sense, they're very exciting. They're a new tool, a new dimension to the work of the cinematographer.

INTERVIEWER: *How involved do you get in lab work?*

MENGES: The relationship between the cameraman and the laboratory is terribly important. As a cameraman, it's very important to constantly be prepared to take risks. But it's also very important that the negative be strong enough to make dupe negatives and prints; if it's not, then there will be a serious problem. I try to have a strong negative, a well-exposed negative, so that the best possible print can be produced. You have to produce a negative that is aesthetically pleasing but that is also strong enough to produce good prints with good blacks.

Of course, when it comes to the grading, the liaison with the lab is vital because all the aspirations of the film depend on the work of the laboratory.

The success of the film is dependent on the lab's excellent processing of the negative and ability to print that negative well. So day by day, the reports that you get from the laboratory are incredibly important. Anybody who is interested in being a cameraman or director of photography should do their homework very well and have a good knowledge of the work of the laboratory, so they can produce the most excellent results. It's no good dreaming and having visions if the work is not printable when it's completed.

INTERVIEWER: *Do you like to use any particular camera?*

MENGES: The camera I mainly use is the Arriflex BL. Because it's small and it doesn't involve lots of boxes of equipment, I find it the ideal camera to work with. I feel it makes you much more mobile than with certain other cameras. Its registration is also very good. The particular lenses I like working with are the Cook lenses because I love their quality—the sharpness and the definition.

INTERVIEWER: *What was your first camera?*

MENGES: The first camera I ever used was a 16-mm Arriflex.

INTERVIEWER: *How did you get interested in film and photography?*

MENGES: My father spent many, many years working as a composer for the Old Vic Theatre in London. So my interest in the theater has always been considerable. And my interest in the cinema has been something that I remember from being very young indeed. I remember as a young lad seeing *Citizen Kane* and marveling at Orson Welles's astonishing film and being totally inspired by Gregg Toland's photography. And the films of Jean Vigo— *L'Atalante* and *Zéro de Conduite.*

INTERVIEWER: *What problems did you face when you were breaking into the business?*

MENGES: When I was about seventeen and had finished school, I was very fortunate in getting a job with an American documentary filmmaker called Allan Forbes. I worked with him for two years, cleaning the camera, running errands, making cups of tea, polishing boots—the same old story. And he introduced me to the cinema and to documentary filmmaking. After I'd been with Allan for two years, he went back to the United States. But he introduced me to quite a few filmmakers in Britain, and I went on to become a trainee assistant editor and then I became an assistant cameraman.

I worked with Allan King* and got involved with shooting a lot of documentaries, all shot hand-held, all shot totally freestyle. If we used any lights, we bounced lights off buildings. These were documentaries where sound was all-important. If you couldn't hear what people were saying, there was no point in shooting them. I learned very early the relationship between terrific sound and good photography, and about the moving, the observing, the hopefully sensitive camera recording events in documentary films. In those days, if I used lights I would always bounce them, always try to make them as unobtrusive as possible.

Then, in 1967, I got my first chance to work with Brian Probyn, who was the director of photography on *Poor Cow*, Ken Loach's first feature. It was quite an extraordinary experience. After I operated that film for Brian, Ken asked me to shoot his next feature film, *Kes*. That was probably the beginning of my career as a lighting cameraman. The thing about working with Ken is that you learn very, very quickly that he wants a very sensitive, quiet camera that isn't going to impose a style on the actors, on the script. It should quietly observe. It was tremendous training. It taught me to be very sensitive to the needs of the script and actors. In that sense, perhaps I didn't have the normal training of being the loader, the focus puller, and of being the operator and then becoming the cameraman.

I also spent two quite long periods with a documentary filmmaker called Adrian Cowell. Between 1963 and 1965, we went to Tibet and to Burma and made a film about the opium warlords and the opium trail in Burma's Shan state. On the first journey, we were away for a year and a half, and I went back again with Adrian in 1973 and spent another year and a half in Shan state, again making a film about how opium is brought from Shan state in Burma down through the jungle into northern Thailand. I spent considerable periods of time trapped in the jungle, working on documentaries, and away from my family.

Also during the period that I worked as a cameraman on feature films, I made six of my own documentary films. It's the only way to stay sane, to stay on an even keel. I feel that after trying to solve other people's problems, to go away and make your own documentary film gives you a lot of freedom and in a sense brings you back down to earth, away from all the razzmatazz of

---

* Canadian director of documentaries such as *Warrendale*, *Who Has Seen the Wind*, and *One Night Stand*.

making feature films. To just go quietly out with a tiny crew, with a hand-held camera, is very satisfying. I am always trying to make films from situations that I would learn from—for instance, a film about a family doctor in Wales, a documentary film about a traveling circus in the Midlands of England, or about a family living in Spanish Harlem in New York, or about a lawyer working in London.

INTERVIEWER: *Do you work on just one project at a time?*

MENGES: I went to an interview the other day with David Lean, who is one of our better directors in Britain, and he was saying that he could only think of one consuming idea for a film at a time. To be a producer, you have to think of about fifteen ideas at once. I feel more like David Lean; it's very hard to concentrate on many ideas at once. He's seventy-six now, I believe, and he's going to do *Nostromo*.

INTERVIEWER: *Who influenced you while you were learning the craft?*

MENGES: During my early training, one of my biggest influences in the style of photography was Raoul Coutard, the French cameraman. I think he taught many of us to look anew. From the United States, the films of Gordon Willis, Haskell Wexler, Conrad Hall, Vilmos Zsigmond, and from Europe, those of Sven Nykvist, Vittorio Storaro, and Giuseppe Rotunno are all very important influences for me, and another filmmaker in Britain, Kevin Brownlow,

> *"Regardless of who controls the cinema, there should be the freedom to create caring, thoughtful films."*

who made *Windstanleigh* and *It Happened Here*. I shot a number of documentary films for him. He used to show me the work of Charles Rosher and Gregg Toland. Kevin employed me to shoot a film for him about Abel Gance, who made, among other films, *Napoleon*. I went to Paris with Kevin to shoot an interview with Abel Gance. Gance was like D. W. Griffith, a giant. I think Kevin Brownlow taught me about the brilliance of the early cinema, about how the cinema could be free, about how the cinema could always be fresh.

The early films of Allan King were an inspiration to me. I remember Allan telling me that when you are shooting hand-held to avoid moving the camera to catch people talking. If you pan across a face and you miss the words, don't always worry about the words, because sometimes what people are doing is more important than what they are saying. Having watched someone doing something, you could always pan back gently to the person who is talking. He used to say, "Think. Listen. Observe. Try to capture." He thought it important to be very simple, to try to be calm and have a rhythm.

From what Allan said and from what other directors have said while I was learning, the style of the lighting and the way you hold and move the camera are questions of listening and observing and feeling what is going on around you. Don't divorce yourself. Don't let the equipment or the technique divorce you from the people whose story you're trying to tell when you are shooting documentaries. And the same thing goes for cinema. When you are on the set, listen to the director, listen to the actors, listen to the words. Feel where you are and let the feeling of what is happening around you dictate how you should go about the job of setting up the camera, where you should put the lights, and how you should perform in a particular situation.

INTERVIEWER: *Do any contemporary cinematographers influence your work?*

MENGES: I'm absolutely sure that many cinematographers have left deep impressions on the work I do. I don't think you work in a vacuum. You are enlivened by the experience of good camera work. There are two of Milos Forman's films that I absolutely adore—*Black Peter* and *Loves of a Blonde*.

INTERVIEWER: *How do you judge the success of your work?*

MENGES: It's very difficult to judge the success of work. I think I've done well when the director's truly pleased. And I'm continuously aware of the fact that I could have done a lot better.

INTERVIEWER: *What has been your most rewarding project?*

MENGES: It's difficult to know what my most rewarding project has been. I've mentioned *Kes* several times. It was the first film I shot, and I remember at the end of shooting that film the sadness of having to go, of having to leave, of having to stop. I think that's probably my most rewarding project. The film is about a boy from a mining community in Yorkshire and about what happens at his school and what happens at home. It was beautifully written by Barry Hines. It was brilliantly cast out of a local school by Ken Loach. The main lead was chosen out of a classroom of kids. There were no actors, but they were the most brilliant performances. Ken's ability to choose actors from among real people is phenomenal.

INTERVIEWER: *What role do you think film plays in society?*

MENGES: I think the cinema plays a vital role in life. Lenin said that out of all the arts, the cinema is the most important. I think the cinema at its best can enrich people's lives. For instance, I love working with Bill Forsyth* because his films do make me laugh. But I think the cinema is very important because some films can enrich people's lives, not denigrate them, and those are the kinds of films I would like to work on. I'm interested in the cinema that cares. I'm interested in the cinema that's passionate. I'm interested in the cinema that makes you laugh and the cinema that's epic.

INTERVIEWER: *Documentaries tend to deal with social and political concerns. Are you involved in any political activities?*

MENGES: Ah yes, politics. I am a member of the British Labour Party. All the films I've shot with Ken Loach—and there are many of them, documentaries and cinema films—are about the struggle of working people. I

Chris Menges and director Ken Loach.

* Scottish director whose films include *Local Hero* and *Comfort and Joy.*

think the cinema has a very important part to play in the development of people's political consciousness. But then I believe you can't live a life without actually making political decisions. If you decide to buy a South African orange, then I think you're supporting apartheid. Every day you have to make political decisions.

INTERVIEWER: *What are your ambitions?*

MENGES: To carry on being a part of telling stories, working with fine directors, and continuing to make films myself. I'm going to direct a feature next year. It's kind of a new role for me, but also an extension of my directing documentaries. I wouldn't want to stop shooting entirely, because I love photography and there are many directors I really like working with as a cameraman. I would love to do both.

INTERVIEWER: *Are you involved in any other creative activities?*

MENGES: Because of the history of my family—my father, my aunt, and my grandfather were all accomplished musicians—I care passionately about music. I read a great deal. I take a great many photographs. I care very much about my family.

INTERVIEWER: *What do you do to relax?*

MENGES: I like to spend time in the countryside near where I was born. I live on a tiny farm in the hills on the Welsh border. There we farm a few sheep, have a few ponies, and run a tiny farm without the use of pesticides. We encourage the wildflowers and plant trees. I live with my wife, Judy, and the children when I'm not away on jobs. The physical part of living on a small Welsh farm is very important to my mental happiness and my physical strength. It's a lot of hard work, too. It gives me the chance to get away from the cinema, to get away from almost the torture of working on a film, because making a film can be a very torturous experience. It gives me a chance for my mind and brain to relax. To be with the sky, the animals—to be with nature is incredibly enriching.

INTERVIEWER: *What would you like to see happen in the film business?*

MENGES: That's such a difficult question to answer, really. Ultimately, I suppose I am hoping that the projects with a lot of caring in them will actually be made. Cinema can so easily exploit people, it can be so voyeuristic and quite demeaning. Yet on the other hand, it can be terribly entertaining, very funny, and very thought-provoking. Regardless of who controls the cinema, there should be the freedom to create caring, thoughtful films.

Carol Littleton

EDITING

*B*orn in Oklahoma, Carol Littleton studied French literature at the University of Oklahoma, where she earned her bachelor's and master's degrees. She spent a year studying in France and was a Fulbright scholar in 1969.

Littleton moved to Los Angeles in 1970; she edited her first feature film in 1974. Her work can be seen in a number of memorable pictures, including French Postcards, Roadie, Body Heat, E.T., The Big Chill, Places in the Heart, Silverado, and Brighton Beach Memoirs.

Littleton is married to cinematographer John Bailey. They live in a modest stucco house perched on a steep hill overlooking Los Angeles, and it was there that I talked with Littleton about her editing career.

When I arrived they were finishing breakfast on the patio. We began the interview there, but because of a neighbor's chain saw we soon retreated to their study, a comfortable desert-colored room full of books and records. The house had recently been remodeled and they were still in the process of settling back in. I commented on the kachina dolls that graced

*shelves in the living room. Littleton mentioned their interest in American In-
dian and primitive art. As we talked about the Southwest, the movie* Silverado
came up.

LITTLETON: *Silverado* was shot at different locations around Santa Fe.
We were there for about four months. That was a wonderful experience. I love
the Southwest, the desert. It's so extraordinary to see such empty country.

INTERVIEWER: What was your last project?

LITTLETON: I worked on *Brighton Beach Memoirs,* Neil Simon's adaptation of his Broadway play, directed by Gene Saks. I finished it about a month
ago, but we're having two previews in August. Based upon audience reaction,
we either go ahead and cut the negative and answer-print it, or we'll make a
few changes first.

INTERVIEWER: Are these the director's previews?

LITTLETON: No, the film was produced by Ray Stark and he wanted to
have a couple of additional previews. We've already had one preview, around
the first of June. The film has been finished for quite some time and it's just
been sitting there. Ordinarily we would be in a hurry to finish, but the studio,
Universal, decided to release the film at Christmastime. In a way, having time
on our hands makes the film more difficult than having a short schedule.
Now, everybody has too much time to dream up ideas to make it a better film.

INTERVIEWER: How do you decide what particular project to work on?

LITTLETON: I hope that every film I do is different. *Brighton Beach
Memoirs* was the first adaptation from a play to a film that I'd worked on. Neil
Simon is probably our country's most popular playwright. I liked having the
opportunity to work on one of his plays, and this is, I think, one of his best.
Also, Gene Saks is probably Neil's best interpreter, so I had an opportunity to
work with both of them.

The most important element for me is the script, because editing is essentially rewriting. It's the final rewrite. If the script I'm offered has too many
problems, then I'll usually pass on it.

And it also has to be material I respond to. If it's something I can't relate
to, I would really hesitate to work on it. I couldn't be untrue to myself and
work on something I didn't believe in.

INTERVIEWER: *Is that because you become so emotionally involved with each project?*

LITTLETON: I don't know how you can avoid it. It's my life for anywhere from six to nine months, and it's very intense work during that time.

There are certain kinds of what you might call exploitative material that I'll probably never do. I'm very sensitive to the way women are treated in scripts, the kinds of roles that they have. I would avoid working on films that would be demeaning toward women. I don't think I could deal with that.

Another element besides the script is, of course, the director, because I work so closely with the director. My involvement in a film is almost as long as his or hers. If I feel we cannot understand one another, or we wouldn't be able to get along in some way, then I shouldn't do the picture. Directors sense that too, and in many ways they cast their editors much like they would cast an actor. They need to make sure it's someone with whom they can be totally vulnerable, someone whom they can trust completely. The editor has an important position. You are asked to do a lot of different

"Editing is essentially rewriting. It's the final rewrite."

things, from scheduling to making artistic decisions. Editing goes from pure mechanics to dealing with performances and restructuring the film, dealing with the heart of the picture.

INTERVIEWER: *How did you become involved in film?*

LITTLETON: Well, I was introduced to the notion of working in film when I met John. While I had always loved film, I didn't ever consider it as a possibility for a career until then. When I met John, he was at the USC cinema school as a graduate student. Listening to him talking about film and meeting his friends, I became more and more interested.

I was a French literature major at the time. I spent a year studying in Paris, and it was at the height of the French new wave. All those films were so exciting because they were so different from American films. I saw the same movie three and four times, ostensibly to hear the language. After a couple of times, I started looking at the movie—how it was put together, what it meant, why the new wave pictures were so different from what I'd been seeing in America. So all of those elements made me more and more interested in film.

When I moved out here in 1970, I decided I would like to work in film. I thought about going to film school, but John discouraged me. He thought I'd been in college long enough; God knows I had been! I just started getting odd jobs. I didn't really know precisely what I wanted to do. I started out as a script girl, then worked in the sound transfer department at a small film company. They did a lot of training and educational films and documentaries. By watching the editor there working, I began to realize that the movie is really made in the editing and I wanted to be a part of that process.

Editing fits my temperament. I was never happy on the set. There was too much confusion—so many people, so much noise. I really never felt like I was accomplishing anything. I rather liked the solitude of the cutting room—having the time to think and to try different things, tinker around with the film. I don't know if I found it or it found me, but eventually I started editing.

INTERVIEWER: *Did you receive all your training on the job?*

LITTLETON: Yes. I learned simply by doing. I had a lot of odd jobs, and each one of those odd jobs seems to have given me a set of very valuable skills. I worked transferring sound effects and became very familiar with the tools one needs for doing sound tracks. Then I worked on a lot of educational and documentary films, which give the editor almost total control over storytelling. They also had all the problems of managing huge amounts of footage.

I also worked as a commercial editor off and on for about five years. I would work just enough so I could save up enough money to do a dramatic piece for no pay at the AFI [American Film Institute]. Then, when I became destitute again, I'd go back and cut some more commercials, then I'd cut another short theatrical film, then cut more commercials, and so on. Commercials not only subsidized my first foray into dramatic filmmaking, but they also gave me a tremendous range of editing problems to solve. Commercials last thirty or sixty seconds, but what you have to know to edit them is virtually everything. Each time you do a commercial, one editor does everything: the music, the sound effects, the picture. And following the film through the laboratory, you have to become familiar with all the optical processes. In commercials, I became thoroughly acquainted with all of the tools an editor needs.

INTERVIEWER: *How did you make the switch from commercials to feature films?*

LITTLETON: I had a career in commercials. At one point I even had my own commercial postproduction company. It was very lucrative, and at a certain point I had to make a decision: Did I want to stay in commercials, or did I really want to get involved in dramatic film? Then one day I just said, "That's it. I'm not doing commercials anymore; I'm doing films now."

I didn't work for about six months, but I had made the decision. I saw friends who were commercial editors dreaming about the day when they would be theatrical editors, and not one of them had made the transition. They were in their forties and fifties and I was in my early thirties, and I could see I was headed for the same thing unless I made the big decision and just jumped into it.

INTERVIEWER: *Why do you think you have been so successful?*

LITTLETON: I would have to say that I've been extremely lucky. I have a husband who is very supportive of my career. John and I have worked it out between us for both of us to have a career. We've been very supportive and very nurturing of each other.

I haven't had some of the problems that a lot of women do have. Many women have had families first and then a career or have tried to do both at once. That's one reason why it's been a little easier for me. But most of all I've been very lucky. I've been at the right place at the right time.

I've been very clear about what I want to do. There's been no confusion about the kinds of films I've wanted to work on. Unfortunately, being obsessive and having a monomania can be terrible personality traits, but insofar as one needs those traits to edit a film, I hope I can be forgiven. When I'm dealing with a problem, I stay with it until it's solved. When I want something, I simply stay with it until I get it.

Another element could be that I'm really not a fearful person. The first film job I got in editing was working on Alan Rudolph's first picture, before he worked with Robert Altman. As an assistant director at Paramount, Alan saved and bought short ends until he had enough film to shoot a script that he had written. Richard Patterson was the editor, and he needed an assistant. I asked Alan if I could be the assistant, and he said, "What do you know about working in an editing room?" He knew very well that I had never even walked into one before.

And I said, "Well, I know nothing about it."

"What makes you think you're qualified to do this?" he said.

"I want to."

And he said, "I'll tell you what—it's perfect. I can't pay you any money and you don't know anything, so I guess it's even, isn't it?"

So I went to Larry Edmund's bookstore, bought a textbook on cutting technique, and the first day syncing dailies I took the book, opened it to where it described dailies, and read the instructions on how to sync dailies. I only had about a thousand feet of film, but it took me all day. When we went to the screening room to look at the dailies, I was sweating bullets—I was so afraid it would be out of sync, but it worked.

There was an old-time editor, Michael Luciano, down the hall from me, and he came in and said, in his Italian accent, "Sweetheart, do you need some help here? Any time you need to ask a question, I'll show you what needs to be done." Which he did. I learned a little at a time.

> *"The days run anywhere from fourteen to sixteen hours, depending on the requirements of the job."*

By virtue of working on that film, *Premonition*, I knew that editing was what I wanted to do. I loved editing films. I really loved life in the cutting room.

INTERVIEWER: *What kind of editing equipment do you work on?*

LITTLETON: I learned to cut first on a Moviola and then, because a lot of commercial directors like to use the KEM, I learned to use the KEM and have used it ever since. For me, it's a more flexible machine to use. There's much less wear and tear on the operator! The upright Moviola is a very versatile machine—there have been great pictures cut on it—but if you can work on a more sophisticated machine, why not?

INTERVIEWER: *What sort of person makes a good film editor?*

LITTLETON: If you were to meet fifty editors, each would be different. I don't know what personality traits they have in common. But as far as one's approach to the material, I think it has to be a good mixture of an analytical approach—understanding characterization, structure, and so forth—and an emotional approach—being able to let yourself go and enjoy the movie as a fresh experience each time you work on it, so that you become a member of the audience, enjoying the picture. You have to be able to have one set of eyes for one set of problems and a different set of eyes for the enjoyment of the project. It's sort of an odd combination, but I think that combination is what makes a successful editor.

INTERVIEWER: *What's the most satisfying part of editing?*

LITTLETON: I like the storytelling part of cutting film. This fits in with my interest in literature that I've had all along. Somehow, editing seems like a perfect marriage of both of the things that mean the most to me—film and literature. Having the opportunity to edit film and being able to use both of those skills and interests has been rewarding.

INTERVIEWER: *Do you still read a lot?*

LITTLETON: As much as I can, yes. I likewise have very eclectic tastes in reading. I love to read. It's my favorite pastime.

INTERVIEWER: *Do you write any stories yourself?*

LITTLETON: I did quite a lot when I was in college, but for some reason I have not had the urge to write—perhaps because so much of what I enjoyed in writing I've been able to use in editing. So I don't feel like I've lost the opportunity to tell stories.

INTERVIEWER: *Do you have any other creative outlets?*

LITTLETON: Well, I love to garden, but I don't know how creative gardening is. I think because I'm enclosed in a dark room for so many hours, I feel liberated when I can get outside. I do a great deal of gardening and I'm very interested in nature and the outdoors. I'm now redesigning and rebuilding the garden that was destroyed when the house was remodeled. There are some vegetables down below, but it's mostly cactus and succulents. I'm very envious of the Huntington Gardens. I'll take a trip to the Huntington Library and look at their cactus garden, then come back and have my reverie, figuring out what I can do with my postage-stamp-size yard. Cacti remind me of little sculptures. They don't look so much like plants as they do some strange accidents of nature.

John and I also have a little cabin up in the mountains north of here, in the high desert. We go there as often as we can. It gives us a chance to be outside, in the wild. The contrast to our urban lives is invigorating.

INTERVIEWER: *It must be a terrific problem in your home life, being married to a cinematographer.*

LITTLETON: It is difficult. We both have made an effort to be home like this at the same time. I finished editing *Brighton Beach* in June, and John finished Paul Schrader's new picture—I think they're calling it *Light of Day*—in May. We decided to create some time for ourselves now, a bit of a vacation to get settled back into our house.

When I work in New York, I am there for six to nine months. When I am on location during shooting, I can be away from L.A. for three or four months. Practically all of John's films are on location. So we can be separated for anywhere from three to nine months of the year. Some years are good, some years are bad. Our last vacation was in 1980. Separation—maybe that's the secret to a successful marriage in the film business!

INTERVIEWER: *Do you ever visit each other on location when things are slow with one of you?*

LITTLETON: When John was working on Paul Schrader's picture in Chicago, I was able to go there on three weekends. I was in New York at the time, and that's a short trip. When John was in Japan doing *Mishima*, I was in New York doing *Places in the Heart*. We didn't get together for about six months. That was a long, long time to be separated.

The best arrangement is to work on the same picture. That way, not only do we have the film in common, but we also have time together. We try to do that whenever possible. Twice, Larry Kasdan has been brave enough to hire both of us on the same picture: on *The Big Chill* and *Silverado*. And then John shot *Brighton Beach Memoirs*. Early on, the first two films I did with the director Karen Arthur, John did those also.

INTERVIEWER: *Is there any type of picture you're partial to, or that you seem to do more than others?*

LITTLETON: Well, if I look at all the pictures that I've done, I've done a fair amount of comedies, dramatic films, blockbuster movies, and little films.

I wish I could say that I'm attracted to one type of film more than others, but I can't. I love to do comedies—they're difficult. But, on the other hand, I enjoyed doing *Body Heat* very much. It was a drama in the tradition of tough dames and tough guys.

I guess I'm very eclectic in my tastes. In a sense, I'm attracted by a film because it's unique, unusual. I'm more likely to get involved with an oddball project because it affords me a new experience as an editor.

Of course, you have to deal with schedules—what's available to do when I'm available, whether or not I want to overlap pictures or take a long break. Being free lance, you have a bit more control over that part of your life. All of those elements enter into making a decision.

INTERVIEWER: *Do you work with one director more than others?*

LITTLETON: Well, I've had repeat performances with several directors. I've worked more with Lawrence Kasdan than with anyone else. I'll probably be doing his next picture, which will be the fourth for me. I like working with Larry very much, and I like the continuity of working in a relationship that is immediately understood.

There are other directors whom I've worked with, like Robert Benton, Steven Spielberg, and Karen Arthur. We have tried to work together again, but for some reason the projects and schedules have never been synchronous.

INTERVIEWER: *Do you ever have a problem keeping a healthy distance from the material you're working on so you can judge it properly?*

LITTLETON: I guess I had that problem on one film. The schedule was so short that I never had enough time to think about the film. I was just so involved with getting it finished. The most valuable time is usually toward the end of the editing process, when a lot of the minor problems have been ironed out and you're able to look at the film several times in projection—show it to audiences and have time to think about it, sift through it. I never had that time on *Silverado.*

"I don't consider the editing room a place where dark, mysterious alchemy is taking place."

It wasn't a question of losing perspective as much as it was not having enough time to think. With Hollywood films, that's the big problem. Schedules are becoming more and more reduced. Producers translate the number of man-hours it takes to get a film finished. But it doesn't work that way. We're not manufacturing tires. We're not stamping out cookies. It's so much more than a mechanical process. You can't just feed it through a hopper and have it be done, although some films look like they were done that way.

INTERVIEWER: *What are some of the biggest problems you face in the cutting room?*

LITTLETON: The biggest problems are all generated by shortened schedules. Whether I have six months to edit a film or nine months, I still work the same way. I don't know how else to do it. I haven't been able to find any shortcuts. If I have to do a film in six months, I end up working seven days a week, twelve to fourteen hours a day. I'll do the same amount of work, just in a shorter time. That becomes very exhausting. How do you make up three months? The only way you can do it is to hire another editor or do all of it yourself and pack the days and hours as tight as you can. You're just running on adrenaline. That's why I'm getting gray hair.

The main problem with a shortened schedule is that you do not have time to think. The time it takes to mechanically put the pieces of film together is actually pretty quick. But what takes more time and effort is thinking about a sequence as an isolated sequence and then thinking about the film as a whole and how it could be more concise, more effective emotionally: what kind of music needs to be used, or concepts of sound that would be more effective for one scene or another; transitions, which always take a great deal of time—how to make the film seamless; which performances are in trouble and need to be helped. There are just a lot of problems that take a great deal of thought. And they're all connected; they're not isolated problems. One performance can be weak and affect the narrative of the film. Many times you'll have to keep scenes in the film that you'd love to drop, because those scenes have essential storytelling points. You are constantly weighing the value of one problem against another problem or the value of a brilliant performance that may take the film in the wrong direction. You have to exert a certain level of discipline.

The other problem is that usually the studio or the producers or the production manager wants you to write out, even before they start shooting the picture, a postproduction schedule. This is a difficult task. In a case like that, I try to tell the production manager, "I know we have to deliver the film on a certain date. But between the time the film is shot and the date we have to deliver it, we may not be exactly on schedule—we may float a few days to accommodate problems. But the film will be delivered on time." I believe in being responsible and making deadlines; I've never missed one. But the feeling that everything must be on schedule every minute can put a stranglehold on a film.

INTERVIEWER: *Do you always work as the picture is being shot, or have you cut pictures after the shooting's finished?*

LITTLETON: I've always worked in situations where I start with the first day of shooting and I'm cutting as closely behind the production as possible. If I'm on location I can have a gap of four or six days, depending on how long it takes the film to get to the lab and back to me, and who has to see the film. If I'm in L.A., I'm usually three or four days behind the shooting. So, the director can look at sequences as they've been cut. Certain evaluations can be dealt with as soon as possible: Is the performance what was intended—does it serve the picture? Do we have enough coverage? Can a scene be dropped? Can scenes be combined?

INTERVIEWER: When you're cutting along with the shooting, what kind of schedule do you keep?

LITTLETON: On *Brighton Beach Memoirs,* the call on the set was usually 7:00. A car would come by and pick me up at 6:30 in the morning. I like to start cutting when the crew starts shooting. It makes my day as long as theirs, and I feel I'm in touch more. We would have a lunch break at 1:00. We would look at dailies and eat lunch at the same time. Then at 2:00 we would be back on the set and work until 7:00 or 8:00 at night. Later the director would come in and I would show him what I had cut that day. By the time I got home it would be 9:00 or 9:30.

Now, on location, it's more involved. On *Silverado,* in Santa Fe, I would start cutting at 7:00 A.M., but at lunch the crew would be out on location away from Santa Fe. When they returned at around 7:00 or 8:00 at night, we would look at dailies, and afterwards I would look at cut film with the director. It would be about 10:00 or 10:30 by the time I'd be finished for the day.

Carol Littleton at work on a flatbed editing machine.

So the days run anywhere from fourteen to sixteen hours, depending on the requirements of the job. When they're shooting, I have to deal with the film as dailies every day as well as the cut footage for that day. Once we're no longer shooting, I'm not concerned with dailies, and the days get shorter, about ten to twelve hours, which is a regular schedule.

INTERVIEWER: *Are you usually the only editor working on a film?*

LITTLETON: I will do everything I possibly can to be the only editor on a picture, not because I'm egomaniacal, but because I have enough faith in my-self and the editing process. A film works best when the director and one editor work on it together. The product of two minds is greater than the product of either mind, but when you have additional picture editors, you start to lose the point of view.

> *"I think we have to take responsibility ethically for what is put on the screen."*

INTERVIEWER: *Is there a certain kind of crew that you like to work with?*

LITTLETON: I like to work with two assistants. I work on a KEM, and there's a great deal of organization needed to get the film into what I call KEM rolls. They are organized with the widest shots—the masters—first, and then all of the two shots and singles. Once the film has been edited, the trims and outs are cut back into the KEM rolls so that everything is kept on its original roll. If there's a lot of film, I also have an apprentice on the crew.

I don't like using more than three or four people, because then there's too much chatter and not enough work. I like to keep the socializing in the cutting room to a minimum.

INTERVIEWER: *As an editor, are you ever caught in the middle of political disputes?*

LITTLETON: That's never happened to me. Either I'm stupid and I don't understand when there are disputes, or we've been able to work in such a way that people feel satisfied, or I've worked with directors who are strong enough to clearly delineate what they want to do before the picture starts and there-fore there are no surprises. It's probably a combination of the above. To date, I've never had a problem with a studio wanting to take a picture away from me, or a producer and director fighting over their cuts.

I think the most important thing in editing is that you never show a cut until you feel you don't have to defend it. If you can show a cut and say, "This is what we are trying to achieve," and talk about it ahead of time, you have very few disputes. Clarity is my best ally.

For instance, in the first cut—the assemblage of all the scenes—nothing is deleted. If the director wants to invite the producer or people from the studio, I find it's the best policy to make it very, very clear what the first cut represents. And likewise for the subsequent cuts—there are anywhere from six to twenty, depending on the picture. Each time it's best to explain ahead of time what you are trying to achieve with the particular cut, what you feel the problems are. In being clear, not only do they understand what you are trying to do, but they also feel they're participating. When people feel they are participating in a project, that nothing's being hidden from them and it's clearly a work in progress, their expectations are not too high and they don't feel they are being manipulated. That's one reason why I've never had any problems.

I don't consider the editing room a place where dark, mysterious alchemy is taking place. I feel that, first of all, there's very little magic involved, and the more people know, the more they understand, the better off everything is. I've known editors who are extremely secretive and use the editing room for power plays and become very egomaniacal about their work. I think that's just not the best way to work. I like a very free, open spirit in talking about the film. If people have ideas, I like them to present those ideas.

I have a role to play as an editor. I am not doing my own movie; I am interpreting the director's movie. There's a great deal of myself in it, undoubtably, but I need to understand the director's point of view—what he or she needs to do—and execute it as best as possible. At any time I will give my opinions, sometimes to a fault. At a certain point directors will get so exasperated they'll say, "You are the most stubborn woman in the world!" Until someone tells me to stop, I will always go for what I think is best. But for the most part, editing is truly collaborative.

INTERVIEWER: *Who do you work with on a film besides the director?*

LITTLETON: Hollywood films are not made by just one editor. In addition to my editing crew, there's the supervising sound editor, whom I work with very closely. He or she has a very large crew, often as many as twelve to twenty editors.

Sound editors are generally not appreciated for what they do. They make an extraordinary contribution to a picture. Have you ever seen a gun-fight without the sound? On *Silverado*, we had several screenings before the sound was actually cut. We put in just enough sound effects to compile a temporary sound track. The biggest surprise was looking at the film after we had our sound mix and realizing how violent the picture was. For the first time, we had all of the gunshots and the ricochets, the body hits, the body falls. It was too violent. The sound made it so much more convincing. It really surprised me. We had to redub certain sequences to tone down the violence.

So much can be brought to a movie through the sound—the score, the sound effects, and very clear, audible dialogue.

Then there's the music. I never underestimate the dramatic value of music. While editing the picture, I always use a temporary score as a guide for pace and rhythm. When the music editor joins my staff, I try to communicate the musical values of the picture.

INTERVIEWER: *How do you feel after a film you've worked on is released?*

LITTLETON: I guess I look at the films I've worked on in a strange way, as if they are my little children. You nurse them along and finally they are on their feet, on their own. There's nothing quite as thrilling as going to a regular movie theater on a Friday or Saturday night a month or so after the picture's been released and just watching people enjoy the picture. It's such a delightful experience. It's very, very rewarding to think that people can be frightened or happy, or be intent or be entertained, reacting to decisions I've made all along the way.

INTERVIEWER: *When you go to the theater, do you watch critically or do you enjoy it?*

LITTLETON: I'm just a sucker; I enjoy it. I don't think of myself as an editor when I go to watch a movie in the theater. I go as a member of the audience—I love it. I laugh, I cry, I get involved, I sit on the edge of my seat. I'm like a kid each time I go to a movie.

To some extent, you need to keep that when you're working on a picture. That's difficult because you look at the film a jillion times. But you are analyzing and looking at different problems each time you look at it. It's a complex process. At the first cut, you're working with one set of problems, and as the refinements progress, you're working with different problems. It changes every day.

A lot of people ask me, "How can you stand to stay in the cutting room for as long as you do? Doesn't it get boring?" Frankly, it doesn't, because I'm not in the room; I'm in the picture. And I'm involved in the problems and, hopefully, in the solutions to the problems. That's simply fascinating to me. I'm never bored.

INTERVIEWER: *How do you feel about the role of film in our society?*

LITTLETON: Film is, as we all know, an extraordinarily powerful medium. It presents so many ideas and attitudes. Our own fantasies create ideas in other people's minds. Governments have used film very successfully as propaganda. It's very powerful stuff. In many ways, I think we have to take responsibility ethically for what is put on the screen. Film is far too powerful for us not to think about that.

"I only have twenty-five more films I can do. I want each one of them to be important to me."

Even now, we're entering a postliterate age when people do not receive ideas from reading as much as they do from powerful images. And it is not only the narrative that is powerful, it's also the juxtaposition of unrelated images. Today's audiences are visually sophisticated; new approaches to editing are becoming accepted as a kind of vocabulary that even two or three years ago would have been considered incoherent.

INTERVIEWER: *You can change the meaning of a picture by changing what you see before or after it.*

LITTLETON: Absolutely. You see that on a daily basis when you're cutting a film. A sequence can be channeled in a different emotional direction simply by either moving that sequence to a different place or cutting to a seemingly unrelated object and thereby creating a new relationship.

There was a great Russian-American editor, Slavko Vorkapisch, who studied film in Russia under Eisenstein. He did a lot of the old-fashioned montages—the calendar pages ripping off to show the passage of time, the travel montages of the train wheels, and all that. He taught at USC and I was able to go to some of his lectures. He talked about and analyzed the power of editing, the power of one image juxtaposed against another. It's more than a theory; a cut controls a connection between the mind and the image.

When you see a movie like *Rambo*, you can see what we are talking about. That's really exemplary of the kind of power film editing has, however primitive the meaning may be.

INTERVIEWER: *You feel that there's a lot of political content in film, then.*

LITTLETON: An awful lot. You could even say American film has been the most powerful tool Western culture has used—as an apology, or as an example of itself. Throughout the world, cultures can embrace our fantasies and accept them for truths; they do that all the time. Or they can see how American–Western culture is exemplified in American film and reject it. It's amazing. You go to a little village in Mexico and they have the TV turned on and are watching *Dallas*. Now what does that do to their minds? What can it mean? Out of social context, it obviously doesn't mean the same as it does to me, for example. I can look at *Dallas* and see it as a pastiche or a soap opera or something else. But in a different culture, what can it mean?

Whether we accept it or not, we have a tremendous social responsibility. I know how editors can manipulate film to get the responses they want. That's what we do. But we have to be very careful. The violence one sees on the screen can breed violence in an unformed mind. For those of us who work on films, the choices we make as to what films to work on *do* make a difference.

INTERVIEWER: *It must be very gratifying when you think you have fulfilled that responsibility.*

LITTLETON: Yes, it is. The thing about film is that it affords the people who work on films a vicarious experience as well. Maybe we're all a bit Walter Mittyish.

Films affect us as well as affecting the audience. I worked on *Brighton Beach Memoirs* and have nothing whatsoever in common with the experience of the characters. And yet for eight or nine months I was able to live the experience of an immigrant Jewish family in New York in 1937. I'm not from New York. I'm not Jewish. I wasn't even alive in 1937, and yet I experienced it. It was a very valuable experience that enriched my life. I'm a better person for having had the experience. I had a great deal of compassion for the family in the movie, and now I can see beyond my own experience.

Personally, it's very gratifying to me. And apart from being wonderfully entertaining and very moving, I would hope a film's ability to open up another world would work for the audience as well.

I'm from Oklahoma, and when I worked on *Places in the Heart*, I was reminded of common experiences. I could relate to the film on totally personal

terms. I understood the film completely. The story of Edna's life is very similar to my grandmother's. I was able to relive my own family's experience. The
film became a kind of therapy. I was liberated from certain aspects of my
early formative years by having worked on it.

So beyond the experience of film editing, there's also the experience of
the film—the actual material. You cannot be removed from it. And it's pretty
exciting to have your work also be meaningful to your life.

I examine very carefully the films I consider doing. I do about one a
year. If I have about twenty-five years of cutting ahead of me, I only have
twenty-five more films I can do. If I have a choice, I want to exercise that
choice. I want each one of them to be important to me.

.

Thom Noble

EDITING

Born in London, Thom Noble was educated at West-minster School. After a stint in the Royal Air Force, he began his film career by reading novels and writing reports commenting on their suitability for adaptation to the screen.

Noble worked extensively in Europe, wending his way through the film editing community, before coming to Los Angeles in 1978. The films he has cut include Fahrenheit 451, And Now for Something Completely Different, The Apprenticeship of Duddy Kravitz, North Dallas Forty, First Blood, Uncommon Valor, Red Dawn, Witness *(for which he received an Oscar),* Poltergeist II, *and* The Mosquito Coast.

The Saul Zaentz Company Film Center resides in a featureless white building in Berkeley, California, not far from San Francisco Bay. I met Noble in the lobby of the studio. We decided to do the interview in his cutting room, amid the clutter of editing paraphernalia and the curtains of celluloid from the film in progress, The Mosquito Coast. *Noble slipped off his long overcoat and settled into a comfortable chair. He wore denim and what appeared to be American Indian jewelry of a modest sort. What sticks in my mind, however, are his bright red leather shoes. At the extremity of such a tall, thin body, they made quite a statement.*

As we talked, Noble often became quite animated. He would sit on the edge of his chair or seem to hover just off it, his arms flailing the air to capture an anecdote's emotional pitch. Periodically, he ran his hands back through his unruly gray hair. He gave the unmistakable impression of someone hopelessly in love with his work. He's an enthusiastic, gregarious person who delights in the sometimes sordid, often exhilarating collaboration that is making a movie.

INTERVIEWER: *Back in England you were originally in the publishing business. What led you from there to film editing?*

NOBLE: I had this affliction—in the dictionary it's called proofreader's delusion. When you go through a book with obvious mistakes, your eye corrects them for you. You just move on and never notice them. At that time, a friend of mine, John Bloom, whom I had known since I was nine—and who won an Oscar in 1984 for editing *Gandhi*—was working for the story department at Pinewood Studios.* He was reading books to see if they'd make good movies or not. He asked me, Why not join him there?

Well, that sounded perfect. It was, except that I had to write the reports. My typing was nonexistent. I would read the books in three hours, and then it would take me three days to type the report. I thought, This is insane. I was making absolutely nothing, as I was being paid by the book.

I called them and said, "This isn't working out. How can I earn a bit more?" They said, "By reading foreign books. What languages do you speak?" I told them French, German, Italian, and Spanish, although actually I only spoke the first two. But having been to a school devoted to the classics, I figured I could get by in Italian and Spanish.

When I realized this wasn't working, I started making up entire stories. At the end of the report, of course, I'd have to put, "This would make a terrible movie. It has nothing going for it." There must be authors all over Europe who never got their books made into English movies simply because I had made up these preposterous stories. I thought, in hindsight, Suppose someone had actually liked one of my stories? And then decided to buy the book! But then I

---

* Located 17 miles northwest of London, it was founded in 1935 by industrialists
Charles Boot and J. Arthur Rank as Britain's answer to Hollywood.

thought, That's what happens with movies anyway. People are constantly buying books for movie scripts and altering them so completely that the author doesn't recognize them.

So I did this for a while. Then John decided to move into editing films. He called me up and said, "You'd really love this." Well, I talked with him about it and then I joined a company. The company was run by a couple of weird brothers who were basically operating hotels and for some reason were making a TV series as well, about a very suave, one-armed detective named Mark Saber.

INTERVIEWER: Did you have any problem getting into the union?

NOBLE: I immediately applied to join the union. My friend had said it would be no problem. He said he could get me in during the summer, when everybody in the union was working. Nonunion people could actually get in. Nobody would oppose you because they needed the staff. But I started in September, and my union application didn't come up for approval until December. These brothers I worked for had figured out that if they fired everybody just before Christmas and reengaged them in the new year, they wouldn't have to pay them for those few weeks when nobody does any work.

> *"Some people in features are totally against working in commercials. It's like the lowest thing you could do."*

The English union has this rule that you have to be actually working when your application comes up. Of course, I was laid off on the eighth of December and the application came up on the eleventh! But everybody said, "Don't worry; by the new year everything will be all right."

Well, the new year came and the union said, "I'm sorry—there are a lot of people out of work now. All the people on the roster have to go ahead of you." The company called up every assistant editor that was on the roster and none of them wanted the job. I called the union and told them about this, and they said, "That doesn't matter; the job has to be circularized through all the people who are affiliated with the guild, in case they want it." They did that, and somebody in a laboratory decided they might like working in the cutting room and took the job. January and February came and went, and I couldn't get a job. I thought this was very unfortunate. I wanted to stay in this business somehow; I was actually enjoying it.

I found a documentary company that didn't worry about unions, and I got a job with them for about six or seven months. Then the film librarian there left, and the company decided to give me the job because I'd be in a branch of the union and would then be able to easily change branches. Well, they circularized the job: "Film librarian wanted with a fluent knowledge of Russian and Swahili." It was brilliant. Naturally, nobody applied for the job except me. So I got the job.

And when it was time to go in and renew my union card for the next year, I told the union, "There's actually been a little error. Here where it says assistant librarian, it should really be assistant editor." They said, "Oh, our mistake." And they put down assistant editor and stamped the thing.

INTERVIEWER: *What sort of things did you work on in those early days?*

NOBLE: From the time I got into the union, things took off. I had met a guy, Kevin Connor, who is now over here directing *North and South* for TV. He was then an assistant editor on a feature film; he was doing a documentary just to fill in. He said, "How would you like to work on a feature when I do my next one? I'll be the first assistant and you be the second." So I did two features as a second assistant.

Then he got a job in Singapore while we were working on a picture. He said, "I'm going to recommend that you get upgraded to first assistant because I have to leave the picture now."

The editor said, "Fine, I'm sure Thom can handle the job. We'll just get another second assistant."

So when this editor did his next film, he said, "Come and be my first assistant." That was great. I think I did about four pictures as a first assistant, all in England.

The last one was a picture with Terence Young. Because *Tom Jones* had been so successful, they adapted a similar novel by Defoe into a movie called *The Amorous Adventures of Moll Flanders*. At one point the editor was off somewhere, and Terence wanted to see something cut together, so the only person who was able to do it was me—the understudy being called up. So I cut it together, and he liked what I'd done.

After *Moll Flanders*, Terence called me and said he had a picture he wanted me to cut. I thought it was amazing! But it would have been impossible for me to leave the picture I was on. I had just started *Arabesque*, a big, big picture with a lot of special effects that I was in charge of ordering.

But toward the end of *Arabesque*, strangely enough, I got a call from the guy who had been the associate producer on *Moll Flanders*, a friend of Terence's named Mickey Delamar. He said, "I'm down here in the south of France with this French director and we're looking for an editor. Would you be interested?" I said, "Who's the director?" And he said, "You've probably never heard of him. His name's François Truffaut." I said, "What!" And he said that the next time they were in England maybe I could meet with them.

About six weeks later, I was working at Pinewood Studios and the phone rang. "I've got François here. We're in the art department, going through some sketches. Why don't you come over and meet him? And just one other thing: He doesn't speak a word of English." I thought, Well, that's no problem. I speak French. So I went over and there was this little guy smoking his Gauloises and biting his fingernails. He was tiny. And he was speaking to me in French, and I was understanding everything. But then I realized that I couldn't think of a sentence to put together in French! I was just sort of nodding, letting him do all of the talking. And this was hugely embarrassing. Everything I wanted to say, how much I loved *Jules and Jim* . . . nothing!

So, we shyly said goodbye to each other, and as I closed the door all the French came back to me. I thought to myself, Well, you blew it. You had the opportunity of a lifetime. You'd have gone from being a first assistant to editing a film by François Truffaut. That was in October. In November I heard that Truffaut was interviewing all kinds of people—established editors like Tony Gibbs.*

Well, on New Year's Eve, the phone rang very late. It was Mickey Delamar and he said, "I'm glad I got you. I just wanted to tell you happy new year and you got the picture." I said, "What!"

"Yes, yes. We've been seeing a lot of people, but finally François decided that you were the one. Get your crew together and I'll see you at Pinewood."

I had something like three weeks to get ready, so I played French tapes all day and spent a lot of time thinking to myself in French.

Then I met Truffaut again and we started working on *Fahrenheit 451*. Finally, the time came when I said, "I have to ask you. It's been in the back of my mind all this time. Why me?" "Well," he said, "you know, I interviewed a lot of editors. They all said how much they loved *Jules and Jim* and my other films.

* Noted British editor whose films include *Tom Jones, The Knack, The Loved One,* and *A Bridge Too Far.*

They were gushing all over me. But you were so nice, so shy, so reticent. I really liked you."

INTERVIEWER: *What was it like working with Truffaut?*

NOBLE: We had a great working relationship. I'd never really cut a film before. But we had a great time. He wasn't calling every shot. He wouldn't pick takes. I'd cut the film the way I thought it should be, we'd look at it, and he'd say, "Oh, that works well," or "I wanted this and this and this." And I'd say, "Fine," and change it around.

> "A lot of people that I know basically live in the cutting room. That's their world."

But an incredible thing happened. He and Oskar Werner fell out. He couldn't even bear to see Oskar Werner on the screen smiling. So when we'd go through the cut of the film, we'd see Oskar and he'd say, "Oh! I can't stand that man! Look, when they sit down and start to speak, let's cut to Julie Christie because I can't bear to see this man."

So the whole film was cut in this way. I thought, God, this is an insane way to be doing this. But, why not? I mean, it's teaching me something, right? That you can actually totally manipulate a picture—cut it on another person entirely when you don't want to see them.

In a way, I know why it happened. They had had a great time on *Jules and Jim*. Then Oskar had gone to America and made *Ship of Fools*, a gigantic film with love scenes with Simone Signoret. His head just became enormous. So when he came back to this little French director, he became absolutely impossible. To Truffaut, it was almost the betrayal of a lifetime.

There was one wonderful occasion—near the end of the picture, we realized we needed a closeup shot of Oskar's hands. So Truffaut decided to go around the crew and pick the person with the worst hands—the ugliest hands, covered in nicotine stains—that he could find to do this insert shot! It was amazing.

INTERVIEWER: *Once you've worked with a particular director, do you continue to work with him or her?*

NOBLE: That's what normally happens, yes. There are people who have made lifetime careers out of working with one director. But in my case, we came to the end of the film, and François was all set to do *The Bride Wore*

Black. It was going to be in English like *Fahrenheit*. Then the reviews of *Fahrenheit* came out and said that the problem with the film was that François did not understand the English language sufficiently to make a go of it. Truffaut felt really upset by this. Yet he thought that they were probably right. Why was he making films in English and not in his own language? So *The Bride Wore Black* became *La Mariée Était en Noir*. That meant it would be a totally French production and I was no longer concerned.

INTERVIEWER: *What was your next project?*

NOBLE: Everyone had said to me, "However difficult it was to get your first film, the second film is a nightmare. Nobody knows you've cut the first one—it isn't out. You can't go back to being an assistant, so you're in an incredible limbo." And indeed it was true. After *Fahrenheit*, there was nothing; nobody called. Then an editor I knew called me and said, "I have a chance of doing a Sinatra picture but I'm in a bit of a bind." He was also in negotiations with some other people who were making a spy picture with a Romanian director, an ex-opera singer. He asked me if I would go and be interviewed. I told him, "Yes, I'm just sitting here waiting for the phone to ring."

So I talked to them and I knew right away that I didn't want to do the film. The more I said, "I don't think I'm the person for this," the more they wanted me to do it. They said, "Is it the money?" I'd done *Fahrenheit* for 55 pounds a week, and they were offering me 120. I kept thinking, I don't want to do this picture; someone is going to call me. But nobody called.

So I whacked the money up to about 150, accepted, signed the contract, and the next week the phone rang. "We've got this big picture with Peter O'Toole, *The Great Catherine*, and we'd love you to do it." From that week on, the phone kept ringing.

I ended up doing the spy picture. It was terrible. But in a way it was wonderful to do, because they didn't know what they were doing and I was always cutting my way out of situations—making things work that should never have worked. It was perfect training.

INTERVIEWER: *What kind of editing problems did you have doing that picture? What did you learn?*

NOBLE: The actor in the picture had a terrible drinking problem. And they couldn't really shoot with him after lunch. His lines were terrible, and he would sit down like a sack of potatoes. So I could never cut to him sitting down, which is what you usually do. People tend to cut on movement. From a wide shot, as the person sits down, you cut into the close-up of them. So I was always cutting to people watching him sit down. Then I'd cut to him, when he got himself together. It was a wonderful lesson in cutting. At the time I didn't even realize it.

And another time, my sound editor came in and said to me, "This is incredible. This is innovative what you're doing here. I've heard of people overlapping sound but never doing it frontward." I had been fooling around, and I thought it would be interesting if, when you heard somebody's dialogue, you heard it first while you saw the person they were talking to. But he said, "It is interesting, but you've got to look out. You seem to be doing it to everything." So these were things I was picking up and learning all the time. It was a real experience.

INTERVIEWER: *Have you ever cut commercials?*

NOBLE: Yes. First I did another picture for Westinghouse, who had done that spy picture after *Fahrenheit.* After that, I decided to fill in by cutting commercials. It was incredible. It was great training. What you have to say in thirty seconds is amazing. You can get away with things in cutting that you'd normally never do in features.

And some people in features are totally against working in commercials—as if it's the lowest thing you could do. It would be better to go down to the unemployment office than take money for a commercial. But I thought it was great. I loved it. I had always been interested in publicity and advertising anyway, so it was fascinating.

I did that for about six months. The people I was working for said, "Why don't you stay on and direct for us?" So I stayed on and directed for a while.

Then the Westinghouse people called and offered me an editing job on a picture in Amsterdam. I told them I was directing commercials. Then they called again and said there was a lot of second unit direction on the picture and would I like to do that? I read the script and thought it could be fun to do. There was a lot of flashback material that would all be silent. I could do some interesting things.

So I went to Amsterdam, and it was quite fun. It was a detective story. A lot of it was an inspector questioning a guy, and he says, "My alibi is so and so." And we had footage of the guy doing something else. We made it quite interesting. He would say, "I was out by the canal doing so and so and so and so." And we could actually cut in bits of him not doing anything like that. But when I showed it to the director, he thought it was too clever for the movie.

The second unit stuff is normally pretty boring. Somebody gets on a tram, so you shoot the tram pulling away—that's it. I decided to shoot it an entirely different way. I got up into the tops of buildings in Amsterdam, and when anybody got on a tram, I'd start up high and zoom very slowly in. The tram would take off, and I'd follow it through the streets. You know, tremendous atmosphere.

At the dailies, the footage was all of the detective interviewing the guy—medium shots, then the close-ups, the over-the-shoulders. The same dialogue over and over. People were bored out of their minds. Then at the end of it, we'd have the second unit stuff. And for my second unit stuff I would put music on! So afterward, everyone would come up and say how great the second unit stuff was. By that time, the director and I were no longer speaking.

> *"For me, it's a totally intuitive thing.... I can't tell you why those two pieces of film really go together."*

INTERVIEWER: *How involved do you get in political maneuvering?*

NOBLE: The editor is in the middle of all the politics. What normally happens is that, at some stage, the producer and director fall out. It's pretty well guaranteed. You're always in the middle. And there are always people saying to you, "Can you talk?"

It's a very fine line that you walk, because basically you're with the director. He's hired you. It's his vision that you're trying to put across. Your input is always with him. You're working closely with him. But there are times when, obviously, you would disagree with him, over matters of personal taste or something like that.

And sometimes you find yourself in agreement with the producer. Now when that happens, the director may think you're a complete turncoat. You've betrayed him, right? And the producer's always thinking that you're just a lackey of the director and he's not going to trust you. When everyone is ganged up on both sides, you're really trying to say, "Now look, there's a middle point here and both of you are right. Let's see what we are doing here."

INTERVIEWER: *You seem to thrive on this interaction.*

NOBLE: I quite enjoy it. A lot of editors work kind of slowly. I tend to work very fast. So I have time for all the nonsense that goes on.

But it doesn't have to be that way. When we did *Witness*, there was none of it at all. Everyone was in love with Peter Weir from the word go. And everybody was in love with everybody else. It was the most incredible picture to work on. Peter and I were in agreement about everything. The producer thought everything Peter did was wonderful. The studio thought everything Peter did was wonderful. I'd never had an experience like that.

After I left *Witness*, I did *Poltergeist II,* which was utterly different. People were really attacking each other on that picture. They were insane at times!

INTERVIEWER: *Doesn't it make a difference if a film is someone's personal vision, rather than just a commercial venture?*

NOBLE: Yes, it does. What happens is that it becomes a personal vision of the director. But when this vision seems to the producers to be getting away from them, seems to be something they can't sell, they get very worried. That's why there is a paranoia about previews.

Directors are very strong these days. They have it written into their contracts that nobody can touch the picture until they've had two previews. The director can do it his way for the preview and if people don't like it, then the producers can change it.

INTERVIEWER: *Does an editor have an incredibly detailed contract?*

NOBLE: It's not all that detailed. My contract says that at the start of the picture, they guarantee me something like fifteen weeks. They can't fire me before fifteen weeks. If they want to fire me two weeks into the picture, they have to pay me for another thirteen. And then the contract just says that if I stay on, I have to be around for the answer print to be confirmed. That's basically all it is.

What tends to happen with me is that I work with people who give me a chance to get my cut together. Otherwise, there's no point in doing this job. You might as well be in a factory putting film together as you are told.

INTERVIEWER: *When did you start working in this country?*

NOBLE: When I first came to the States, I was working with a director named Ted Kotcheff. We did four pictures in a row together. I did *The Apprenticeship of Duddy Kravitz* with him in Canada. And on the strength of that, he came to Hollywood. All the producers loved that picture because they all thought they were Duddy Kravitz.

Then Ted did *Who Is Killing the Great Chefs of Europe?* It was filmed in Europe, but since it was a Lorimar film, they wanted to finish it in Hollywood. So they took me and my assistant to Hollywood, and we were there for six months, though I couldn't get into the guild here. On *Chefs*, I got screen credit for it because I had been on the picture for the five months in Europe before we came to Hollywood, and it was established that I was the editor.

Ted's next picture, *North Dallas Forty*, was a Paramount picture on the Paramount lot and another story entirely. My screen credit was some weird thing like "editorial consultant." Ted kept on making pictures in the States and I kept on coming over and cutting them. Eventually, it made sense to get a green card and try to get into the union.

INTERVIEWER: What kind of problems did you encounter getting into the union here?

NOBLE: It was like a nightmare. No way was I going to get in. When Ted did *First Blood*, we went up to Canada and it was no problem; it was a non-union picture. But after that, I did *Uncommon Valor*, which was another picture for Paramount, and it was the same problem—no screen credit, that sort of thing. I was really getting upset. Film critics like Pauline Kael were complimenting the editor on some of these pictures and it was somebody else's name, not mine. I was going to get lawyers, bring up the right to work, the Taft-Hartley Act, all that sort of thing. Eventually, everything worked out. After taking up residence in L.A., paying taxes, et cetera, the union finally relented, and I got in while I was cutting John Milius's film *Red Dawn* in Las Vegas, New Mexico.

INTERVIEWER: How did you get hooked up with Peter Weir?

NOBLE: Well, after *Red Dawn*, I was going back to London to sell my house and get divorced. I really had no ties with London anymore. My wife and I had been separated for five years. When Paramount called and asked if I was going to be available, I said, "No, I'm going to England for six weeks and I really can't do it." And they said, "Well, we can't tell you what the movie is. We can only tell you if you're free."

So two weeks went by and my ex-agent, Larry Mirisch, called me. He said, "The thing that Paramount called you about is a Peter Weir movie. I remember from when we were together that you had two people you really wanted to work with, Peter Weir and Roman Polanski. Do you want to meet him?" I said, "I would love to meet Peter Weir."

So I met Peter and we got along incredibly well right from the word go. He told me about the history of *Witness*. He had had an editor that he wasn't happy with and they had finished shooting the picture without an editor at all. Now they were in L.A. looking for an editor to go to Australia with them and finish the film. So Peter said, "Well, what do you think?" I said, "You know, I'd love to work on this picture." But I told him I was trying to get back to England to do all that stuff. He said, "Is there any way you could put it off?" I said, yes, there probably was. But I told him that I'd only do it if, say, I cut a sequence for him here that he liked, because I didn't want to go out to Australia and have the same thing happen that happened with his first editor. He said, "Great."

> *"Being out on the set is a terribly bad idea.... You lose any objectivity you might have."*

So I called my wife and said I had a chance to do a Peter Weir picture, and she knew it would really mean a lot to me. I said maybe we could just put things off a bit longer, but I told her, to show my good faith, "I'll give you the house. You can have the house, but I really need to do this picture if I can." She said, "OK. Fine."

So, that weekend I was waiting to cut a sequence together for Peter. I waited the whole weekend for the phone to ring, and nothing. On Monday I was back in the *Red Dawn* cutting room and Peter called. He said, "Hi, Thom, I'm at the airport. Listen, I know you're the right person for this picture. You don't have to cut anything for me. How quickly can you get out to Australia?" I said, "Probably by the end of the week." He said, "Great. I've told Paramount that I want you. Fix the deal and I'll see you out there." So I flew out there Sunday, and Monday morning I was in the cutting room.

INTERVIEWER: *Tell me something about how you worked with Peter Weir on* Witness.

NOBLE: Well, when I got to Australia, the first thing we did was look at all the film for the first third of the picture. And we talked about it in very general terms. No specific takes were chosen; we just ran through the first third of the picture in a day. And that's quite a lot.

He said, "How long do you think it will take you?" I told him, "Well, about ten days."

So the ten days passed and I put the film together and I realized, What happens if he doesn't like it? It was a whole third of the picture I had now cut together. And in the opening were some very tricky sequences. I was actually very happy with it. I was thinking to myself that I'd really done an amazing job. But if he didn't like it, then I'd just have to pack my bags and go because I didn't know any other way of doing this. I really didn't. I thought, This is my best. I can't do any better than this. So we ran the first reel. There was absolute silence. We were both sitting on a couch near the editing table, and I was sitting forward like this and I was actually shaking! I was really worried. I was thinking, This is pretty good, but if Peter thinks it's terrible, I might as well open my veins, because this is it!

So we got to the end and he turned to me. And with a great beaming face he said, "It's great!"

From that moment on, everything fell into place. We're on the same wavelength. The picture was an absolute joy to do.

INTERVIEWER: *What's different about your work now that you've received an Oscar?*

NOBLE: Now I'm getting a lot of scripts coming to me and they're all absolute garbage. Everybody's making the second version of something. And I think this is terrifying! All these are "go" projects. People are actually going to make these films, no matter what I say or do. Then I got one called *Poltergeist II*. This is really what I needed like a hole in the head.

But I started to read it, and it was all basically the teachings of Don Juan in the Carlos Castaneda books. I had read those books in London and, like many other people, I'm sure, dreamed of meeting Don Juan and studying with him. But it all had seemed a million miles away. However, at the time the *Poltergeist II* script came my way, I actually was studying with an apprentice of Don Juan's in L.A. and had gone through all sorts of ceremonies and vision quests. So as I turned the pages of the script, I said to myself, This is a film I have to do. I'm so thrilled!

So I went to the interviews and I got to do the picture. We finished the film, the actors had said all these Castaneda lines, and we were all in seventh heaven that we were getting this out. We all thought this film was wonderful—so different, an adult picture.

Then the executive producer came down and said, "This picture's a piece of garbage. It's totally useless. I would hate to show it to the studio in this state." Then the fear of God had been put into everybody, and no one knew what to do. The writers, who were also the producers, started to get nervous, and they didn't know what to do. People were going insane.

And in the middle of this, I was having rows with the director and with the producer. I said, "You just don't know a good picture when you have it. Let's show the picture like it is. Let's take a chance. We've all loved it up until this madness took over."

So we showed it to the studio and they loved it. Now everybody loved everyone else again. We all went off for the Christmas holiday and everything seemed to be fine.

Then, over Christmas, the head of the studio started thinking about it. He thought, It's wonderful, but it's 93 percent wonderful. If we spent another million dollars, we could put a few jolts in it to make it even better.

Because of my commitment to do Peter Weir's *Mosquito Coast*, I had to leave *Poltergeist* before all the insanity was resolved. I've subsequently seen the film, and I really thought about having my name taken off the credits, because what that film turned out to be was nothing like the film the writers and director, in their hearts, wanted to make. It's been hacked up in a way you cannot believe.

The resolution of that film was that the love of the united family produces an extremely potent force in the astral plane. When they came to do final battle with the beast, an aura was produced around them that was so powerful that the beast was destroyed on impact. The studio thought that love defeating evil was too wishy-washy. So in the final version, the beast is defeated by the father thrusting an astral spear into him. So much for pathos, as Monty Python used to say.

Also, the film was really hacked to pieces by a variety of uncredited hands while I was in Belize cutting *Mosquito Coast*. By the time my agent had gotten me a video of the final version, it was too late to do anything, even remove my name!

INTERVIEWER: *Do you think the film would have been different had you stayed there?*

NOBLE: It wouldn't have made a difference, because the decisions are made at a level that you can't fight. If somebody says, "It's not working and we're going to spend one million dollars more," they're going to believe that it works that way.

INTERVIEWER: *When do you usually join the production?*

NOBLE: The editor is normally hired on the first day of shooting. Before that, you've read the script and had discussions. You usually go on location. Wherever they are, they set up a cutting room for you. You are really with the director and seeing material with him every evening. You are putting it together as fast as you can because on location, obviously, they might want to pick up an extra shot that they can't when they're back at the studio.

INTERVIEWER: *Is it more difficult working on location?*

NOBLE: Locations are always tough for editing, in a way. Because nothing quite works. Your equipment is constantly breaking down. And in Belize there were power cuts all the time. We had coding machines that would suddenly pack up and not code the film properly. If you can't code the film, you might as well go home. Those numbers that we put on are the only way we can actually stay in sync. The machines are terribly sensitive, beautiful machines. But they are nightmares. You're always up against the elements. At the same time, there's something nice about being with the crew.

"There are people who have made lifetime careers out of working with one director."

INTERVIEWER: *Do you ever go on the set?*

NOBLE: Being out on the set is a terribly bad idea, I've found, because you lose any objectivity you might have. If you're on the set and you see them lining up a shot that finally takes four hours to get, when you get that shot in the cutting room, you think, Oh, this took them four hours. I better use this. If you just look at the film for the first time in the cutting room and think to yourself, This is useless—it probably is. It's a much more intelligent way to work. So I always try to keep away from the set.

INTERVIEWER: *How do you work with the director to express his vision yet make your own contributions?*

NOBLE: There's a way that the director has it visualized and a way that I have it visualized, but we really don't talk about it until later in the production of the film. When we watch the dailies, it's obvious, most of the time, which one is the best take. They really come screaming at you from the screen.

What usually happens is that there are maybe seven moments in each scene that are brilliant. But they're all on different takes, different shots. My job is to try and get all those seven moments in and yet have it look seamless, so that nobody knows there's a cut in there.

The director knows how he sees it when he shoots it. When I cut it, I cut it the way I see it. Then, if he has another viewpoint, we can discuss it, and he can make his decision.

INTERVIEWER: *When does the sound enter your editing process?*

NOBLE: In Hollywood, you get the director's fine cut of the picture. If it's a twelve-week shoot, that comes at about eighteen weeks. By that time, we've pretty well got it down.

At that point, an army of sound editors comes on with a supervising sound editor: dialogue editors; Foley editors doing the footsteps, clothes rustling, et cetera; and the effects editors. They then make several black-and-white copies of the picture and prepare to record all the ADR—automated dialogue replacement—all the lines that cannot be heard properly on the original track because of backgrounds like passing jets, steam hammers, waterfalls, and so forth.

The Foley editors then re-record every footstep, clothes rustle, and glass clink that appears on the screen. Dialogue editors strip out everything unusable in the original track, and the effects editors go to work conjuring all the atmospheric sounds that go into making the final track.

At this time also, the composer is discussing when the various sections of music should start and finish, and the music editor gives him a detailed breakdown of every incident in that section, accurate to one-third of a second.

INTERVIEWER: *Do you have a certain routine when you work?*

NOBLE: I try to work in very concentrated periods. When I get in, I immediately go to the machine and I work from, say, 9:00 to something like 12:30 or 1:00, absolutely solid, no breaks for coffee, no wandering in and talking with people. I have lunch away from it. Then I come back and work in an absolutely concentrated bout until about 6:00 or 7:00. And I work fast. I have a reputation for working amazingly quickly.

I never work in the evenings. Except, for example, when we're putting Peter's cut together, the hours tend to expand. But when I'm putting my cut together, I really don't. I try to get the space in. Otherwise, if you're never away from the picture, you have no perspective on it whatsoever. You can't see the wood for the trees. You need that time to step away from it. And if they're shooting six days, you're working six days, and that seventh day off is never long enough.

INTERVIEWER: *But you make time for outside interests?*

NOBLE: There is a life outside the movies. In the evening I like to see a movie, eat Thai, Indian, Japanese, or Chinese food, see friends, study Zen and shamanism, read, write letters, or play racquetball.

A lot of people in editing don't ever realize that. A lot of people I know basically live in the cutting room. That's their world. They don't work in concentrated bouts, they work in fits and starts, but slowly. They talk to people on the phone, and the cutting room becomes their home.

There's a certain paranoia that creeps into cutting rooms. When you think about it, editing is really kind of an anal-retentive thing to do, and it attracts a lot of introverted worriers and fussers. Also, a lot of the top editors love to have so many assistants and apprentices on the film that gaining access to their inner sanctums becomes quite a task.

People either work out of fear or out of love, and there is a tremendous amount of fear in the cutting room. And producers really love that about editors. If they think an editor is actually there until midnight every night working on their film, it's a tremendous ego thing for them. And the point is, the editor's already given away his power, such as it is, by doing that. The producers think, This guy's really great, he's so dedicated. At the same time, they know they can walk all over him.

INTERVIEWER: *What equipment do you like to work with?*

NOBLE: There are two schools of editing. There's the moviola, which I use. And the KEM, which is the table—the flatbed. I tend to be happiest with the moviola simply because I feel much more in contact with the film—the fact that it's running through my hands, I can stop it just like that and mark it. When I work on a table, I never feel that much in control.

But I use the table in conjunction with the moviola. The strength of the table for me is when you're fine-cutting the film. Because it has two heads on it, you can run all the outtakes as well as the takes you've used. You can say, That may be a little better than what we have in. So, I would look at it on the KEM, then make the changes on the moviola.

The moviola is the machine I'm really comfortable with. It hasn't changed in God knows how many years. But they're also always breaking down. The sound heads break down. We had two of these machines in Belize that were brought down from Hollywood, and they were constantly going wrong. It's fine in a studio because they just wheel in another machine and off you go. But on location there's usually no one to fix them.

INTERVIEWER: What kind of new technological developments are there in the editing field?

NOBLE: Well, some people are trying things out with video editing. It's so expensive and it's so new that nobody I know has thought it works well so far, although I'm sure we're going to see a lot more of it. It's used more in TV than in features at the moment. However, certain feature directors—Francis Coppola and Hal Ashby, for example— put all their material on tape and edit that. Then they match the 35-mm negative to it later.

"Film is an incredible medium, and we're still using it in pedestrian ways!"

The closest we got to video on *Witness* was having a copy of the work print transferred to video for Peter. He didn't have to be at the KEM; he could just skip through the video, seeing what I had and comparing it to what I hadn't used. That was quite a good idea. I think video will be used more and more. If you can preview opticals on video—dissolves and things—that can be very useful.

A lot of people are using computers for logging all their material, which is a great idea because it's painstaking what we do; there are thousands of numbers. But the people who have come up with the programs are keeping them very much to themselves.

INTERVIEWER: Most people would consider you very successful.

NOBLE: Yes, I suppose. I really served a hard apprenticeship, as you know. I could never have cut a film like *Witness* without having cut a lot of absolutely dreadful pictures before that.

For me, it's a totally intuitive thing. Friends of mine connected with film schools have often asked me, "Come along and talk to the students." But I have nothing to say. I mean, I can't tell you why those two pieces of film really go together. If you run it through the machine and it doesn't work and you ask, "Why?"—well, obviously it's a bit too long on that side and a bit too short on this side. So long as you know it's wrong and you can put it right, that's all I know about. It's a feeling. People have come to me and said, "How do you do this?" I have no idea. The only rule is there's no rule.

INTERVIEWER: What do you think is the worst part of this business?

NOBLE: There's one thing I find that occasionally makes me really angry. Say you're working on a film and you feel the director's gone out and shot a pile of garbage with no idea of how it's going to go together. You go through 6,000 feet of film, and all you can think is, I've got to make something out of this. There's a certain resentment that creeps in, and you say, "Why?"

I remember a sequence like that on *First Blood*. The second unit went out and shot literally 5,000 feet of a wild boar. And the thing is, the boar wouldn't even move! I found out they had taken this pig out and it had gotten away from them. They had to chase it all morning to get it back, so the boar was exhausted by the time they started shooting. They kept jabbing it to try to get it to move. So, I was going through all of the material and all I could see were these sticks coming in and the pig just standing there! How dare they do this! But you just have to let it go. If you attach yourself to those sorts of feelings, it can build up and build up and become very bad. You just have to step back from it all and say, "OK, this is ridiculous."

Actually, working with a director like Ted Kotcheff, you can laugh about it together. Because at some stage, he is going to be sitting with you going through all 5,000 feet of it again. At least on the KEM you can run in warp speed, and when you're through it's usually a perfect time to laugh.

INTERVIEWER: Is there anything about editing that gives you trouble?

NOBLE: Well, say it's been a month between pictures. I go to cut the first two pieces of film and I know it will be a disaster. I never get it right. It's like the rhythm is totally wrong.

And the assistant I always work with says that I can never get people going through doors. And it's absolutely true. It's basically an easy editing principle. But I can never get it right! If you look at my pictures, at the people coming through doors, they're always a little bit off. I don't know why that is.

It's stupid things that you worry about. Like the first time you put a film together, you're worried about a person's left, right, left, right, as they're walking through a series of shots. When you see it in the final film, you see that it doesn't matter. You don't even need most establishing shots anymore. You have a lot of freedom to play around.

And I always have said this about the cutting room: When it stops being fun, we should stop doing it. I've had a lot of fun and been all over Europe, Canada, the States, and, of course, Australia to do the fine cuts of *Witness* and

Mosquito Coast. It's wonderful to end up doing something that you really enjoy by what appears to be a series of accidents. That is, if you believe anything is an accident. It took me fifty years to realize that everyone creates his or her own reality.

The next step for me would be directing. I've had opportunities in the past, but I didn't feel I had anything I wanted to say. But it's different now. I have something to communicate.

INTERVIEWER: And what do you want to communicate through film?

NOBLE: Everyday reality is only one of many realities; there are innumerable possibilities and probabilities. I want to explore them on film, to try and break some new ground. I'm tremendously excited! Film is an incredible medium, and we're still using it in pedestrian ways! I'd love to change that. I can't wait to start.

Chris Newman

SOUND
PRODUCTION RECORDING

Chris Newman was born in New York City in 1940. He grew up in Brooklyn and, at sixteen, attended MIT (Massachusetts Institute of Technology), where he studied metallurgical engineering. About this time, he made some little films with friends who were getting involved in the theater and movies. In the early sixties, influenced by his interest in music and technology, he began working in a recording studio, initially for no pay. The studio got an occasional recording job for a film and he broke into the business that way. He learned quickly, getting all of his training on the job. He met lots of people, got into the union, and it wasn't long before Newman was on his way.

As a sound recordist, Newman is responsible for capturing the sound on a movie set—the dialogue as well as the ambient sounds that contribute to a film's atmosphere and realism. He has received Oscars for his work on The Exorcist *and* Amadeus, *as well as Oscar nominations for* Fame, The French Connection, The Godfather, *and* A Chorus Line. *His sound recording can be heard on more than two dozen motion* _pictures, including_ Medium Cool, The Landlord, Hair, Klute, Little Murders, The Taking of Pelham One Two Three, Sophie's Choice, Ragtime, All That Jazz, The World According to Garp, Tender Mercies, The Mosquito Coast, Brighton Beach Memoirs, _and_ The Unbearable Lightness of Being.

Newman lives with his wife and children in a New Jersey beach community, where he recuperates from the filmmaking experience by tending three dozen rose bushes and indulging his passion for classical music and jazz.

INTERVIEWER: What criteria do you use to decide whether or not to become involved with a particular film project?

NEWMAN: My interest in movies goes way beyond just the sound recording. I'm interested in making good movies. The first question that I ask isn't, Who's directing it? What's the scheduling? What kind of money's involved? Is it being shot in a war zone or in the studio? My first question is whether this picture will have some kind of impact, substance, some kind of potency.

Now, in some cases I'll pick pictures that will suit my personal and family schedule. In other situations I will pick a picture because of the director. But most of the time I'm looking for pictures with some potency.

INTERVIEWER: So you're looking for some satisfaction beyond the sound work itself?

NEWMAN: What happens is that after you've been doing this for a long time, the recording problems become, for the most part, very similar. There has to be something that transcends the recording problems. Not a hell of a lot is to be gained by doing safe jobs all the time. I think it's important to do jobs that absolutely stretch the film, yourself, and the other people right to the limits of what they can do.

INTERVIEWER: Which of your films have been the best experiences for you in that regard?

NEWMAN: That's a very difficult question to answer. Up until recently, one of the best tracks I ever made was on a picture that no one ever saw! A picture called _The People Next Door,_ made in 1969, directed by David Greene, it played only very briefly. The first feature film I ever worked on, _Medium Cool,_ was a very rewarding experience because we got through it using tons of wild tracks. Another one of my best tracks was _The French Connection._ It was a street movie with street tracks at a time when we weren't supposed to be able to make tracks like that. But almost every picture is rewarding in one way or another.

On one job it might be that we got a good sound track in spite of the people who made the movie. In some cases we got a good sound track *because of* the people who made the movie.

Certainly the best pictures I ever worked on would be *Amadeus* and the first *Godfather.* The tracks for those pictures were very good because people took the time to make them good. It's not just because you do a good job on original recording. It's because people like Walter Murch and Francis Coppola and Milos Forman and Saul Zaentz and all the re-recording people took the time and the care to develop the tracks, to let them sing. *The Godfather* is an example of a picture totally fraught with executive and control problems. But anybody who looks at that movie today can't help but feel admiration for it. I don't know exactly how *Amadeus* will stand up to the test of time, but certainly it's a damn good movie.

"In addition to entertaining people, I think films should help broaden people's experience."

INTERVIEWER: *What role do you think film should play in society?*

NEWMAN: In addition to entertaining people, I think films should help broaden their experience. Anything I can do to help make a picture is important to me. I enjoy the collaboration a great deal. I enjoy all of the give and take; I enjoy helping to make the movie.

INTERVIEWER: *Did you enjoy working with director Peter Weir on* The Mosquito Coast?

NEWMAN: You won't find many directors like him—so intelligent, so thorough, and so thoughtful as well. It's a very unusual combination. The intelligent ones are usually ruthless, and the thoughtful ones are usually dumb. You know, it's very hard to find the combination of someone who's a decent human being and also a good director.

INTERVIEWER: *There seems to be a tremendous amount of luck involved in this business.*

NEWMAN: There is. At one point, I turned down a picture because it just seemed like the job would be wrong for me. Three hours later, the phone rang and it was a production manager calling to ask if I would do a picture called *The French Connection*. And after *Little Murders*, the producers wanted me to do another movie with Elliott Gould. But, just by chance, I ended up doing *The Godfather*, because Francis Coppola's favorite sound man was teaching in college at the time. And it turned out that, for some reason, the other picture stopped shooting.

You really have to have a great deal of luck. A lot of good sound recording is luck. Did the airplane go over exactly when the director got the best take? Or did the airplane go over on the next-to-the-last take?

INTERVIEWER: Do you ever get involved with picking locations?

NEWMAN: With *Mosquito Coast*, I went to Belize while they were scouting locations, about six or eight weeks before they started shooting. But it's very unusual for a sound man to do that kind of scout. If it was in Los Angeles or New York, they would take you around and show you the various places. But to go down to Belize for ten days made a big difference to me because it helped me prepare the equipment for the job.

One of the big things for a sound man is to get the equipment right. The equipment is at least half the battle. It has to be suited for the job; it has to work all the time. We're always having stuff modified and fooling around with it. My kids opened the refrigerator the other day and found a piece of microphone cable in the freezer. I wanted to see how stiff it would get. Then I gave it to the kids and let them try to pull it apart.

INTERVIEWER: What kind of equipment do you use?

NEWMAN: I always use the Nagras tape recorders. They have been, without question, the standard used in the film business for some time now. We are always using stereo machines now. And I always use mixing consoles when I'm on location.

In the old days, the mixer would work on the set right near the camera, and we would run lines back to the truck or wherever the noisy mag recorder was. When the Nagra came out in the early sixties, people worked directly into the Nagra on the set. Then they began adding mixing panels. And as the panels became bigger, it wasn't always practical for the mixer to be on the set. If you had a situation where you knew what the boom man was going to do and what the action was, you didn't necessarily have to see everything. But more and more situations are occurring where the mixer has to see what's going on, so he has to be fairly flexible with the equipment.

INTERVIEWER: *Did you have to have any special equipment for the locations on* The Mosquito Coast?

NEWMAN: Very often, before a job begins, I will make some big changes in the equipment. I decided that the mixing consoles I was using were too big and heavy for the conditions in Belize. I got two new mixers made by a Swiss company and had some modifications done to them. They're very well made, rugged, and they're much smaller. I had done some preliminary work with them, so I wasn't using them cold.

All the carrying equipment was made so that it could be slung over the shoulder, and all the bags were waterproofed. So we didn't have to think too much about weather conditions. I must say that I was the best prepared I have ever been. Because I saw the conditions, I was able to get a handle on what was needed and then change the equipment to suit the conditions. There were fewer problems with humidity than I had anticipated. It makes a big difference to be that well prepared.

I also devised a little tripod to carry the recorder and the mixer in a relatively small profile. If the camera can be on a tripod, there's no reason why the mixer and recorder can't be on a tripod. That's what we used in the jungle. We could just pick up the thing and carry it.

INTERVIEWER: *What do you do when things break down on location?*

NEWMAN: I always carry a lot of equipment with me. There's a great deal of redundancy. There are two of almost everything. When something breaks, we simply take out a new one and have the old one repaired.

In Belize, we did have one disaster. One day we were walking and I slipped. The tripod with the mixer and the recorder went up in the air in one direction and I went in the other direction! The equipment went up in the air and described a perfect arc, and the whole thing landed in the mud. It was a small miracle, because it could have come down on a tree or a rock and have been smashed beyond hope. I smashed my face against some wood and broke some cartilage. But in the final analysis, everything was OK. One switch needed to be replaced, my nose healed, and we went on.

INTERVIEWER: *Being on location, how do you deal with not having the production services that are available to you in L.A.?*

NEWMAN: In the case of *Mosquito Coast*, we even did our transfers on location. They were done at night. In a situation like that, there's an enormous advantage to doing it that way.

First of all, they were cutting the picture as we went along. So we could do additional pieces of sound right then and there. It gives more of a feeling of security. If you're thousands of miles away from the transfer house, no matter how well you know what you're doing, you really can't judge a hell of a lot on headphones. In a situation where you listen to it on a speaker, you can hear what you've done and you know where you're at. And if you're running multi-track stuff, where you might have one microphone close and one microphone in perspective, and you have to make mix downs for the rushes, it's not practical to get on the phone in the mornings and call the transfer house. If you're in the middle of nowhere, you can't have a phone on a tree.

"One of the big things for a sound man is to get the equipment right. The equipment is at least half the battle."

INTERVIEWER: *You mentioned that on* Mosquito Coast *they were editing as they went along.*

NEWMAN: They were cutting as much as they could. In fact, before we finished the filming, we were able to see the last hour of the picture. That was very good because it gave some food for thought; it showed how stuff was going to work, and I don't mean only in the sound area, I mean in general. It certainly is good for morale for everybody to get an idea of what they're working on and whether it has any substance or not.

INTERVIEWER: *How do you go about picking your crew members?*

NEWMAN: On long jobs out of the country, you pick people as much for their expertise as you do for their ability to survive psychologically. You don't pick people who are brilliant technicians and very unstable or unpredictable. You don't pick a guy with family problems, or a guy who's going to drink himself under the bar every night. You really do have to pick the people very carefully. You cannot do a good job unless you have a good boom man and good assistants.

INTERVIEWER: *How many people are usually on your crew?*

NEWMAN: Usually two other people. One is the boom man, and the third guy is the jack-of-all-trades. He'll do maintenance and he'll do booming and he'll have a sore shoulder from my hitting him and saying, "Why didn't we do this?" and "Why didn't we do that?"

INTERVIEWER: *Do you have a certain daily routine on the set?*

NEWMAN: We come in anywhere from 6:00 to 8:00 in the morning and set up the equipment. Either I'll set it up or the third man will. The boom man goes ahead and takes a look at what we're doing. Somewhere in the middle of this someone is getting the breakfasts from the caterer. Most of the time, it's fairly slow in the morning. Even if the people are well prepared, things don't crystallize for a couple of hours. Then things go fairly quickly. Some directors will be ready to go first thing in the morning. In that case, we do it differently. We set up first thing, as quickly as we can.

INTERVIEWER: *Do you go to the dailies?*

NEWMAN: I do. I go to the rushes day in, day out. It's the only chance I have to see what I'm working on. I don't necessarily go to see if the sound is going to work, because I usually know when the sound is bad and when the sound is good. I'm not often surprised. It's like coming out of an exam—you usually know what grade you got, if it's hopeless or not.

INTERVIEWER: *What kinds of things do you have to be careful of as a sound recordist?*

NEWMAN: I think you have not really lived, as a sound person, until you've erased a take! I've done it twice. On *Ragtime*, we did a big crowd scene adjacent to Madison Avenue, where Elizabeth McGovern comes out of the courthouse. We had a radio mike very cleverly mounted on her so that it was very low in her cleavage and all the people around her, who were chattering at her, were picked up on the same microphone. We had another mike for background effects on a separate track. It was a fairly sophisticated setup.

We did eighteen takes, and each one got better and better. I set up the eighteenth take to play back for Milos Forman and we broke for lunch. Well, when we came back I must have neglected to play it for him, because we went on to something else and I recorded right over it! When I called the transfer house the next morning, there was no eighteenth take, so I knew I had erased it. I didn't know what to do. I discussed it with the assistant editor, and we decided to print take seventeen twice. We didn't tell Milos, who gets very excited about things like this, naturally. When the rushes came up, take seventeen was there twice, but Milos never knew. I don't know what take they ended up using, but when the picture was finished, I told him. By that time, he was laughing.

Years ago, I worked as somebody's third man and at one point, he was running out of tape. He did something I wouldn't have the courage to do. If there was a take that was no good, he would back up and erase it, just record right over it.

INTERVIEWER: *What makes a good sound track?*

NEWMAN: Well, I can point out pictures to you where the sound is really mediocre but you wouldn't realize it. And these days, the sound is never terrible. It's a question of how good it is going to be. With the level of competence, with the level of radio mikes now, with the level of re-recording the way it is, and with the level of ADR [automated dialogue replacement] the way it is, you rarely go into a theater and hear a bad track. You just don't hear it anymore. In the final analysis, if the dialogue track is mediocre, it doesn't necessarily affect the picture.

A number of years ago I worked on a movie called *Mikey and Nicky*, directed by Elaine May, with Peter Falk and John Cassavetes. Elaine decided to have Peter and John improvise the entire picture. They used two and three cameras; they printed a million feet of film. There was a tremendous amount of material. And I really didn't know how to do the sound. I decided to use a two-track technique, which had never been used before on the East Coast. We used the stereo Nagra with radio mikes on one track and an open mike on the other track. But we didn't really know what we were doing. We didn't even know how to transfer the material properly. Initially we transferred it to two separate strands, and when it was lined up, it was out of sync, there was phasing, there was every conceivable problem that you could have with multitrack.

In addition, Elaine had broken every rule that we had specified in the beginning about not stealing lines from different takes. She did what she had to do to make a good, effective movie.

When I went in to see the screening of the picture, I was absolutely terrified. Usually I'm concerned with whether the movie is going to be good. In this case I was terrified because I thought the sound track wasn't going to be any good.

A friend of mine said, "Don't be concerned." And I said, "Why not?" He said, "If the picture's no good, and the track's no good, it doesn't matter. If the picture's mediocre, and the track's good, it doesn't matter. If the picture's good and the track's mediocre, it doesn't matter either."

In terms of the dialogue, unless the track was totally unintelligible, it would not have a substantial influence on the efficacy of the picture. That's probably true. The point is, the sound track can really influence the movie.

There's no question that a good sound designer/supervising sound editor can really influence the emotional state of the audience by where he or she places the effects, by doing sophisticated backgrounds, and by choosing and moving the dialogue. But film is basically good storytelling.

INTERVIEWER: *How involved do you get in postproduction?*

NEWMAN: I get involved as much as I can, as much as they'll let me. On some pictures, I am absolutely not involved, either because I'm away or it's not my place. Obviously, I'm not a re-recording mixer and I wouldn't tell any re-recording mixer how to do the job. But I do have a very good sense of what seems correct in terms of what the director wants.

INTERVIEWER: *Who do you work most closely with, outside of the sound crew?*

NEWMAN: My orientation is primarily around the director. The job might come to me through the producer, but my loyalties are going to be to the director. The director is the one who sets the tone of the picture for the whole crew. If there are any questions, they all go to him: Do we need to cover this? Is this going to work for you? Is this a situation where we hear every pristine syllable, or can it be a very general track? We discuss a lot of different questions. Most of the people that I want to work with are those who are willing to take the time to talk with the sound man. There are directors who don't give a damn about sound, and they

> *"On long jobs out of the country, you pick people as much for their expertise as you do for their ability to survive psychologically."*

don't need to have me there. I'm a strong personality, and while I certainly don't want to dominate a movie, I want my input to be accepted. If it's taken and rejected after some thought, I'm perfectly happy with that. The thing that puts me off the most in terms of working with the director is to go and ask about something and the director doesn't want to hear what I have to say.

INTERVIEWER: *When do you prefer to become involved with a picture?*

NEWMAN: In most cases, I won't get involved with the guys who want to bring me on the picture at the last minute. I try to avoid the jobs where the production manager calls me and says, "We have a film that's starting in ten weeks. Are you interested?" And I'll say, "Fine, who's the director?" And the production manager will say, "Well, we haven't got a director yet."

That already tells me what the project's about. Occasionally, you have to do them. You can't always pick. Those movies are already disasters for me. If they're hiring me before the director, what the hell kind of movie can it be? It doesn't mean it's a bad movie, it just means it's a movie that's not suited to the way I want to work.

INTERVIEWER: Is there anything that really bothers you about the whole movie business?

NEWMAN: There certainly is something. It bothers a lot of other sound men as well. Most sound men that I know are pretty responsible. They try to bring pride and craft to their work. Most of the problems that you run into in sound recording are scientific problems. Someone makes a sound and someone has to record it. You can't just stand there and wave the microphone around and hope that the recording is going to be perfect each time. You need to have a good boom man; you need to have good equipment, you need to know how to use it; you need to know how to deal with the crew—getting the boom man what he needs, getting the set quiet—millions of things. As you become more experienced, you become almost computerized in the sense that the information comes in and you spit out an answer. You are getting paid to digest a lot of information quickly, come up with an answer quickly, and execute it as quickly as you can.

Nothing makes me angrier than when a production person, particularly after you have made all these considered judgments, comes over and starts to second-guess you or even first-guess you. Nothing is more annoying. It is a total insult to why they have you there. If they have hired you and are paying you all these thousands of dollars a week, why are they standing around discussing things that *you* are getting paid to make the judgments for? And nobody knows anything about sound. Even sound men barely know anything about sound.

INTERVIEWER: What would you like to see happen in the film business?

NEWMAN: Well, two things. I would like to see better scripts. I would also like to see responsible people treated responsibly. One of the reasons I work for Fantasy Films is that they give me what I call responsible carte blanche—in terms of hiring practices, in terms of preparing for a movie, in terms of how I approach a picture.

It's ridiculous to have to argue about somebody getting paid five or ten dollars more a day. There are other things to worry about. If people are going to spend a lot of money to hire you to be the head of the department, the least they can do is give you the respect that goes along with the job. And I've found that if you're given a license to steal, you don't. You begin to protect the producer's money. If you're told, "Don't do this, don't abuse that," you become very annoyed and resentful. And this affects the picture.

INTERVIEWER: I imagine there is quite a possibility for conflict when you have so many different people working together.

NEWMAN: Yes, there is. There is a lot of conflict under the surface that comes out very quickly. Just go and try to put a furniture blanket on a camera when it's making a lot of noise, and the camera operator and the cameraman and the focus puller will all get annoyed because it makes their job more difficult. It's interesting that cameramen often take the point of view that camera noise is not a camera problem but a sound problem. I find that kind of contradictory. They expect the sound men to solve the camera noise problem. And in fact, no one is to blame. People are being victimized by either poor design or by nickel-and-dime considerations.

In some cases they aren't so nickel-and-dime. I was on a job in England

Chris Newman on location in Belize for The Mosquito Coast.

where I was hired just before shooting began. When I arrived I discovered that there was an Arriflex BL being used in a studio situation. And the Arriflex BL is not a studio camera; it's too noisy, no matter what Arriflex says.

I went to the production manager and the director after the first day of shooting and said, "Listen, this is a nightmare. I don't know how we can make this work for twelve or fourteen weeks. The actors are speaking very quietly. You don't like to loop. I don't know how to get rid of the camera noise. If I begin to put blimps over the camera, then the camera people are going to complain. I know it would have been nice if I had spoken up about this several weeks ago, but I didn't know I was doing this job several weeks ago and no one thought to ask me. So what do we do?"

> *"I think you have not really lived, as a sound person, until you've erased a take!"*

They went through the economics of it, and in this particular case, it was something like $40,000 cheaper to rent this camera rather than the Panaflex. It was a nightmare for me. So I spent every day making what I thought was a really good dialogue track with this curtain of camera noise behind it.

If that were to ever happen to me again, I would quit. It's absurd, but it's absolutely the essence of the business: You have a big, multimillion-dollar production, with very experienced people making the same mistakes over and over again.

INTERVIEWER: *When have you laughed the hardest in this business?*

NEWMAN: It's lots of laughs, mostly having to do with people screwing up. Most of our laughs are when something rather subtle will go wrong and we'll notice it.

I remember one time going to a director and saying, "I couldn't hear the actors because they spoke so quietly." And he said to me, "Well, I could hear them perfectly." I found it wildly amusing that he was so naive about how microphones worked and how sound-recording techniques worked.

INTERVIEWER: *What was one of your more embarrassing moments?*

NEWMAN: I remember one time we were shooting in the middle of the night on triple-time. We were being thrown out of the location, a big stone-floored garage. The owner of the garage was yelling and screaming at the production manager in the background while we were trying to make a take. So we finally got everything quiet, they rolled it, the take was going great, it looked like it was going to be the take, and we could wrap. I stretched my leg out to relax during the take and all of a sudden I heard a tremendous crash! I was so angry! I got up, tore my headphones off, and I yelled, "Who the hell made that noise?" Then I looked down and there was a jug of water that I had knocked over with my leg, and it was rolling endlessly over the cement floor!

Another time, in the sixties, I was working in India on a picture called *Raga* with Ravi Shankar. It was financed by The Beatles. I went out to Ravi's house to record a wild track of some music. When I arrived there, I had all the equipment except I had forgotten the tape recorder! I didn't say to him, "I forgot the tape recorder. I'm a jerk." I just said, "Look, I forgot a very important piece of equipment. I'll be right back." So an hour and a half later I returned with the tape recorder. They didn't seem to care. They were playing their music and having a good time. It wasn't a situation where you had actors waiting around, but I was pretty embarrassed. It happens.

INTERVIEWER: *Do you see many movies?*

NEWMAN: I see them in fits and starts. If I'm working in some exotic location, I don't see many at all. Then I'll go and see a big burst of them. In the summer, I manage to see all the summer releases—most of which I cannot stand—with my children.

INTERVIEWER: *Which other sound recordist's work do you admire?*

NEWMAN: I admire all of them. When I see a movie and I divorce myself from the story line and think about the sound, I have no idea how they did it. Sometimes the sound is amazingly good, and I have no idea whether it's dubbed, or whether it's studio, or whether they've got wonderful radio mikes that no one knows about or terrific techniques that I haven't caught up with yet. Even with some of my own stuff, if I look at it today, I don't always remember how I did it.

INTERVIEWER: *What kind of technological developments do you have to keep up with?*

NEWMAN: In the last ten years, I haven't really observed any major technological changes in the microphones. What I call open microphones—ones that are either hidden or put on fish poles and microphone booms—are all directional microphones. It's just a question of how tight the pickup pattern is going to be, how they sound, and how they hold up physically. I don't really know if there will be any dramatic changes in that area, simply because of the physics involved.

The radio mikes have improved dramatically in terms of their reliability, in terms of their immunity from radio interference, and in terms of how they sound. On location in Belize, for example, I was using Microns, which are made in England.

And as the radios get better and better, there will be more and more emphasis on them. The radios are real easy to use when they work. But you are still confined to what they sound like on the person; you still have problems with clothing noise, so you're always pestering the actors. The other limitation is the way they sound. They don't sound great. You have to use another track to make them sound pretty good.

Re-recording techniques are getting more sophisticated. It's now possible to remove more background than ever before with new filtering techniques and with the digitization of the material.

INTERVIEWER: *Have you used digital recording equipment?*

NEWMAN: I don't really view digital set recording as being a major change. I can see the advantages in using it. You don't have to worry about the dynamic range of an actor, for example. You're probably gaining a great deal with digital recording, but you're also buying the potential for a lot of other problems. I wouldn't have gone to Belize with a couple of portable video recorders and an outboard digitizer like a PCMF-1, because of all the physical problems. It was more advantageous for me to have two small, high-quality analog recorders.

Also, most of the people I know who are using digital equipment on the set are also making analog protection. It's still in a very formative stage. But I can see it coming. I toyed with it on *Amadeus,* in the studio. I think it's particularly well suited to any kind of static situation, because of the current hardware limitations.

When I record, I don't listen off the tape, I listen direct. I go back and forth off the tape periodically. With digital recording, I wouldn't have that option. I'd have to stop and play the stuff back. There is a way to overcome that, but it means even more hardware.

INTERVIEWER: *What do you do when you're not making movies?*

NEWMAN: I'm raising children and listening to music and growing roses. It's taken me twenty-odd years, but I'm learning how to relax. It's very hard to do. I do it by convincing myself that nothing has to be kept clean or put in order and that it's OK not to feel guilty about looking at the clouds roll by. You know, making movies is like playing professional football—you come out every morning and you're ready to go. When you're at home with your family, you may come out and you're ready to take them somewhere or go do something, but it shouldn't have the same intensity.

INTERVIEWER: Having the beach house must be a good way to get away from it all.

NEWMAN: It is. It's marvelous. I go around fixing things, some of which need to be fixed, some of which don't. I have a garden and grow flowers. I'd never really done it before. I didn't learn it any more than I learned how to do sound recording, except from books and from experience. And the roses are exquisite! Anne and the kids help me plant them and pick out the colors. There are about three dozen bushes.

It's a marvelous entertainment for me because I don't cut them, I just watch them grow. I never realized this, but with roses, you can see them responding on a day-to-day basis—to being watered, to being talked to, to being trimmed and sprayed. I've never seen a plant that was quite so responsive. If you water them very deeply in the morning, by the afternoon the foliage gets darker, the plants look fuller; I don't think I'm imagining it. It's really the most amazing thing.

"For me, music is really what makes the world go 'round."

When I was in Belize, and I was absolutely nuts near the end wanting to go home, one of the things that kept me going, outside of my family, was thinking about my rose bushes! I kept thinking about how great it would be to get home to them and spend a couple of months just tending them.

INTERVIEWER: What kind of music do you listen to?

NEWMAN: For me, music is really what makes the world go 'round. Whether it's music the kids play or music that I play, all of it is really very important to me. I have rather eclectic tastes in music—a lot of jazz, although to me the world of jazz ended in 1965. And also I listen to a lot of classical music of all periods.

My son and daughter have introduced me to a lot of rock, or whatever contemporary composition can be called. And there is always music in the house, whether it's my son's bass guitar or his friend's flute or guitar. There's always a lot of sound in the house.

I read voraciously—a lot of potboilers interspersed with some fairly heavy stuff. The books I read are almost all fiction, with a smattering of the *New York Times*. Believe it or not, by doing some manipulating, I was able to get the *New York Times* in Belize, flown out of Miami with the film courier, every day for sixteen weeks!

Bill Varney

SOUND
RE-RECORDING

Born in Massachusetts, Bill Varney spent the early part of his career on the East Coast, as a disc jockey and sound engineer. He moved to Southern California and spent five years working in sound for educational films before starting Producers Sound Service with two other sound technicians. Seven years later, he joined the sound department of Samuel Goldwyn Studios. In his fourteen years there, he supervised the re-recording of films such as Hair, The Black Stallion, Grease, Animal House, Ordinary People, The Jazz Singer, Star Trek: The Movie, Poltergeist, Twilight Zone: The Movie, *and* Iceman.

In 1985, Varney moved to Universal Studios, where he is now sound director. Besides being involved with recent films like Back to the Future *and* Young Sherlock Holmes, *he has overseen the introduction of stereo television sound in several of Universal's television shows.*

Varney has received Oscars for his work on The Empire Strikes Back *and* Raiders of the Lost Ark, *and Oscar nominations for* Back to the Future *and* Dune.

He lives with his wife in Los Angeles. They have a daughter, who also works in the film business.

It strikes you as soon as you walk onto the lot at Universal: There must be some mistake. This isn't where they make movies. From the hulking, hangarlike buildings, you expect to see airplanes or new railroad cars rolling out into the San Fernando Valley's hazy glare.

But it was strangely quiet. A golf cart glided down the studio's tidy street, and a few ordinary-looking people strolled past carrying boxes of file folders or doughnuts.

"They make magic here?" I asked myself.

The security guard's directions led me to the sound department. I found Bill Varney's large, windowless office on the second floor at the end of a Kafka-esque maze of stairs and hallways.

It's from here that Varney directs the gargantuan effort of producing a film's final sound track. This final track is the product of the re-recording mixer and involves an extraordinarily diverse group of talents who combine the sound recorded on the set with the music, sound effects, and atmospheric sounds, as well as any additional dialogue and effects needed to replace unsuitable recordings from the set.

Varney has done his best to dispel the 1950s hospital atmosphere of the studio buildings with comfortable furniture, bookshelves, and a stereo. An Oscar stood amid the clutter on a credenza in a dark corner.

Varney is an imposing man physically, but warm and friendly. He gave me the impression of being slightly uncomfortable in the spotlight.

INTERVIEWER: Tell me something about the things you're doing here at Universal now.

VARNEY: First of all, since I've come here, we've opened a brand-new re-recording room that features a new Harrison PP I re-recording console. With this facility, we can do about any conceivable motion picture or video sound-recording format in one room. This doesn't sound unique, except that this room is totally automated—the console is totally automated. It's probably the most advanced state of automation available in the world of motion picture sound, at this point.

INTERVIEWER: *It's quite an intimidating experience to see all those formidable consoles and the people, obviously intent upon what they are doing, performing those strange rites with the dials and knobs.*

VARNEY: Yes, yes, it can look a bit confusing. I always have great difficulty trying to answer people when they ask, "What is it you do for a living?" It seems like it should be easy to explain, but it really isn't. As you say, people are at a loss when they walk into a re-recording room or into one of our rooms where we do the voice looping or into one of our Foley rooms where we do the sound effects. People think, "Wow, those guys and gals look really strange doing that work. What is it that these people really do for a living?"

> "*...making motion pictures is compromise.*"

INTERVIEWER: *Where did the term "Foley" come from?*

VARNEY: Foley is named after a Universal Studios sound editor by the name of Jack Foley. He started the process of adding sound to a scene after it had been shot. So in the Foley rooms we go in and literally rewalk all of the movements of the actors and the actresses on the screen—walking on the right surfaces, opening doors, moving and handling all the props, and so on. We then record this new material under ideal conditions.

INTERVIEWER: *Why is this necessary?*

VARNEY: The reason we do that is because there is so much material that we have to throw away from location recordings—it's just not usable. So the actors go into a looping stage and redo their lines.

Well, when you use these newly recorded lines in place of the old production track, you lose all the movement—the footsteps and the shirt rustles and the taking hats off and putting them on and so on. So we have people who stand around and do that, all day long. And then we take those tracks, the Foley tracks, and play them along with the newly recorded dialogue tracks and hopefully it sounds like the real thing. We might also add a little background—traffic noise and so on—if it's appropriate.

INTERVIEWER: *How many studios like this do you have?*

VARNEY: We have here, basically, four major re-recording rooms, studios where we do films and television. And there's a fifth, smaller studio where we do some of our smaller video projects. The two big feature rooms are now being upgraded to the best, state-of-the-art, automated systems available. The studio is truly committed to doing that.

We've also totally redone our scoring stage with one of the finest new consoles that's available in music recording. With its full automation capabilities, we've turned it into a class triple-A scoring facility. We're also bringing new people in. We're having a good time. Building is fun—you know, spending money and such.

INTERVIEWER: Tell me about your scoring facility—what types of things do you do there?

VARNEY: Well, as far as our scoring facility is concerned, we just finished one of the biggest orchestral scores we've done here in a long time. We had a seventy-five piece orchestra on our scoring stage. It was fun. I think that from the day I came to Hollywood, the scoring facility has always been one of the most exciting things to work with.

I remember, when I had been here only a short time, I went into one of the independent studios and found that David Rose* was conducting there that day. The orchestra was just arriving. Everyone came in and sat down. They opened up their instrument cases and did a little tuning up and stuff. And all of a sudden, the director said, "Well, let's take a look," and David Rose stood up. He put the baton up in the air and the film started playing on the screen in front of him and here was the downbeat! That phenomenal orchestra and its beautiful sound! It was a big orchestra, and I was overwhelmed by how well it worked!

And two days ago, we did a big score for Steven Spielberg's *Amazing Stories* television series with a relatively large orchestra, and the same thing happened. Every time, it never fails to amaze me; that first downbeat and the gorgeous sound.

But it happens so seldom anymore, because we're seeing less and less of the full orchestras, since many of the scores are now synthesized. You go into the rooms now and all you see are giant racks of synthesizers, and a few men are hidden behind them cranking out the scores. I still tend to like the full orchestral sound, the real rich and airy orchestral sound. There are times, certainly, when a synthesized style of music is wonderful for a particular show. *Miami Vice*, which we do here, is a good example. I don't think there's any better way to approach that. But with Steven's things for *Amazing Stories*, the orchestral material works well. We just finished *Sweet Liberty* for Alan Alda, and

---

* Emmy and Grammy award-winning composer/conductor, and musical director at NBC since 1946; his film scores include *Please Don't Eat the Daisies.*

that was a giant orchestra. Our scoring facility stays very busy. It's a nice-sounding room. We're very proud of it.

INTERVIEWER: *Who designs the sound in a movie?*

VARNEY: It's a strange term, "sound designing." That term came about in the San Francisco Bay area around the time *The Godfather* was being produced. Up there, you're a sound designer. In the Hollywood or New York world of filmmaking, you're a sound editor or creator. I don't think that any one individual designs a sound track. It would be nice to think that someone sits down and has a very concise idea, from the beginning of reel one to the very end of the movie. But all these things get compromised. Obviously, the director's looking for something, and we try to deliver it.

The art of making motion pictures is in compromise. Unlike carving a statue or painting a picture, the artist who conceives the film idea never truly gets exactly what he envisions, because each person who contributes also distorts the original idea slightly. I've worked with some of the best sound-effects people—creators, editors—that there are. I've been with people who wind up with a credit on the beginning of the film or the end of the film: "sound design by so and so." But when it was all over and done with, I realized that no one had truly designed it. No one sat down and wrote it out and had it all planned. We talked it over and it was a collaboration between the sound-effects people, ourselves, the dialogue people, and so on.

INTERVIEWER: *On a film like* Raiders, *for example, there are various peripheral sounds—often complex atmospheric sounds—coming from the sides of the theater. Who comes up with those?*

VARNEY: Well, those were the work of Ben Burtt, who's a sound designer—or sound creator, I think is a better word—for Lucasfilm, and Richard Anderson, and a bunch of really top-notch sound-effects creators and editors down here in Hollywood who worked on the project with us. With a film of that magnitude, we'll go through and build what we call predub after predub. We go in and we first work with only the ambience. What should the scene feel like?

Ben, utilizing his sound lab, may have already created that sound. Maybe he's already decided that off to the left of the picture there should be the sound of dripping water. Or maybe he's already looked at the film carefully and noticed that the camera pans to the left and water is dripping. So he says, "OK, let's start the sound early." Or he knows we're going to see those rats off to the right, so he says, "Let's, once in a while, hear a few pebbles dropping."

Then we implement those sounds on the re-recording stage; Ben's sound lab will supply them and we go through and manipulate the levels and spatial placement. It's truly the fun part—creating those environments. Most of the sound will be dictated by the visuals—the gun shots, car crashes, lightning cracks, et cetera. So it's the little nuances off to the side and in the surrounds that you don't see that are the fun things to do.

> *"It's the little nuances off to the side and in the surrounds that you don't see that are the fun things."*

INTERVIEWER: *What makes a good re-recording mixer?*

VARNEY: I have found over the many years I've spent in this business that very seldom do the highly trained and educated electronics engineer types make very good and creative re-recording mixers. By the nature of their education and training, they tend to get a little too much into the numbers technique of what they're doing, rather than going with the gut instincts that one learns—the creative gut instincts. And I think I've always operated that way. I've never looked down at my console and said, "My goodness! Gee, I can't believe I'm pushing 6 decibels at 120 cycles in this particular track," and get too worried about it. Because the bottom line to anything you're doing when you're manipulating sounds is, Is it working? Does it sound right? Is it doing exactly what you want it to do for that moment? Numbers are sort of irrelevant.

You know, truly, you can go from here to any facility up north or in New York, and all sound facilities can record relatively good sound. They are all tuned within certain parameters as far as the technical setups are concerned—the machines, the distortion, and all those things. But it's what the people bring to it that's most important. Not only what they bring to it in a technical sense, but in a creative sense. I have always tried to have trusted engineering people around me. That way, I can concentrate solely on the creative side of my job and not become encumbered with the technical side of things.

INTERVIEWER: *Certain people have said that sound is half the movie. Do you see it that way?*

VARNEY: I wouldn't be that bold. I would never dare make a statement like that, because I think it quite obviously depends on the motion picture.

Let's see if we can cite some examples. I did a motion picture years ago called *Ordinary People,* which was a very successful film directed by Robert Redford. *Ordinary People* epitomizes the good, but average, sound track. In this particular case, it happened to be a nightmare for me. No one will ever know, except myself and an editor and a couple of other people, that what we did was miraculous. We had tracks that just didn't work. They were badly recorded in production. We made them work. So to anyone in the theater seeing that movie, it sounded fine. The point is, it's a dialogue movie surrounded with some fine music and a light and unobtrusive sound-effects track. Truly, we needed to hear the words in that movie, but I don't think you could say that the sound was half the movie.

Now, compare that picture with a movie like my favorite, *Raiders of the Lost Ark.* Without its sound track, *Raiders of the Lost Ark* would not have been the movie it was. And certainly here, the percentage that sound contributes to the movie starts changing dramatically. *Raiders of the Lost Ark* is my proudest achievement and will probably go down in history as being—and maybe I shouldn't make a statement like this—probably one of the best stereo sound tracks ever done. And that's credit not only to me but to all of the people involved. It's a beautifully constructed sound track that's often ripped apart and studied in cinema schools. It was an Academy Award winner for sound.

And interestingly, this year's Academy Award winner was *Out of Africa.* That was also a brilliant sound track. Many people leaving the theater said, "Gosh, that was a beautiful sound track," and it truly was. Yet the percentages would start changing again. I mean, the sound track in *Out of Africa* was—I'd hate to use the word *ordinary,* but it was. It was a fairly simple sound track: Good dialogue, good sound effects, and beautiful music, all craftily interwoven into a marvelous sound track. But in terms of the true drama of the movie, *Raiders* leaned heavily—very heavily—on its powerful and dynamic sound track to make it into the truly successful adventure film that it was.

INTERVIEWER: You've been at this for a long time and you've been tremendously successful. Does anything worry you anymore?

VARNEY: Not really, though one of the great fears that I've had in my career is that each time I'm nominated or pick up an Oscar for my work, I might say, "Uh-oh, am I going to get the attitude now that I've climbed my mountain and there's nowhere to go?" I've been lucky. I've found it works the opposite way. It pressures me because now people are looking to me and saying, "He's an award winner, so he's going to give us something special." So I keep trying to come up with something new and unique all the time.

INTERVIEWER: *What is new and unique? How do you judge?*

VARNEY: I gave a speech recently at the Cinema Audio Society awards banquet. That's the re-recording mixer's organization here in Hollywood. And one of the comments I kept hearing there was that there's a lot of good sound being done now. Previous to this banquet, we had gone to the Academy sound-effects nominating screenings. There you look at seven films, ten-minute excerpts of them, and the decision's made as to what's going to be nominated. I used to go in there feeling very cocky—you know, "Boy, my stuff's going to be the best-sounding stuff here." This year I walked out and I found my shoulders were kind of drooping and my tail was between my legs. I said, "Wow, there's a lot of great sound being recorded now." There's not only a lot of good sound being re-recorded, but the sound-editing teams are doing incredible work. So it's really tough to pick what is best anymore. There's so much good stuff going on. It's great.

INTERVIEWER: *Why do you think that is?*

VARNEY: Well, part of it is the technology. I'm glad we have the technology that's been available in the last few years. It gave us the opportunity to advance the quality of sound tracks to where we are today. The real tragedy is that you have to go and listen to movies in these bowling alley kinds of theaters, the six- and seven-plexes. I don't know if we'll have a quality industry left after awhile. You might as well be home, truly, in the comfort of your home, rather than seeing films in some of these environments. It's really sad.

INTERVIEWER: *How many people do you have working on the sound for a feature film?*

VARNEY: No one realizes the number of people it takes. We had 155 people involved in the postproduction sound track of *Back to the Future*. That's a lot of people. That's just on the sound track, now. That has nothing to do with the picture editorial or the camera crews or drivers or carpenters or anything like that. It was a very complex sound track. Now add to that the fact that it did get into a slight time crunch, so we had to add people, but it's a safe bet that, had we not been in a time crunch, we still would be looking at 120 or 130 people. Still a lot of people.

INTERVIEWER: *Do you find the collaborative process of filmmaking exciting, or is it frustrating?*

VARNEY: It's a wonderful chance for people in various crafts to come together and enhance one another's work. However, it depends a little on who you're collaborating with. Hopefully, the mixing crew has worked together for a long time.

First of all, there's the supervising re-recording mixer. I think I have the toughest goal of all. The dialogue work, the basic sound, the sound concept are basically my responsibility. I have with me a man or a woman who's handling the music and another one or two if it's a movie with extensive sound effects. Hopefully, I've got a good team there. Between us, there has to be a sort of magic, a chemistry. Because if we don't work really well with each other, it affects the movie.

The effects people and the music people have to know how and when to get out of the way of a very important line of dialogue. Even though they might be in the midst of a giant battle or whatever it is, those sound effects have to come down; they have to get that music out of the way, but without stopping the motion that's being created by the whole scene.

> *"One of the most overused expressions in Hollywood is 'We'll save it in the mix.'"*

Then, there's obviously the collaboration with the director, the producer, editors, and all the other people who are directly involved.

It can be great if you have a team of people who are truly interested, if they are striving for something new and unique all the time. That's what keeps me going, I think. If I had to go down and do routine, mundane kinds of re-recording with people who have been doing it forever and are tired of it, people to whom Thursday, payday, is the only thing that is truly important to them, I think I would have stopped doing this a long time ago. But I still get charged with it; I still like it; it's still fun.

It can also be very frustrating sometimes because obviously it's a very subjective sort of thing. Everyone looks at it in a slightly different way. Someone wants the music a little higher and the effects a little lower and so on.

I find that, and I will probably regret saying this, the best sound tracks I have ever been involved with are the ones we have the least guidance for. I think the most successful ones are made when the people in charge have such faith in you that they let you be your most creative, and they are just a nice, gentle, guiding force to keep it all on track. Obviously, we can't go in and do the re-recording on a motion picture if we don't really know what the director's after, unless it's an *Ordinary People*—a very straight dialogue and music kind of film. If a director's going to be utilizing sound in a strange way, the way Martin Scorsese will use it sometimes to try get into people's heads, then you need strong input.

INTERVIEWER: *Which way do you prefer to work?*

VARNEY: I like the films where the director and the producer say, "Here, dub our movie, and then let's play back each reel." We work in segments—ten-minute reels. Then, after recording and playing back the reel, we get together and talk about it—"Gee, don't you think you've got a little too much music? That's not really what I had in mind. Let's keep the music a little lower here because I'm trying to go for something a little bit different." Or, "Wow, that's great. I really like that electronic sizzle in there. Can we get a little more of that at one point?" Then we'll make the minor corrections and sort of finesse it. That's a nice way to do a movie. Good people. Good collaboration. People trusting each other.

INTERVIEWER: *How often does that happen?*

VARNEY: I've been lucky. I would say probably 60 or 70, maybe 75 percent of the movies. And the worst sound tracks I've ever done are the ones with which I was simply an extension of somebody who says to you: "No, I've got to have that louder."

"But it doesn't work. It's not going to have the effect you want."

"I don't care, that's the way I want it." Those pictures never, ever work. And I think I've seen some good examples. Now you're going to ask me what they are, but let's not get into that.

INTERVIEWER: *How do you find working with the very powerful people in this business?*

VARNEY: The bigger they are, generally, the better they are to deal with. When I say that I mean that their egos aren't such an issue. They've found their place, they've found their niche, they've found their success. They don't have to prove anything to anybody.

If I ever get to produce my own motion picture—which we all dream we're going to do, but we're probably never going to—I certainly hope I would go out and hire the best possible craft people I could find and let them do their thing, with my guidance—letting them know what I wanted.

I see so many people, and some of them very successful, too, who insist, "Oh, I've got to have all the Academy Award winners. I don't care what it costs." And then, when they work with these people, they reject every suggestion. It becomes very frustrating. And I believe it doesn't make for good moviemaking.

INTERVIEWER: *What's the most difficult part of your job?*

VARNEY: It might be hard to accept this, but it's true: The most difficult part is probably the politics—working with people, the collaboration, the political aspects. The actual movement of the knobs or the change of the sounds or the change of the picture or cleaning up the noises in the dialogue track becomes second nature.

The real magic is making everybody totally happy and convinced that what you've given them is the best possible thing that could be given to them. You've got to have them understand that you've extended this particular medium as far as you can extend it. That you can't go beyond that point, whatever it is, whether it's volume, equalization, or whatever. That to go any further would be a mistake. Some day, before I retire, I'll decide what the percentages are—the balance of technical prowess as opposed to the diplomacy or whatever word we want to use for dealing with people, the human element. We become the referees and the mediators between the directors and the producers and the editors and all these people with all their opinions. You have to size people up quickly. Do they want a strong person? Do they really not want a strong person? Do they want my input? Do they want me to keep my mouth shut and do what they tell me to do? You have to quickly make those determinations, so that everybody's happy and moving in the right direction.

The people that falter in this business are the people that don't know how to make those determinations quickly. They start forcing themselves and their opinions and ideas on everyone else. Somehow, we have to take all this information and these opinions and say, "Here's who we should pay attention to on this one." And that's tough. It's the toughest part of the job. You win some and you lose some, you know? I've won and I've lost with some of the biggest people in this industry, and I'm sure I'll win a few more and lose a few more. Over the years I've wished I could publish that list. Here are the guys you should let have their way and here are the guys who want you to contribute and want you to dub their movie for them. Being able to quickly and successfully sort out the kinds and types of supervisors and directors comes, I guess, with age, experience, and keeping your eyes and ears constantly open.

INTERVIEWER: *What originally got you interested in the field of motion picture sound?*

VARNEY: My interest in the world of communication came shortly after I left high school back in New England. I worked in radio and television as a disc jockey, newsman, combination engineer—did just about everything you could do. And I had the opportunity to work during the very last days of network radio, which I think was probably one of the best things that happened to me. Network radio was a sound medium, and it was a wonderful opportunity to experience its unique use of sound. Sitting there at night in a lonely radio station in New England and listening to all of those old radio shows, I think I learned a good sense of timing and a good sense of balance—things that people coming into this industry today simply don't have a chance to do.

> *"It's a strange term, 'sound designing.' In the Hollywood or New York world of filmmaking, you're a sound editor or creator...."*

I worked in independent radio and rock music and news for a good many years. It got a little overbearing after nine or ten years. I wasn't enjoying it. It wasn't fun.

I'm a New England boy; I came out of the Boston area. So I went home to gather my thoughts, and I found out about a film project that was beginning as part of a physics series at MIT. It was a government-funded project, during the later part of the fifties. The United States thought the Russians were going to surpass us in the sciences. There was a tremendous amount of money infused into programs to promote science in the classroom.

When I found out about the MIT project, I just walked in one day and said, "What are you doing here?" and the fellow in charge said, "Well, we're building this studio. We're going to make educational motion pictures. What can you do?" And I said, "I can do anything." Luckily, he had based all of his success on the premise that a person can, in fact, do anything if he applies himself. So I was hired and I spent two good years there working with topnotch New York film crews on an exciting set of films with some of the top physicists from MIT.

And like all young filmmakers, we were off making our own private little films on the weekends because we had the use of all the equipment. I did a film with the folk singer Joan Baez. Her dad was part of the series as a physicist at MIT. She was just starting her career as a folk singer in those days.

Someone saw that film—it was just a small thing we shot in a coffeehouse in Boston—and liked it. They were coming out here to the West Coast to do a six-month project with educational films, and they asked me if I'd be willing to come out and do the sound on those. I said sure, I'd take a chance. So I came out here and that project went on for about five years. I had the opportunity to do not only sound, but to do everything—editing, directing, producing. It was a great learning experience.

INTERVIEWER: How did you make the transition from educational films to features?

VARNEY: By keeping my fingers crossed and talking and listening a lot. I was using facilities here in town to do our educational films, and I got to know the people there and pretty soon I got accepted by different folks and got into the union. Basically, I did it just by meeting people. It's much tougher today even than it was then.

Once I was established, I went into partnership with two other fellows, and we opened a company called Producers Sound Service in Hollywood. I was with them for seven years, and again it was a good experience because we did everything. We did all the engineering, built consoles and equipment. I helped in the design, did mixing, recording, projecting, swept the floors—everything. I also got into the administrative end later on. After I left there, I hunted around a little bit. Don Rogers, at what was then the Samuel Goldwyn Studios, hired me as a re-recording mixer. And the rest of it's history; I was there fourteen years. The final six or eight years with Goldwyn I was the lead re-recording mixer there—heavily booked and sought after.

Then, about a year and a half ago, Universal approached me and offered me a position here with a dual role of continuing on as a re-recording mixer for a short while and also running the department—reshaping it and creating a whole new image. We're having a terrific time here.

INTERVIEWER: Your training was all on the job, then.

VARNEY: No formal training. I think on-the-job training is still one of the best ways to learn, particularly in a business like this. I found this out when I first started in radio, years ago. I came out of a little, tiny, hole-in-the-wall school of radio and television in Boston. I was there about six months and got my first job on my first audition.

Later, I started bumping into a whole bunch of kids that came out of Emerson College in Boston, which is truly a fine college of drama and radio and broadcasting. I learned an interesting lesson. All of them came from the world of their FM stations—the classical music and so on. And they were tossed into a strange world of rock and roll and commercials selling Hallmark greeting cards and vacuum cleaners. All this articulation they had been taught—speech patterns and so on—it didn't work.

I think, in many ways, that the same thing happens often to the people who come out of cinema schools. We're lucky, here in L.A., to have such really fine ones, both USC and UCLA. But there's almost an unlearning process that has to take place. You step out of that environment and whoops—all of a sudden you're in the real world of filmmaking and sometimes it's a real culture shock.

INTERVIEWER: *Are your children following you into filmmaking?*

VARNEY: I have a twenty-year-old daughter who started in the industry two years ago. She's been serving as an apprentice. She chose that rather than going on to college. She had the opportunity to go to any college she wanted, anywhere in the world. She simply said, "No, I want to do like you did, dad." And of course, how do you argue with that? She said, "You learned the hard way. You learned the right way. You're good at what you do and I want to do the same thing." And she already is sought after and is going to be very good at what she does.

My wife also, though she's now retired, spent almost ten years in film sound recording, having been, as a matter of fact, one of the first women to break the "male only" barrier of the sound union. The men made it real tough in those days, but she soon became a respected sound recordist who was much in demand.

INTERVIEWER: *Is this a tough business to break into?*

VARNEY: Yes. But it looks like there's just been a ruling handed down or there will be in the next couple of days, here in Hollywood, that the seniority system probably is going to come to an end. This will inspire younger people with talent who are out there now and can't get a crack at this kind of work. They might have a better chance at it now than they have had in the past because the seniority systems unfortunately protect the incompetents rather than doing anything for the people who are truly gifted and do a good job. Those people always work.

INTERVIEWER: *What do you have to say to new people coming into the sound business?*

VARNEY: One of the difficulties with bringing new people into the industry today is that most of them seem to come to us never having experienced any of the other steps in the sound process. Very few of the people I employ now in postproduction have ever worked in production, have ever truly been out there and recorded on a set or on location. Our people don't know about the problems the mixers and the sound recordists and the boom men out on the set are going through. And it's the same the other way around; I think the two groups truly don't understand each other's needs. Some of these people don't understand how movies are made because of their very narrow vision. That's a tragedy.

"Without its sound track, Raiders of the Lost Ark would not have been the movie it was."

And strangely enough, just today, I started the first notes of what will be some way to reconnect the production and postproduction people. Whether it's through manuals or seminars or letting the production people visit with us in the postproduction areas and vice versa, I don't know. But this is the kind of thing that I'm trying to bring to the studio. Rather than let these chasms widen, let's see if we can get back some kind of communication.

INTERVIEWER: *When does the producer bring the re-recording people on board a project?*

VARNEY: [He chuckles.] It depends. If you're in television, that's one thing and if you're in feature work, it's another thing. But let me tell you how serious the television problem is. And it's not unique to this studio. We have been in situations lately where the show that will air on a given Saturday night is handed over to the editorial people on the previous Monday. And those people have to edit the sound—try to put it all together soundwise—within two or three days. It will wind up in our re-recording stages sometimes two or three days prior to going on the air! There's literally no room anymore for any kind of mistake.

And many times now we're doing satellite feeds to Canada. The Canadian air dates are always slightly ahead of the U.S. air dates. So very often we'll satellite to Canada and then we'll just barely get a print together good enough to get to the network before they go on the air. One thing that helps a little is that we don't need the lab as much anymore because, for example, almost all of the stereo television we deliver is on 1-inch videotape now with two tracks of stereo information on it. Although it's created one new process, it's eliminated a whole bunch of others. So it's a little faster getting the product to the network that way.

Now in an ideal schedule, the episode would be turned over to the editing people about two weeks ahead of time, the scoring and all the looping having been done. Then the editors have enough time to get it prepared and we have a whole day of dubbing, and a day to get an optical negative made, get it to the lab, get it processed, get a print made, and probably deliver it to the network three or four days ahead of time. That would be nice. I don't know when the last time we worked like that was. The only show we work with that way now is *Amazing Stories*. It's way ahead of schedule all the time.

With feature work, the film used to be turned over to the sound editorial people weeks, sometimes months ahead of when it went to the re-recording stages. But now that's changed too and our feature postproduction schedules are beginning to look more like TV schedules.

INTERVIEWER: *Do they ever come to you when the film is still in conception, to involve you in the project early on?*

VARNEY: Once in a great while. We'll get people who will want some advice on crews, or maybe they're going for something special and they want to try a new process, or they'll want to try the new digital recorders. We sometimes get involved, although not as much as I think we should.

You see, there's less time for everything now. They are shooting faster, moving quickly from location to location, and you never have much of a chance to get that second or third take you'd like to get for sound anymore. They've got to move on. If the shot's good for the camera, that's it; let's go.

Unfortunately, we're in that part of the industry where, whatever problems we have in the field, they *can* be solved later. You can't solve the camera problems on that film later. If it's out of focus, it's out of focus. If the actors look stupid, they're always going to look stupid. You can't change that. But everything we record on a set can be changed later. If the director doesn't like the way the actor or actress read, they come into a looping stage and he or she redoes it. Literally just re-records it, watching and listening to themselves again. But that's the way film is, and it creates headaches for us. You say, "But gee, the tracks are no good." And they'll say, "Well, that's your job. You fix them. You make them work."

One of the most overused expressions in Hollywood is "We'll save it in the mix," or "We'll save it in the dubbing." And it's true, we finally wind up trying to save it in the re-recording stages.

INTERVIEWER: *What's a typical postproduction schedule?*

VARNEY: We have a major film that I start on next Monday. It originally had a postproduction schedule of about eight weeks. Now, for a whole bunch of reasons, it's been crunched into four weeks. So I and the crew will be down there for four seven-day weeks trying to get this film put together. Not just put together—we also want it to sound good. It's getting harder and harder for the craft people, because when you get into those crunches, the creative things get cast aside. I worked with a man years ago who had a wonderful expression. He said, "Well, we're back in the business of creating reasonable combinations of sound and shipping it." And that's what you do. With so little time, all you're doing is trying to make the dialogue at least intelligible, let the music dance around and do its work, and hopefully the sound effects are creating the right environment.

But to really get in to polish it and to make it special and unique—that's hard to do these days. There are very few filmmakers who give you that time. Spielberg gives you that latitude, Lucas still does, and there are others. Sidney Pollack had a fairly realistic postproduction schedule on *Out of Africa.* But there are fewer and fewer people like that.

INTERVIEWER: *Do you generate all of the sound effects here at Universal?*

VARNEY: Some of them. The independent sound editorial companies in town now have synthesizers and other equipment to create certain sound effects. With *Back to the Future,* for example, when the actor Michael Fox made his trips in and out of the various environments, the editorial people were hunting for some unique sounds, and they came to us with a massive, really terrific selection of sound elements to work from.

INTERVIEWER: *How many of the sound effects are synthesized now and how many are the old "coconuts on the desktop" type of thing?*

VARNEY: Sound effects are still pretty much the coconuts—recording the real material or something that sounds like it. A hatchet through a watermelon; those things are still being done a lot. Not a lot is being done in terms of synthesizing everyday sound effects. In terms of synthesizing sound

119

effects for space-age kinds of films, a lot is being done. We need to create the environment, create the sounds of the various devices in the room, and so on. A lot of that's being done with synthesizers. With the synthesized stuff you can store it all digitally and call it up on a keyboard like a piano. The stuff can be easily stored and easily manipulated.

INTERVIEWER: *Are most movies recorded in Dolby stereo these days? Is it the standard now?*

VARNEY: Yes. I don't know exactly what the percentage is, but it's kind of silly not to do it anymore. Many of the technical restrictions we have we sort of encumbered ourselves with from the early days of photographic sound tracks. Neither the film stock nor the processing allowed us to extend frequency response much either way, at either the low end or the high end. So someone decided on a set of standards and said, "Okay, we'll work inside these parameters." And they weren't very good, when you think of how sound tracks rolled off in the 6kHz region and made a tremendous dip from there on.

> *"The real tragedy is that you have to go and listen to movies in these bowling alley kinds of theaters."*

Then the Dolby people came along and said, "Wait a minute guys. You've got fine-grained films. You've got real good processing now. You can extend the range. It's easy to do it." That was the start of the Dolby film process, when they realized we could in fact get better sound tracks. Dolby stereo is basically three things. It's the utilization of the Dolby noise-reduction process in the making of a motion picture, so we can keep the generation buildup of noise to a minimum. It allows us an extended frequency response we never before had available to us, both in the re-recording and in the presentation in the theater. And last but not least, it gives us the ability to carry a four-track stereo sound track on a single piece of film. There's nothing unusual about the track if you look at it. It looks just like the old optical tracks unless you look very carefully.

And the Dolby system, over the years, has improved. We've improved in the utilization of it. We know how to use it better than we did before. Also, most of the re-recording mixers I know have achieved what we call good mono-compatible dubs. That means that the stereo tracks we make, on the final released product, if played on a mono projector, in a mono environment, work and work very well. In the early days of Dolby they didn't. We didn't know how to make it work.

INTERVIEWER: *Yet people still make films with mono sound tracks?*

VARNEY: A lot of people will justify it by saying, "Well OK, I've got a film and it's not a *Star Wars* or *Raiders of the Lost Ark.* It doesn't have to be stereo." That's not true. If you've had a seventy-five-piece orchestra in and you've got a gorgeous score, why not utilize it to its full value? Why dump it into the center speaker and roll it off at 6kHz and make it sound terrible? And Dolby doesn't cost any more, except for a little licensing fee. It seems I say this every year—"Well, it will only be another year or two and everything will be stereo." And I still believe that one day that will be the case.

There's another thing you can do if the producer wants to keep costs down. If you don't have a lot of sound effects that need to be spatially placed, you can keep the dialogue in the center speaker and keep the sound-effects track simple; maybe spread the background sounds a little bit but basically just let the music be enhanced by the stereo. That's a quick way to do it, and it works really well. That's what I think everybody should be doing, at a minimum. Because with the techniques we've evolved, stereo dubs don't take any longer to do now.

INTERVIEWER: *And you've begun working in stereo television.*

VARNEY: We're making tremendous inroads in stereo television now. This past year about half of the studio's television output of some ten or eleven hours of television was in stereo. And this year it will be even more. Tremendous advances are going to be made there. Some new decoding boxes are going to be made available for your home—really good systems, not Mickey Mouse junk. You'll be able to enjoy full four-track stereo in your living room, if you can get the kids out.

INTERVIEWER: *What about some of the newer technologies—the compact disc, for example?*

VARNEY: We're seeing some compact discs now that are beautiful. Not only do they have music, but they can have another channel with a thorough discussion about the artist or composer. We're just scratching the surface, and we seem to say that every year, "Oh my God, we're just scratching the surface!" But it's true.

The technology is changing so fast. That makes it difficult for a company like ours. How do you stay of top of all the new technology? It's not very cost-effective. Today you go to this process, and six months down the line someone comes out with a new one. So you have to assess each major change very carefully. We just came back from the NAB [National Association of Broadcasters] convention and the SMPTE [Society of Motion Picture and Television Engineers] convention. It's startling what we saw. There's a lot of good stuff on the horizon. The high-definition television is unbelievable! There's no reason why, very shortly, we would ever deliver prints to a theater again. Within two years certainly, we're going to be able to satellite-feed theaters throughout the country and we'll see the image projected on the screen from those feeds, the source having been some kind of digital environment.

INTERVIEWER: Have you looked into what the Japanese are doing with television technology?

VARNEY: We've seen the Japanese digital, or high-resolution, TV at some of these shows. I'm just staggered by the quality. I've seen it on every size screen you can imagine. I've seen every kind of transfer, from television to film projected on huge screens, from film to video. I've seen it every way you can imagine and it is just mind-boggling. There's no such thing as a line. It just doesn't exist. Every screen you walk up to looks like somebody's literally painted it, it's just so beautiful. It's really breathtaking. We'll go to that system later than the Japanese because they're developing the technology and can make the conversion more easily than we can. But it will happen.

INTERVIEWER: I imagine there are similar advances in the equipment that production recordists use.

VARNEY: Yes. When I started out in this business, when we went out in the field to record a motion picture in production, we went out with giant trucks, with batteries and generators and converters and sprocketed film equipment. It was amazing—tons of equipment.

Then, in the past fifteen or twenty years, we've been going out with the little Nagra, the Swiss recorder that's as small as a briefcase. And everyone says, "Boy, is that really trim." But there will soon be some amazing tiny, new digital field recorders available. We were looking at some things that Sony's designing right now. I just saw a prototype for a machine that will soon be on the market that makes the Nagra look big and cumbersome. And it will have twenty times the features that the Nagra has. So these are exciting times.

In some ways I would like to have come to this industry ten or fifteen years earlier. Maybe I'd have had the chance to work with the true moguls—the Goldwyns, the Mayers, and those people. But on the other hand, in a technological sense, this has been a very exciting twenty years for us in the film business. And it isn't going to stop.

INTERVIEWER: *What do you see down the road for sound?*

VARNEY: Well, I think we will see some more slightly different stereo processes on the market. I think we'll see a swing toward digital recording formats. That's about to happen. The Dolby people are putting forth new techniques in their area.

But, rather than answer that question, I have a wish list. On the top of the list is my desire that theater owners go back to presenting films the way directors and producers intended them to be presented—a big environment with good sound systems, well projected, in focus, plenty of light on the screen, clean floors, good popcorn and good pop, and people not yakking and talking throughout the whole movie.

I would also like to see a better release format, although I don't know what that would be. I think we've extended the optical process as far as we can extend it. Whether the next step is a laser technology, sound tracks still on the film, or a satellite feed, I don't know. We turn out a magnificent product here, yet it suffers terribly before it's presented to the audience.

And I hope that movie audiences don't get so disgruntled with the way films are being presented now that they stop going to the movies. Staying home and watching films like *Back to the Future* or *Out of Africa* on a little box in your den or living room is not the way they were intended to be seen.

Eiko Ishioka

PRODUCTION DESIGN

A native of Tokyo, Eiko Ishioka is part of an artistic family. Her father was a graphic designer, as is her sister. In fact, she and her sister are the only women members of the Tokyo Art Directors' Club. One of the most eminent designers in Japan and an honored and accomplished woman, Ishioka is best known for her contributions in graphic design and art direction.

She began her career in the art department of the Japanese cosmetic giant Shiseido, becoming the art director there and winning several awards along the way. From there, Ishioka moved into the free-lance field and expanded her work to include design for books, posters, packaging, museum exhibitions, stage design, and production design for television commercials, documentaries, and feature films.

Much of Ishioka's work can be seen in a large retrospective book entitled Eiko by Eiko, *published in 1984. In 1985 she won an Award for Artistic Contribution at the Cannes Film Festival for her set design in the Paul Schrader film* Mishima.

Ishioka now spends as much time in New York or Europe

*as she does in Tokyo. I met her at my Manhattan hotel on a bright afternoon.
She is a petite woman and was dressed in layers of subtle, dark Japanese fabrics.
We found a secluded corner of the hotel's mock Edwardian lobby, behind a folding screen and potted palm. It was an appropriate setting. We sat down in plush,
high-backed chairs and talked across a ponderous gilt table, surrounded by
bookshelves, books, and paneling—all painted on the walls like a stage set.*

*As she spoke, her lively eyes belied the typically Japanese lack of expres-
sion, and her sentences were occasionally punctuated by a bright smile that lit
up her entire face.*

INTERVIEWER: *What you are doing in New York now?*

ISHIOKA: Now I am involved with projects for two great artists here in
New York. One is a composer, Philip Glass, and the other is the jazz musician
Miles Davis. They're completely different musicians, and both of them are
great. I received an offer from Philip Glass last year to be involved as a production designer for his new opera.

INTERVIEWER: *For the entire production?*

ISHIOKA: Yes, to include sets and lighting and costumes—everything, in
fact. His new opera will come out next fall in France and will play in several
important cities in America and Europe. On this trip to New York I had the
second meeting with Philip Glass.

INTERVIEWER: *You've worked with Philip Glass before, haven't you?*

ISHIOKA: Yes, I worked with Philip on *Mishima*. His first project com-
posing for a movie was *Koyaanisqatsi*, directed by Godfrey Reggio. *Mishima*
was the second one. The music was very well done, and the music itself helped
the visual approach—the editing, my set design, et cetera.

I like Philip as a person. He is such a complete talent, and his music is
unique. This is my first chance to collaborate with Philip on an opera. It's very
exciting. The opera is based on the novel *The Making of the Representative for
Planet 8,* written by the British author Doris Lessing.

INTERVIEWER: *Has any of her work been translated into Japanese?*

ISHIOKA: Yes, several have been translated, but this one has not been
translated yet. Philip read her book and he was amazed. He wanted to make
the opera, so the two of them worked together to make a, how do you say it . . .

INTERVIEWER: Scenario or script?

ISHIOKA: Scenario, yes. But for operas we don't call it a scenario. We call it a libretto. They worked together to make a libretto. Then, afterwards, I become involved. Now they are waiting for my design work. I haven't finished yet. It's a very difficult project.

INTERVIEWER: Will you do all the drawings yourself?

ISHIOKA: Yes, I am doing the drawing by myself, at least the basic concept. Sometimes I hire illustrators, but in this case I'm drawing by myself. Afterwards, when we decide on some ideas, I'm going to build a miniature, a model. This is the best way to communicate with each other, instead of using a two-dimensional drawing. The sets are, of course, three-dimensional, so this is very important.

INTERVIEWER: Will you meet with Doris Lessing also?

ISHIOKA: Yes, of course, but not this time. I had a meeting with Doris and Philip and other key people last December. It was our first meeting. Each person has started to compose the music, to design the sets, and so on. This is the beginning of the process. I'm going to see Doris again when my ideas have formed more completely.

INTERVIEWER: Tell me about what you are doing with Miles Davis.

ISHIOKA: Miles, after more than thirty years with CBS, has moved to Warner Brothers. This project is his first album with Warner's. So he needs new, sensational artwork for his album and music video. Warner Brothers presented several artists to Miles, but he wasn't satisfied with them and asked for me. The creative director at Warner Brothers also agreed to hire me.

It's a wonderful situation when artists can work with other artists they admire. I had two meetings with Miles yesterday and the day before yesterday, and we talked about basic creative concepts.

He is a kind of genius still, you know, developing new music. He is a very innovative artist. When I was a student, he was a superstar in Japan and all over the world. But he is still a superstar, because he is trying all the time to develop new music. At the same time, he is competing with other new, young musicians. He is probably fifty-nine years old. He mentioned that his birthday is coming next month, he's almost reached his sixties, but he is wearing very fashionable clothes, and is still competing with younger musicians like Michael Jackson and Prince. He has a driving force to develop new music, and his music is so artistic.

INTERVIEWER: *How is he to work with?*

ISHIOKA: As you know, this is our first collaboration. Many people said Miles is such a difficult person to work with. But he was very nice. I cannot say if I have become a friend of Miles or not. But two years ago he called me up and since then we have had several meetings and we talked, talked, and talked. He wanted to collaborate in some way on this new work.

He has so many ideas. In his conversation, his ideas jump this way and suddenly jump that way, this way, that way. So my attitude must be very careful; I listen to his voice and ask myself, "What does he want? What is he thinking?" always being very careful to listen to everything.

Then I want to build my own ideas based on his. And then I show him my ideas and discuss them—which ones does he like, how do they relate to his ideas, or why I did this idea and not that one.

INTERVIEWER: *This must be very difficult, because as artists, you both have your own strong aesthetic ideas.*

ISHIOKA: I understand Miles's approach to new ideas. He wants to be a new, innovative artist, not just doing the old things over again. So this I understand very clearly and I agree with him. If my ideas are not fresh, not innovative, he's obviously not satisfied, so this is very simple. During our meetings in the last few days, I was very careful to listen to what he wanted to say, what was on his mind.

INTERVIEWER: *Do you enjoy collaborating with other artists?*

ISHIOKA: Oh, yes, but to collaborate you have to work very, very hard and try very hard to get along together. Most of the time producers are very scared of two strong artists collaborating. They are afraid it won't work. But if it's successful, it's very, very strong, and it's innovative and very exciting.

INTERVIEWER: *And in film there are so many different people trying to work together.*

ISHIOKA: So many different people. It's difficult, but it's normal. Between two people, there are personal complications. Among a hundred people, even communication becomes extremely difficult.

If you must work with several people on different levels and with different talents, there is always a lot of misunderstanding, and it can become very difficult.

INTERVIEWER: *Who else have you worked closely with?*

ISHIOKA: I worked with Francis Ford Coppola at the end of 1984. I worked as a production designer for his production of *Rip Van Winkle* for American television. It was part of a series for children. Several big-name people volunteered to work on the series, like Francis and Mick Jagger. I like that kind of attitude.

Francis was also executive producer for *Mishima*. After the editing process for *Mishima*, Francis called me in Tokyo. He asked me to work with him on this television production to design sets and props, if I was interested.

Before I met him, people told me about Francis—that he is such a difficult man. When I received the phone call in Tokyo from Francis, I told him I was a bit frightened of working with him. But he said to me, "No, don't you worry; let's work together, let's study together, let's learn together for this production."

> *"Most of the time the most difficult part of the project is the budget."*

So he sent me the screenplay. And during my collaboration with Francis he wasn't at all difficult. His direction was very clear; it was perfect. He knows what art is, what collaboration is, what a movie is, what teamwork is; he knows a hundred percent. After working with him, I couldn't understand why people criticized him so much.

So this close collaboration helped me a great deal. My creativity blossomed into something ten times greater than if I had been left to work with only my own talent. And because *Rip Van Winkle* was a fairy tale, it wasn't so difficult to do.

Before *Mishima*, I designed two big posters for his *Apocalypse Now*, the Japanese version for the Japanese market. Francis liked my posters very much. He framed the two posters together and hung them in his living room. Since then we have worked very closely.

INTERVIEWER: What kind of artist do you consider yourself?

ISHIOKA: My background is in graphic design. After my book, *Eiko by Eiko*, came out, film producers, art directors, and composers like Philip Glass looked at my book and recognized that Eiko is a unique artist that does not belong in any special area.

So my position in the movie business and the theater is very special, almost like that of an outsider. I'm not a specialist for the movies and I'm not a specialist for the stage, and I don't want to be. I want to maintain my independence as a free-lance artist, art director, or designer.

In this way, if the producer or film director needs some special artwork, something extraordinary for a movie or a play, they are going to hire Eiko. Because for the typical film, the ordinary film, they are better off hiring a film professional—an art director or costume designer from the movie field. Their minds are completely movie, movie, movie. But in my career, I don't need or want any kind of specific title.

INTERVIEWER: *You are very versatile.*

ISHIOKA: Yes. Many things, and using many experiences. I embarked on many different courses as an artist, and I can use all these experiences to create something totally new for a movie or for the theater. I have a cross-cultural view because I'm not limited to working only in movies or only in the theater. I relate to many different areas, so I can combine very two-dimensional kinds of things with three-dimensional kinds of things to create something completely new.

INTERVIEWER: *Can you give an example?*

ISHIOKA: Well, for *Rip Van Winkle,* Francis needed a new approach, not just the ordinary parent-child type of expression, because nowadays a kid has a very rich imagination from science fiction movies or television. If we create an ordinary kid's type of production, they will get very bored. Francis knew this, and I agreed with him. I needed to create something new. But the costumes were done already, and they weren't very interesting costumes. I couldn't touch them. I could touch just the sets and the props. I created all my set ideas in about five days in Francis's house just before they began shooting. It was a very quick job.

INTERVIEWER: *Did you enjoy working in Hollywood?*

ISHIOKA: I was amazed—in Hollywood there is such a very strong union system. I guess I wasn't comfortable with the union system. There were so many people standing behind me, just drinking a beer and having nothing to do, just watching, not involved. I was very uncomfortable.

INTERVIEWER: *Is the situation different in Japan?*

ISHIOKA: In Japan, I can work with everybody from my position. With the carpenters, painters, or the prop men, the assistants to the prop man, I can tell them my idea, for example, "Please come here; your way of painting is not so good. You must paint this way." I can give very precise directions for everybody, if I want.

But in Hollywood I cannot do that. I was so surprised. In one sequence, one of the young men was making a spider's web. He was making an artificial web for one of the sequences. Well, I could see that his way of making the web was no good. So I went up to him and said, "Excuse me, this is no good. I have this image; I need it this way."

Then suddenly, his face was getting mad; he was getting angry. I said I couldn't understand why, so he told me that if I had something to say, not to tell him directly. I must tell my assistant art director and he must tell him. A terrible situation.

I love to work with just a very few good people, collaborating together, people with similar points of view. If a person needs assistants, they must control them very strongly. In this way, my ideas, my design philosophy can be expressed as I intended. As far as my experience with the Hollywood system, I really can't criticize. I had only one experience, but I was so surprised.

INTERVIEWER: *Were you able to work that way?*

ISHIOKA: Yes, because it was a short, volunteer project. I donated my energy and talent to create a wonderful experience for American children.

But it is a terrible system. The producer was always saying, "Eiko, you are over budget, over time, over, over, over, over, over." We couldn't make much progress; their main concern was not with the work but with keeping under the budget and keeping to the schedule.

I didn't want to push too much, you know, because I must work in Hollywood; it's in America, and I'm just a Japanese who must work on an American project. But the first few days I was so shocked. I finally said to myself, as an artist, "I have to adapt to the Hollywood system."

INTERVIEWER: *They didn't care about the quality?*

ISHIOKA: They didn't care about the quality, and they didn't know what good quality was. But Francis is a real veteran; he doesn't listen to such meaningless noise. He cares about the importance of the work and tries to not get involved in pettiness.

INTERVIEWER: *Do you have craft unions in Japan?*

ISHIOKA: In Japan we still don't have such unions. If many artists, workers, and laborers want to get involved with a small-budget, volunteer project like *Rip Van Winkle,* they shouldn't care so much about the schedule, the time, and the budget. They must involve themselves completely, make the project a labor of love.

I think this is also true with commercial feature films. Many union workers still care only about money, and just the key people, like the director, the art director, the actors, and so forth, care enough to devote themselves to their work.

And on a small, volunteer effort, it can be disastrous. The crew are the only ones getting paid. If they don't care about the project, about doing a good job, about the final result, and they run one hour overtime, they ask the producer, "Give me more money, give me more money." And this destroys the wonderful, volunteer situation. They are doing important jobs and it destroys the teamwork.

Many people have told me this is not true of all American film. I've studied it very much—the good ways, the bad ways. I want to try, of course, a project with such an independent, very strong, tiny group, like Philip's project.

Of course, in Japan we have a million problems that an American artist, an American Eiko who comes to Tokyo to work on a Japanese project, would have to face. They would have the opposite problem, I guess. They would not be comfortable working with the Japanese carpenters or workers, because the point of view is completely different.

But I recognize that it is important, from now on, for American and European and Oriental artists to collaborate to create something new, a new culture. A new culture, not belonging to America, not belonging to Japan. I want to explore and look into what this new culture is.

INTERVIEWER: *What is the most difficult part of the design process?*

ISHIOKA: Most of the time the most difficult part of the project is the budget. Most of the time I come up with many ideas, like ten ideas for each sequence or, if it's necessary, fifty ideas. But my ideas have to relate to the budget, right? If the budget is very small, then I must give up many ideas. This is the most difficult thing—to program my creativity for each budget, whether it's a movie or play or video.

Before I started to work on international projects like *Mishima* or Philip's opera or Miles Davis's album cover, my work was directed only toward a Japanese audience, oriented toward Japanese society. So the market was very

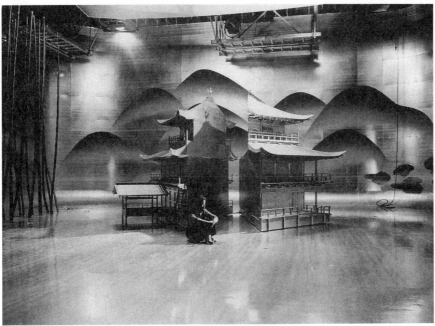

(above top) Eiko Ishioka with Paul Schrader, director of Mishima.
(above) Ishioka with her "Temple of the Golden Pavilion" set for Mishima.

tiny. And for just the Japanese market, the budget is usually more limited. If I had millions of incredible ideas, it was just impossible to do them. It was very frustrating.

Now, for instance, I'm going to direct a video for Miles Davis. I'm doing a design for his album, the newest one. This is for an international audience and the budget is realistic. But now I realize, being involved with these international projects, still the budget is not enough.

So all the time the budget is the basic condition for design. I cannot have a hundred percent freedom. When I create my ideas, I always have to take the budget into consideration. When people look at my designs, they are surprised: "Oh, how can Eiko spend so much money?" But it isn't true. It only looks like there was a big budget.

INTERVIEWER: *When you sit down to work, where does your imagery come from? Have you been influenced by Japanese history, French impressionism . . . ?*

ISHIOKA: Everything. Everything from the past, I guess. When I'm looking for ideas, I always try to come up with something entirely new. The director or producer wants something new and innovative. That is why they want to hire me.

It's very hard as an artist, but it's a very challenging opportunity to be involved with these projects. Most of the time when I am getting my ideas, I am looking for something beyond what has already been done. If I find someone has done it already, I must give up the idea and go on. If I recognize this can be an innovative idea, I keep working with it.

Also, as a designer, my work is different from the work of the painter or sculptor. I have to care about the client's purpose. My ideas have to express the client's message, and my message, my ideas, have to fit a budget, they have to be appropriate for the technique, and the ideas must work within a schedule. There are so many factors I have to consider.

INTERVIEWER: *And they all influence your design.*

ISHIOKA: Yes. But when I was growing up and training to become a professional, I looked outside of Japan, not inside of Japan, for ideas. And now I like to use material and motifs from all over the world. But it depends also on the subject. For example, with *Mishima* I had to use some of the very traditional Japanese motifs in my own way.

INTERVIEWER: *What other designers do you admire?*

ISHIOKA: Artists? Oh, I wasn't influenced by a certain kind of designer or artist in my career. I was influenced by people like my parents, my friends, and my relatives.

When I was traveling in Africa, I was influenced by the Africans' spirit of art. I was amazed when traveling in Italy a long time ago, more than twenty years ago, by the art of men like Michelangelo and da Vinci.

I was influenced by them, not practically, but ideally. They were total men, Renaissance men. Michelangelo I preferred over da Vinci. Of course, I didn't know him personally. If he was a very political man or pure artist, I don't know. But Michelangelo created all his art for clients, right? He was like a designer.

And he had his own spirit. The same spirit goes through all his work. Each project showed a different style, but they all have the same deep spirit. It's something I can feel, I can touch. That period had so many painters and sculptors working for the church or a client, but most of the work is just painting for religious purposes. Nothing with any real feeling. But Michelangelo's work is different—it feels very sensual, erotic. His spirit is original. By sensual I mean very human. I can easily imagine Michelangelo as a male artist. But the others—the technique is great but I can't feel anything. Michelangelo was my hero, but I wasn't influenced by him technically or practically.

INTERVIEWER: What kind of difficulties have you encountered in choosing the life you have and being a woman in Japan?

ISHIOKA: It was a very difficult choice, but fortunately, I had wonderful parents and I had wonderful friends, mainly male friends, and they've always supported me.

My father, who died three years ago, was one of the pioneer graphic designers in Japan. He was born in the Meiji period. But his mind was always very modern. He was an example of the ideal man for me, as a woman, because he had very natural, equal relationships with women, with children, and with friends. He was a wonderful man. He wasn't too ambitious to become successful in Japanese society. He was very quiet, his life was very quiet.

"Until Mishima, American movie people never thought of doing a serious movie about a modern Japanese subject."

He took good care of his family—his children and his wife. He was one of the best male friends in my life; he never asked me at a certain age, "Eiko, why don't you get married?" or "Why don't you have a family?" or "Why don't you have a baby?" That was out of the question for him. He never thought about it. Whether you are a woman or a man, you have to choose your own life. That was his attitude as a father.

INTERVIEWER: *You're very lucky.*

ISHIOKA: Yes. So, my sister and brothers have also chosen their own lives. We grew up in a very comfortable and free family situation. It was very unusual to find this type of man at his age. It was wonderful growing up with him. He taught me about what freedom means, without using any words, but with his attitude.

INTERVIEWER: *What about your mother?*

ISHIOKA: My mother is still alive. She's a good friend of mine. She's a typical housewife, but she wanted to be a professional woman. When she was a young girl, she wanted to become a novelist. So after she graduated from high school she told her mother, my grandmother, "I want to go to the university to study literature."

My grandmother said, "Don't go. If you study literature at the university, you will become an intellectual woman and no Japanese man will want to marry you." This was my grandmother's advice for my mother.

My mother was not strong enough to reject her mother's suggestions, so she gave up because she was worried about not being able to get married. She gave up studying literature, but she didn't want to marry just a salaryman; she wanted to marry a creative person. Fortunately, she met my father.

So they got married and had four children—two daughters and two sons. When I was seven years old, right after World War II, my mother said to me very seriously, "Eiko, you should have an occupation." I said, "Why?" And she told me, "Women's situation is changing. I don't mind if you get married or you don't get married or if you have children or not. But you have to have a job. This is very, very important for you as a woman." I looked into her face— she had never looked at me with a more serious face—and I knew then that she was right. Because even though I was only seven years old, I had already looked at her daily life and thought, "Wow, such a boring job every day." I respected her as a mother, of course, but her work—the cooking, the cleaning, the ironing—every day she did the same thing. I knew I didn't want that kind of a life. I agreed with her very strongly.

And she is very happy I didn't follow the path she did. My mother is like my father—she never criticized my ambitions, never imposed her point of view. They helped me so much, not only by giving me such freedom, but also by giving me such good advice.

INTERVIEWER: *What kind of advice did your father give you as a designer?*

ISHIOKA: For instance, at the university, I studied very hard, sometimes going several days without sleep. Well, one time my father came into my room late at night and he said, "Still working?"

And I said, "Yes." I had three design ideas and I couldn't decide between them. So I asked my father for advice. I explained the three different ideas and I asked him, "Which idea do you prefer?" He said, "Well, this idea is great because of so on and so on and so on." So suddenly my mind got very clear about which one I really wanted to do, and I chose one of the others. Then I said, "OK, I've decided on this one." My father said, "That's really you, that's really your character."

INTERVIEWER: *What kind of friends do you have? Are they all designers?*

ISHIOKA: I enjoy having male friends more than female friends. I've had such wonderful male friends from different fields, like photographer, film director, architect, and composer. I don't have as many close friends from the graphic design field.

I've always been curious about other creative fields and have tried to expand my work beyond the tradition of graphic design. And my friends have been a kind of family too. They have always supported me, no matter what I wanted to do, saying, "Eiko, do it, do it, do it." It's been wonderful. And an unusual situation in Japan.

INTERVIEWER: *Did success come early to you?*

ISHIOKA: In my mid-twenties I received the most important design award in Japan. I was the first woman to get such an important design award. So suddenly, after the ceremony, many journalists came to me—TV, newspaper, magazine—and they were all men. My name became suddenly famous in Japan; I had a ticket to do whatever I wanted, to try anything, and I was actually pretty cool about the whole thing.

Then, right after that, I saw another designer, a man, in a restaurant. He said to me, "I envy you." I said, "Why?"

"Because you are a woman."

"Oh yes? Why?"

"Because if you weren't a woman, the journalists wouldn't have gone crazy about your award."

I said, "I see; I understand." I was only twenty-some years old, and I learned a great lesson. If my talent is just so-so, like many other graphic designers, they will always criticize. Eiko is a woman and the producer is a man, the client is a man, and they like Eiko oh so much. Eiko is like a geisha, you know? So I recognized very strongly that I must be a super artist. If I cannot be a super artist, people will always want to criticize me. It was wonderful advice for me; he gave me wonderful advice without knowing it.

"My sets have a spirit like a human being. Sets have a spirit and a voice."

INTERVIEWER: *It must be hard to be one of the only women in your field in Japan.*

ISHIOKA: There has been terrible pressure from this male-dominated society. It's not just Japanese society, not just Japan, but all over the world I think this is true. Still, good women designers in Japan are very, very few.

You know, when I was young in Japan, I had a dream about America—it was a country of freedom, and New York was a city of freedom where anybody could do anything. But when I traveled in America and Europe—I spent six months traveling in the mid-sixties to observe the design situation—I was shocked. Women's position was nothing. It was nothing. All the famous architects, all the leading graphic designers, all the leading moviemakers, film directors—they were all men.

It's not just the men's fault and responsibility. Women always give the excuse that a woman's body is not so strong. Or they shout, "Women must be equal, equal, equal!" But that has no meaning. They have to get out and do it, try it. When women can do a good job at something, or do it better than men, then they will be equal. Just shouting won't do it. This is particularly true in Japan, where women are very weak.

I belong to the Tokyo Art Directors' Club. When I became a member, there were fifty members, and forty-nine of the members were men. I was the only woman member. My sister became the second member just a few years ago. She became my rival in a friendly way. My former assistant, a woman, became a wonderful designer. I'm very happy they are following me, but when I look at Japan, there are still very few successful women.

INTERVIEWER: How did you decide to become a graphic designer?

ISHIOKA: I entered Tokyo National University of Fine Arts and Music and studied four years. It was general design—basic study like industrial design, graphic design, furniture design, and so on.

Just before I graduated from the university, I had to decide which design field I wanted to work in. So I asked my father, "What do you think?" He suggested to me, "Eiko, don't choose graphic design, because from my experience, it's too competitive for women. It's much better for you to become a fashion designer or pastry designer or shoe designer." So I said, "OK, I am going to become a graphic designer." I wanted to compete very much. So I became a graphic designer. My father knew my character very well. I think he was not very surprised.

INTERVIEWER: What was your first job?

ISHIOKA: I entered the biggest cosmetic company in Japan, Shiseido, because I thought that if I worked for a large company I could study the entire range of design technology with that company. If I had started out as a free-lance designer, I wouldn't have been able to learn about printing technique, photo technique, and other design techniques. I wasn't interested in advertising cosmetics, but Shiseido was one of the companies creating good designs in advertising. I became the main art director and also did outside work, like book designs, on my own time. I worked there for seven years and then became a free-lance designer and began doing projects for film, theater, books, advertising, and other things.

INTERVIEWER: What design work have you done for the theater?

ISHIOKA: In Japan, I worked for several stage plays. I did set design, costumes, props, and lighting design, because their relation is very important. The first time I designed for a contemporary dance theater production— dance, singing, theater, and poetry reading combined together. It was a very strange and unusual kind of production. I designed the sets, costumes, and lighting. Then I designed for a Japanese *Hamlet*, and I designed for a Japanese version of *Salome*, based on Oscar Wilde, and several others.

INTERVIEWER: Is there more freedom in the theater than in film because it's more abstract?

ISHIOKA: I don't think so. It depends. Some plays allow you quite a bit of freedom, and some moviemakers do the same. But movies need much more money than the theater.

It's also more difficult for moviemakers to create their own ideas because producers push film directors all the time. They are under such tremendous pressure to succeed at the box office because they spend so much more money on movies than on the typical play.

INTERVIEWER: *In film, don't you think there is a stronger tendency toward visual realism?*

ISHIOKA: Yes, but many artists use video and film media to create just such an expressive, sometimes weird, avant-garde art as you often find in the theater. But people don't want to see that, so it's not good business. Those films don't ever achieve commercial success. Their audience is very limited.

INTERVIEWER: *Your sets for* Mishima *were very theatrical.*

ISHIOKA: Very much, yes.

INTERVIEWER: *How did you go about translating the ideas in his novels into set designs?*

ISHIOKA: Basically, I had to be concerned with the question: Who was Mishima? My sets were part of the answer to that question, part of the expression of his character. And if you feel that my sets look kinky or tacky or kitsch, Mishima himself was that kind of a person.

Of course, this is Paul Schrader's movie, so it is mostly Paul Schrader's answer to who Mishima was. It's not a general answer or a complete picture of the man Mishima. This is necessary, I think. Sometimes audiences become confused when they see a movie about a famous person. Audiences expect the faces to be the same and the voices to be the same as the real person. This is a ridiculous reaction.

When I saw the movie *Gandhi*, I felt doubtful about its reality. The actor in the film had the same face as *Gandhi*, the same build, the same body movements, but I didn't feel the same spirit. I felt then that with movies that portray actual figures in history, the harder you try to duplicate exactly the person's face, his style, his voice, the historical background, the more you lose that sense of reality. What's more important than the details is expressing the director's point of view.

(above top) Eiko Ishioka conferring with Mishima*'s director of photography, John Bailey.*
(above) With George Lucas, one of Mishima*'s executive producers.*

At the press conference for *Mishima*, Francis Coppola, the executive producer, said, "If you're going to be really particular about the casting, the only actor who can play *Mishima* is Yukio Mishima himself. This film is Paul Schrader's vision of Yukio Mishima."

But sometimes the audience's attitude toward *Mishima* is wrong because they are expecting the same look, the same voice, as Mishima himself. It's wrong. As Francis said, this is Paul Schrader's vision of Mishima. So, the audience must listen to what Paul Schrader has to say.

If someone knew Mishima himself or knows him from a picture, or from his novels, they have their own image of Mishima. When they look at Schrader's vision of Mishima, they often look only at the differences from their own view and they say, "I hate this movie!" This is very narrow minded.

INTERVIEWER: *How different were your and Paul's visions of Mishima?*

ISHIOKA: This was my first experience working on a major feature film. When I met with Paul in New York, he said, "I need your work for my movie *Mishima*." So I said, "Why do you want to make a movie about Mishima?"

He told me his reasons for wanting to make the movie. But before I gave him my answer, I read his screenplay. And the structure of the screenplay was very interesting, not the details of the Mishima character. I did not have a chance to see Mishima himself before he died, so I didn't know him personally. But, from what I knew of him, I didn't like the man. So, I told Paul, "I am not the right artist to work on your movie. You like Mishima, you probably love Mishima, but I didn't like Mishima." He said, "Eiko, you are the right person." I said, "Why?" "Because," he said, "it's not necessary for all the key people working on the movie to fall in love with Mishima. It's only necessary for me. You know this is my Mishima, not Eiko's Mishima."

So this was the perfect answer for me. I understood that he needed me as an artist, and that he was being honest. So I said, "OK, I'll do it." When we met and talked about the film, he told me his image of Mishima. Then I read the three novels that appeared in the film. I read them very precisely, very thoroughly. Then I understood why Schrader wrote this kind of screenplay. The next time we met, we talked all night until the next morning. Paul and I talked, talked, talked, and most of the time I was the listener. He explained why he had chosen these three novels from many other novels—why he chose *The Temple of the Golden Pavilion* and *Kyoko's House* and *Runaway Horses*. I asked him many questions, including what was his image for the sets and the artwork. And he explained things in great detail, very precisely.

So after the meeting, I went back to my studio and started to design ideas that were concerned with Paul's image of the sets. Well, it wasn't Eiko. It was Eiko's idea, but relating very much to Paul's vision.

When I completed the first two ideas for *The Temple of the Golden Pavilion* part of the film, I called together my assistants, the assistant director, the line producer, and several others, but not Paul. I explained my ideas, and I explained to them that I wanted to follow Paul's basic concept but that my own ideas were different. If Paul could give me complete freedom, my own set ideas would be completely different from this, I said, but I recognized I must follow the film director. They were all film professionals, part of the Japanese crew. I was the only outsider. After I finished the presentation, they all said, "Ishioka-san, you must try your ideas instead of following his ideas; his ideas are normal. They are good, but they are conventional film ideas. Paul Schrader needed you as an outsider because of your fresh ideas." They were all expecting my own ideas. Otherwise, they thought, Paul should have hired a regular film production designer.

This opened my eyes very strongly. I said to Paul, immediately afterward, "If you don't mind, I want to create my own ideas for the sets." He said, "Go ahead and try it." So I worked on my own original designs and the next presentation I did was for Paul Schrader, the cinematographer, John Bailey, and the Japanese crew. It was a very challenging presentation. If two key people like Paul and John don't like my ideas, it's my job. I'm not so important to the project. They can always find another artist. So it was a very important presentation for me. After I finished my presentation, Paul and John and everybody said, "Congratulations." Paul didn't like two of the set ideas, so I went back and reworked them, but fortunately he liked the overall concept.

Afterward, working from my basic designs, Paul added some suggestions from his director's point of view and John Bailey needed some small changes for his camera angles. The three of us discussed every detail of the set designs very precisely. I was very satisfied. I enjoyed collaborating with them very much. It was wonderful.

INTERVIEWER: *Well, the result was certainly wonderful.*

ISHIOKA: I am very happy to hear that. It is very difficult to develop sets that are unmovielike. There are so many different pressures. And people want to criticize—"Eiko is not a professional production designer. She doesn't know anything about camera. She doesn't know anything about direction," and so on, and so on. If I gave up fighting with those attitudes, I couldn't develop my ideas and also develop as a designer.

But I had the confidence from my experience. I had done the art direction for many TV commercials and many plays. I had never done a feature film before *Mishima*, but I had the confidence as to what art direction is, what production design is, and what innovative ideas I wanted to see happen.

> *"The set designer has to have an important statement to make, like a film director, like an actor, like a screenwriter."*

Fortunately, I also had wonderful people to work with. Especially Paul Schrader, because he always wants to challenge the audience and producers with innovative ideas and new forms of expression. The final result is not one hundred percent perfect, but I respect him very much for trying to break away from the academic movie style.

INTERVIEWER: *How do you see the role of production design in relation to acting?*

ISHIOKA: In most films, even serious artistic or intellectual movies, the producer or the director isn't interested in using a new style of art direction. Most of them are very scared that a new style of art direction will disturb the acting. Art direction has to always be in the background, in the shadows, to support the acting.

But my attitude is the opposite. Good art direction should, of course, not disturb the acting. But the challenge is to make a wonderful harmony between the acting and the sets or between the acting and the location sets. And, through this, show the audience something exciting, stimulating.

If sets are always like this room here, around us, familiar, then I just see you sitting there and the background does nothing to relate to you. The audience is very comfortable, the background is familiar, but also dead; it does nothing to stimulate the audience, nothing to relate with you, the actor. There is nothing about the relationship between the background and your circumstances—the cup and the table and the chairs. It just relaxes the audience and there is nothing new.

So in designing sets for their visual effects, I want to give the actors and

On one of Ishioka's sets for Mishima.

actresses a challenge and create a fifty-fifty relationship between them and their surroundings. If the acting is very weak, Eiko's sets are too powerful.

My sets have a spirit like a human being. Sets have a spirit and a voice. They interact and challenge the actors and the director. My visual approach is very competitive. Eiko is behind all my artwork, and Eiko is shouting, "Eiko is here! Look at me, look at me, look at me!" This kind of production design is too bold, too challenging for many films—films like science fiction, like *E.T.*, even for more intellectual films. Most film directors are not interested in my type of sets, my visual design, because they are frightened by it.

INTERVIEWER: *With* Mishima, *did you work closely with the director of photography?*

ISHIOKA: John Bailey was wonderful. He helped me all the time like a partner. There was a short scene in a white room with a strange kind of shadow. I designed it first of all as a completely black room with special lights. But because of the preceding and following scenes, Paul wanted to change the room to some other new idea. I liked the idea of a black room very much, but I had designed a black kendo hall for another scene and Paul said it was too much black.

So John Bailey helped me to come up with something new. I finally decided on a white room instead of a black room, but I couldn't come up with any good ideas for lighting the room. John showed me some very old still photos that were done in the twenties and he asked me, "What do you think of this kind of lighting for your white room?" I told him I liked it, and it turned out to be very effective.

Also John is a wonderful man as a person. All the Japanese crew respected him. I'll tell you why. One day John told me, "When I arrived in Tokyo and began checking around for camera equipment for the film, I was so surprised. Japanese camera equipment is so poor. Most of the equipment is from the fifties. It's very old-fashioned and in bad condition." I told him that I knew that was true. Japan's movie industry is not so large and doesn't have the budgets that American films do. He is one of the top cinematographers and he can use any of the most modern equipment.

So, I asked him, "What are you going to do?" "Well," he said, "I'm going to use this old equipment. It will be a challenge. Many great Japanese filmmakers have made wonderful films with this poor equipment."

And he did it. It worked wonderfully.

He was the director of photography, and all the camera operators were Japanese. But sometimes, because he needed to do a special dolly or a difficult shot, he wasn't afraid to operate the camera himself. And he studied the Japanese language every day—one phrase or one word, every day for six months. And he spoke it in the studio. The whole Japanese crew became very friendly with him. It was wonderful. He was the most important person I collaborated with.

INTERVIEWER: What kind of problems did you have with a mixed Japanese and American production team?

ISHIOKA: I was one of a very few of the Japanese crew who could speak English. Yet I was amazed by John and Paul. They were so patient, so patient. They never shouted. The first few months it was almost like they were handicapped people. They could not move anywhere because of the language. But they decided they had to adapt to the Japanese way of moviemaking. They were very patient in learning to work with the Japanese crew. It's very different from the American way of filmmaking, but they did it. It was amazing. After the movie was finished, George Lucas and Francis Ford Coppola said to me, "Making this same quality of movie in the United States would cost four or five times as much."

"Technology is like my paint, my brush; it cannot be my concept."

INTERVIEWER: Why do you think that is?

ISHIOKA: It is all passion. The American and Japanese crews were all passionately involved in the project. It was a wonderful experience. Until *Mishima,* American movie people never thought of doing a serious movie about a modern Japanese subject.

I'm not sure if you have seen *Shogun.* It was a hit in the United States but completely failed in Japan. I went to see *Shogun* the second day after it opened in Tokyo. It was a big theater, but there were only twenty people in the audience. Less than twenty minutes into the picture, my friend and I were the only people in the theater. Everyone got so angry. The movie was terrible; it was like a souvenir.

Mishima was the first feature film with a serious attitude that Americans have made about Japan. So when the Japanese crew felt strongly that the American crew had a very serious attitude and a love for the Japanese

147

people and wanted to work with us as equals, we understood that *Mishima* wasn't going to be just a souvenir of Japan, like *Shogun* or *Madame Butterfly.*

INTERVIEWER: *So in that sense,* Mishima *was an historic movie.*

ISHIOKA: This is a very important movie, an historic collaboration between American artists and Japanese artists. We worked together in a very equal relationship and with love. And on a certain intellectual level. It's very easy to criticize a movie like this but very difficult to make that kind of movie, especially with an American director.

Paul Schrader, who is American, did a great job directing this film in which all the actors and actresses were Japanese and all the dialogue was in Japanese. When I first saw the completed film at the Warner Brothers screening room in L.A., I was greatly impressed with the high quality. But what amazed me even more when I viewed the film as a Japanese audience was that I didn't find anything strange or unnatural about the dialogue. After the screening, I called Paul right away and thanked him for giving me the wonderful opportunity to participate in his film, a rare collaboration between American and Japanese artists.

Of course, the ordinary audience doesn't care about what's happening behind the screen, they only care about whether the movie is interesting to them or not. Japanese audience, American audience—it doesn't matter. But it is very difficult to collaborate successfully on this kind of project. And I have hope for the future that there can be more projects like this. It's necessary.

INTERVIEWER: *Is it difficult for you to keep the technical and emotional parts of your work in harmony?*

ISHIOKA: Difficult, yes, but I enjoy it. I'm working in so many fields that my technical knowledge is very poor for each field. In graphic design, I am an expert, but in movies, the theater, in video, I don't have enough experience.

So when I receive an important job, most of the time I work with a technical consultant. I create the concept, the idea, I put in my emotional feeling and spirit, everything, but I need a technical consultant to advise me, to help me to express my ideas and designs.

Nowadays, many artists are involved in developing new techniques for movies or computers or video and they forget about instilling it with important emotions, important ideas, or important concepts. They just play with modern techniques instead of using them to say something. There's often too much talk about technique instead of making a statement. For me, technique is second, not first. If I have a certain message or a statement for a particular audience, then I need to find the right technique for that concept. Of course, as an artist, I am very curious about new techniques. But technology is like my paint, my brush; it cannot be my concept.

INTERVIEWER: *What's the most important thing that contributes to a set design's success?*

ISHIOKA: It's very difficult to say just one thing. This is my own philosophy: A set designer has to have his or her own statement. A set designer is not just a translator. The set designer is not just a slave for the film director. The set designer is not just a technical assistant or consultant. The set designer has to have an important statement to make, like a film director, like an actor, like a screenwriter. This is the most important thing.

Patrizia Von Brandenstein

PRODUCTION DESIGN

*B*orn in Phoenix, Patrizia Von Brandenstein spent her childhood on her grandfather's Arizona ranch and in Europe with her parents. She developed an early affection for the theater, and as a child put on shows in her backyard.

During her teenage years in Europe, Von Brandenstein served as an apprentice in the French National Theater. Back in the States, she studied at the Art Students' League and the Studio and Forum of Stage Design, planning a career as a stage designer.

Von Brandenstein worked as a designer in the theater until she was almost thirty, when she became involved in her first film—Woody Allen's Play It Again, Sam—as an assistant to art director Ed Wittstein. She received her first screen credit for her work as a set decorator on The Candidate. Since then, Von Brandenstein has worked on many films and television programs, gradually moving into production design. She served as assistant art director for Smile and then as art director for Hester Street. She was costume designer for Between the Lines. Her debut as production designer for a *feature film came with* Heartland. *She then went on to do costume design for* Saturday Night Fever *and was art director for Milos Forman's* Ragtime *before devoting herself exclusively to production design. The films she has worked on in this capacity include* Silkwood, Amadeus *(for which she received an Oscar),* Beat Street, A Chorus Line, The Money Pit, No Mercy, *and* The Untouchables.

Von Brandenstein's husband, Stuart Wurtzel, is also a production designer. They spend the little time they can spare from their demanding careers together at their home in New York City or their country house in Connecticut.

INTERVIEWER: *What are you doing in Chicago?*

VON BRANDENSTEIN: The project is called *The Untouchables*; it's a Paramount picture and the director is Brian DePalma. It's set in 1930, and is about the fall of Al Capone. It's an original script by David Mamet, and the producer is Art Linson.

INTERVIEWER: *How did you get involved in this project?*

VON BRANDENSTEIN: The producer's office phoned me when they were putting the picture together. I was just finishing up my last project, a film called *No Mercy*, with Richard Gere in North Carolina, so I went to see them when I got back to New York. I saw some very exciting location pictures from their scouting trips to Chicago, and we talked about different ways to do the film. It was an extremely attractive project for me because, although I had done a lot of period work, I had never explored that particular aspect of society. I thought, This might really be very interesting.

INTERVIEWER: *Have you ever worked in Chicago before?*

VON BRANDENSTEIN: Yes, I spent a month in the city in January on *No Mercy*. When I came out and started working, I absolutely fell for Chicago! It's a great town to make a movie in. And there's so much of it that's unexplored, as far as locations go, especially for period films. Doing research for *The Untouchables*, I really became fascinated by Capone, who was far, far more influential in a very negative way on our society than you might imagine. He was quite an amazing person. He's not a sympathetic character by any means, but there was a vitality about him that was fascinating. It's illuminating about the American character. We're in full swing here and will start filming about the eighteenth of August.

INTERVIEWER: *What makes a film project attractive to you?*

VON BRANDENSTEIN: The first question I ask is, Have I done it before? The only way you can continue to grow artistically is by always looking for a fresh approach. I would hate to come to the point where I would use a bunch of tired, old solutions. I felt that this project was something I hadn't done before, hadn't explored before. Brian is very unusual—he's an action-oriented director who uses the physical world in a very different way. He's a skilled director who knows about doing things from a designer's point of view.

INTERVIEWER: *What does your work entail at the start of a project?*

VON BRANDENSTEIN: On the kinds of films I do, the production designer is one of the very first people who comes onto a project, sometimes even before the deal is solid. First of all, the producing studio will want to know what the scope of the picture is—what it will cost and all of that. You can offer some good advice by reading the script carefully and doing a sort of preliminary breakdown and by deciding how to approach the thing. As one of the very first people involved in the project after the producer and director get together, the production designer can advise them on what is possible and what is not. As more and more people come on staff and begin working on the production, your work also expands.

"The great attraction for me has always been... to be in another world, in another time."

INTERVIEWER: *From there, do you do research?*

VON BRANDENSTEIN: Well, in a picture like this, a period film, one would want to have a very thorough background in what the time was actually like. That doesn't mean you're going to use it—in the case of this picture, it's all out of our hands anyway. But you want to have a very, very thorough understanding of what the time was like and what really happened in the events so that you can be free to go off artistically from there. Research is a kind of immersion process I go through, becoming immersed in a particular period. When that time begins to live for me, there will be art directors and others on the project. We will then create an artistic approach together— what I call finding the soul of the picture. You then proceed in very concrete ways: plans and drawings and models and any other way you can use to convey information to the director. You take it on every tack. I have used every sort of thing—a photograph, a sketch, a painting, a piece of music, a newspaper article, a piece of cloth, a view from a window, a quality of light. Artistic ideas flow from any kind of stimulus imaginable. That's where the artistic concept comes from.

INTERVIEWER: *Which people do you work most closely with?*

VON BRANDENSTEIN: At the beginning, I work closely with the director. He has story needs—just the traffic of people walking back and forth in front of the camera, the staging of the piece. You need to incorporate his needs into the set designs; his needs are paramount. You need to help him find his vision of the film. By the same token, the cinematographer also has certain concerns of film and light. You want to accommodate his problems as well. You need to work on all these fronts at the same time so you can come to a consensus with all these creative people. After all, all these concerns have to proceed from the director. Because if the director isn't in charge, we are in trouble. You also have an obligation to the producers. They have contracted to do the film at a certain figure and you must live up to that if it's at all within your power. The production design department is responsible for achieving the physical look of the film for an agreed-upon figure.

As the actors come on and the rehearsals begin, the director is going to be much more concerned with his performances and with working with the cinematographer. It's important for the production designer to have the relationship with the director at the very beginning. You establish that understanding to see you through.

As the production process continues, you work with the production manager, who is responsible for seeing that everything runs smoothly and everyone gets paid on time, and not too much money and not too little money is being spent, and the equipment is all in the right place at the right time. You work with him too, coordinating.

You also have an extremely close relationship with your art directors, the costume designer, your set decorator, and the hair, wig, and makeup people. These are people you see every day. They help you achieve what you decided upon.

INTERVIEWER: *What is the difference between a production designer and an art director?*

VON BRANDENSTEIN: A production designer has more responsibility

Stages in the development of Von Brandenstein's design for "Capone's Suite," a major set for The Untouchables:

(above left) Von Brandenstein sketched this sunburst design—inspired by a diamond brooch, "an emblem of a person whom the world revolves around"—to reflect the idea of a "Gangland Sun King."

(above right) Drawing of a room (overhead view), incorporating the sunburst symbol into the floor pattern.

(right) Photo of the finished set—the haunts of the gangland Sun King Capone.

over the whole picture. On a picture of this size, there is a production designer, an art director, and then several assistant art directors and draftspeople. The art director's job is to closely supervise the sets as they are designed, to coordinate the shop and the building of all the sets. He makes a creative contribution in the actual physical design. Conceptually, these things come from me, but in practical terms he does a great deal of work in that area. He is responsible for an enormous amount of detail. The art director acts as my right arm, my second in command. If I should vanish, he would be able to take over completely.

INTERVIEWER: *How many are on your crew? Do you usually work with the same people?*

VON BRANDENSTEIN: Well, the size of our crew varies, obviously, from project to project. Certainly, a project the size of *The Untouchables* needs a full complement of assistants. The cast of characters changes sometimes. After all, people do want to do things on their own as well. Sometimes the person you would very much like to work with isn't available. And sometimes you might feel that they aren't suited for the job. They might be absolutely wonderful on another kind of picture, but maybe there's a particular project that they're not suited for. You need to cast your department in the same way that you cast the picture. You want people to be happy in their work, to enjoy it, to be creative, to be a part of it. You don't want it to be a task, you want it to be a joy.

INTERVIEWER: *Do you have any kind of daily routine when you're in the thick of it?*

VON BRANDENSTEIN: When the shooting is going on, I always go to the set early. I arrive with the cinematographer and talk over problems. I always have a lengthy conference with the art director and my staff. At this time, I'm working closely with them. They are responsible for the smooth operation of the sets, and you want to coordinate your activities with theirs.

INTERVIEWER: *What's a typical day like for you?*

VON BRANDENSTEIN: In preproduction, I'll go to my office and speak with the art director. I generally will make a trip to the shop. I'll visit various locations with the location people. At this stage of the game, part of the day I'll be with the set decorator and his staff. They will be selecting furniture, bringing me pictures and pieces for my approval. Sometimes I'll go out and visit a certain vendor with them. I'll be talking with my research person, asking her to try and find me material on, for example, Irish bars in Chicago.

On one occasion, they also researched a painter named Sir Lawrence Alma-Tadema, collected photos of Capone and his henchmen from the police museum, and went to survey several locations. It's a long day—twelve hours at the absolute minimum. Once we are into production, that will extend to something like a fifteen-hour day. You have to go to dailies. You have to have conferences with the director.

INTERVIEWER: *What are you doing when they are shooting?*

VON BRANDENSTEIN: Most typically, standing. But when they need you, they need you, if you know what I mean. Perhaps the cinematographer needs another light and you have to change the set around—you need to mask a light or take walls out and put them back again. A certain prop might not work or doesn't look right. Sometimes you might be able to give a suggestion to the director or the cinematographer about some period artifact or piece of architecture. There's a lot of "hurry up and wait." It seems very tedious unless you're behind the camera. I am not on the set at all times, but I like to stay on the set until the first shot is set up and they are into a scene. Then I feel free to go about my business, go prepare other sets that are coming up.

INTERVIEWER: *When does the production designer's involvement in a picture actually end?*

VON BRANDENSTEIN: After the principal photography is completed, hopefully you can go off to rest somewhere. But you retain an interest in the film. You're interested in going to see various cuts of the picture as it's all going together.

INTERVIEWER: *Have you developed a particular strategy to recuperate from these projects?*

VON BRANDENSTEIN: Oh God! When you're in the midst of it, sometimes you feel a rest home would do the most good! I like to go to my house in Connecticut. We have a house in the country that I love very much. Sometimes I go to Europe and recuperate there. On this picture I've been away from New York for so long; I'll be going back to New York in November. So I'll stay in my house in New York and enjoy the autumn there and go up to the country on weekends and be with my family.

INTERVIEWER: *How have you coped with being away from your family for such long periods?*

VON BRANDENSTEIN: Well, it's very, very difficult. My daughter is now married and has a home of her own, but certainly I miss my husband and my

daughter and my friends very, very much. And my house and cat and my favorite skillet and all those things. I do try to get home as often as I can. My
husband does the same work as I do and is presently involved with shooting a
film, but we do try and spend together whatever weekends we can.

INTERVIEWER: *Do you pursue any other creative activities?*

VON BRANDENSTEIN: I enjoy playing the piano very much. I've just taken
it up. I studied the violin when I was a kid, but never seriously. When I was
doing *Amadeus,* I was so impressed with the lead actors learning the piano.
They both literally learned to play the piano! I was so impressed with this, I talked with the musical director and
told him, "This is something I've always wanted to do." He
said, "Well, why don't you do it?" So I have. I have rented a
piano, which is sitting here, and I plunk away and I take
lessons and I enjoy it very much.

> *"Success is when everyone believes—if you believe my world that I've put up there."*

INTERVIEWER: *How did you get involved in film?*

VON BRANDENSTEIN: I was a theater designer for a
long time. I designed costumes and props and sets. I was
never on a movie set until I was thirty years old. I just had
an opportunity to do a film with a theater designer I had
worked with before. Then I fell in love with movies; I was a
goner from the first day. So I slogged my way through
union categories—I decorated sets, designed costumes, was a scenic artist,
and eventually I became an art director.

INTERVIEWER: *What's the most exciting part of being in film?*

VON BRANDENSTEIN: The great attraction for me has always been to go
to another world that is not your own, to be in another world, in another time,
for a period of your life. I think that's incredible. There are reasons why I do
the kind of films I do. It's personal. It's immensely seductive. After a time of
studying it, immersing yourself in it, you really can slip into another world.

INTERVIEWER: *Are there any worlds you like better than others?*

VON BRANDENSTEIN: Yes, I do like to immerse myself in a particular
style or time, but as far as the films I do, I want them always to be different!
You see, there's the problem.

INTERVIEWER: *If you could do any film, what would it be?*

VON BRANDENSTEIN: Oh, there are a couple of stories. I like the novels of
Peter Matthiessen very much. I was very fascinated by one of his books. It has

to do with a certain feeling about America and various things about this country—religion and many different aspects of American culture. There is also a fabulous book called *Time and Again,* by Jack Finney. It has the premise that if you create a world perfectly enough, you could slip into it. It's a very, very complex novel. For years, people have tried to think of ways to do it on film. Quite honestly, I think I know how to do it! And if that were ever made, I would love to work on it. And, you know, I'm not alone in this. I think every art director in the business wants to do *Time and Again.* It's their dream project. And lately I've been thinking that I'd love to work on a film about the Irish famine in the 1830s and 1840s. When I was doing *Ragtime,* I took a trip to Ireland and I became entranced with a novel called *Famine.* It was published in the twenties, a very old book. No one's ever done anything about that particular time. I think it could be really interesting. It was such an immense human tragedy. And because of the tremendous number of immigrants, it had a lot to do with events in this country. It's a fascinating time, a story that appeals to me very much.

INTERVIEWER: *Do you think these historical stories have any relevance to audiences today?*

VON BRANDENSTEIN: Well, if you talk to anyone who understands the history of this country or the world, you'll see so many parallels in other societies. Artistically, history appeals to me for lots of reasons, but on a social level I think we can learn from the past. Films can illuminate events for people. We can become aware of certain things. For instance, *The Killing Fields* brought an awareness of very recent events that many of us had no idea of. My favorite example from my own career is *Silkwood.* Doing that film illuminated certain things about industry in our country that are fascinating and brought them to a wide audience. And, of course, *Amadeus*—my God, Mozart hasn't been this popular for 200 years. Although he's a very well known and revered musician, *Amadeus* made that music accessible to a whole group of people who otherwise wouldn't have given it a thought. To make the eighteenth century live again like that was a great honor and a great privilege. I loved it.

INTERVIEWER: *Is it important to you, then, that a film be not only artistically fulfilling but also have some weight or substance?*

VON BRANDENSTEIN: I don't know. I also think that film is entertainment. Like that wonderful song Donald O'Connor did, "Make 'em Laugh." To work on a comedy that people love is just terrific. The reason I wanted to do *The Money Pit* was because it had all sorts of hilarious scenes about people trying to renovate an old house, and so many of those experiences were my own. But to go and see the film and have people laughing all around you... it's wonderful. One wants to entertain. Every film doesn't have to be socially insightful.

INTERVIEWER: *Can you think of any particularly hilarious events from your career as a production designer?*

> *"The most valuable thing you can cultivate is a kind of curiosity, a quality of observation about the world."*

VON BRANDENSTEIN: I've had awfully good laughs working on pictures. It seems every film has those moments. The thing is, these events are not especially funny to anyone who wasn't working there. They are funny in the context of what is happening. There's always some hilarious incongruity that arises. I remember watching the first dailies of *Ragtime*. We had all done months and months of planning and labor for these beautiful historical scenes. We'd re-created old New York on East Eleventh Street; there were horses and wagons and what appeared to be an immense vista of old shops and tenements; the immigrant people were everywhere, and right across the front of the screen came this lady wearing bright red sunglasses! We all fell down and shrieked! It was hilarious.

INTERVIEWER: *Is there anything that really riles you about this work?*

VON BRANDENSTEIN: Well, there are problems. Any artistic enterprise is filled with a lot of grief but, on the whole, I love this business. In American films, I would love to be able to work without concerns about union jurisdiction and things like that. That's hard to deal with sometimes—not the unions themselves, but the jurisdictional disputes that arise.

This is a hard business because there is so much involved in it. I consider myself immensely fortunate because there is such a tiny minority of people in the world who can say they do what they really want to do, what they love. I am one of those very fortunate few. It seems churlish to complain, somehow.

INTERVIEWER: *What about the budgets you have to work with?*

VON BRANDENSTEIN: Everybody always says, "Wouldn't it be wonderful to have all the money you needed to make a project?" I think that it would be wonderful to have not quite enough money to do a project. Just enough to make you struggle. You're better off with too little than too much. You've got to hustle a little bit. It makes you work a little harder.

INTERVIEWER: *What kind of goals do you have in your work?*

VON BRANDENSTEIN: I want to improve my skills. I want to draw better. I want to paint better. I want to communicate better.

INTERVIEWER: *What would you suggest to a young person who wanted to become a production designer?*

VON BRANDENSTEIN: Quite honestly, I don't think you should study this per se. I think you should have a very thorough art background. Studying theater design is very useful because it orients you very strongly to the story, the needs of the play. You should try to perfect your physical skills of drawing, painting, model making, et cetera. I really wish mine were better! To make an art director takes a very, very long time. Because it's social—you're studying whole eras and classes of people. The most valuable thing you can cultivate is a kind of curiosity, a quality of observation about the world.

INTERVIEWER: *How would you define being successful as a production designer?*

VON BRANDENSTEIN: It's pretty subjective, but I suppose success is when everyone believes—if you believe my world that I've put up there.

Kristi Zea

COSTUME

*K*risti Zea was born in New York City in 1948. She received her bachelor's degree from the Columbia University School of General Studies, and then spent over ten years as a stylist for commercial photographers in New York City.

Since 1975, her work as a costume designer has been seen in many motion pictures and television productions, including French Postcards, Fame, Tattoo, Endless Love, Shoot the Moon, Exposed, Lovesick, Best Defense, The Little Drummer Girl, Terms of Endearment, Unfaithfully Yours, Beat Street, Birdy, Silverado, and Dead End Kids.

Zea has also designed costumes for the theater, such as the American Repertory Theatre's production of Jean Genet's The Balcony.

Recently, Zea has expanded her filmmaking role to include production design. It was in that capacity that she contributed to Lucas and Angel Heart. In addition, she was design coordinator on Woody Allen's Interiors.

INTERVIEWER: Tell me about the process you go through as a costume designer for a film.

ZEA: Some people work with storyboards, though I never have. Each film has a different set of requirements.

On *Silverado*, the director, Larry Kasdan, and I sat down and had a discussion about what we wanted to do in the film. It was really a synthesis of all of the westerns that were ever made. The time frame was a thirty-year spread, from the 1860s to the 1890s. From the costume point of view, there was a very big change in what women wore during that time. Bustles were very much in evidence towards the end of the 1800s. But we wanted to stay away from anything that would really pinpoint the date; hence, no bustles.

After looking at a slew of westerns to see what kinds of themes in dress there were, I then went back to photographs of the period. Fortunately, there are quite a few wonderful books about cowboys and expansion in the West in the pioneer days. They were invaluable as a reference. The black-and-white photos didn't give us the colors, of course. We decided that, from the photos, the colors looked quite dark. Even the light colors were probably never pure colors because of the kind of water people would have washed the clothes in—when they washed them, which wasn't very often! They washed the clothes in rivers full of mineral deposits. We realized that the colors of the clothes would never stay pure; they would be muted. Also, the dyes they had then were often natural dyes made from berries and roots, and so forth, so the colors would be natural ones.

But in not such a specific sense, the costume designer's "process," as it were, is to analyze the script and talk with the key creative elements—the director, the actors, the production designer, and the cinematographer—then to create the physical package that will best suit the needs of all those people, while also influencing the style of the film.

INTERVIEWER: Do you ever go to museums to look at the old clothes?

ZEA: Yes, I have. Of course, at the Metropolitan Museum of Art there is a very fine costume collection. I found out after *Silverado* that there is a textile museum* down in Texas with a fantastic collection of American costumes and textiles. I had an opportunity to go down there because somebody wanted me to design a line of western wear as a result of the film. I met the

---

* The Museum, Texas Tech University, Lubbock, Texas.

curator there and she had examples of all kinds of costumes I could pick up and hold. I was just kicking myself that I hadn't been able to see them before we made the film. It was very consoling, though, because it turned out that the work I had done, at times instinctively, was for the most part correct.

INTERVIEWER: *When you do this research, do you make drawings?*

ZEA: I like to find photographs and then put together a kind of collage of the different elements that I want to see represented in the film. Then, quite often I will create it on the person, the actor. If it's a modern-day film, of course it's much easier to do. In the case of the western, *Silverado*, it was a lot more difficult, because none of the clothes were in existence. All of the clothes in that film, at least for the principals, had to be made. Which meant that I had to do sketches. Sketches give you an overall mood and feeling for the character. Yes, we want him in dark tones, and he should have a coat and a vest. You can become extremely detailed, but when it came down to, well, what kind of collar, and do we want this to have a yoke, should this be a full sleeve, or what kind of pant leg, then it became a question of simply draping it on the figure to decide what looked the best.

> *"Sometimes a garment will trigger a whole new concept of who the character is."*

INTERVIEWER: *When you have finalized your ideas, how do you find the actual clothes for the film or have them made?*

ZEA: It depends on the budget and it depends on what I can afford to have done. In the case of *Silverado* and *Terms of Endearment*, we had things made at Western Costume out in California. If you need to have things made, you find qualified seamstresses or costume shops.

For modern films, you can go out and find pretty much anything you could possibly want. And you should, because if you are talking about a contemporary individual in a film, that person would go to certain places to buy their clothes. It's part of their characterization. You might say, this guy is a completely fastidious dresser. He loves everything out of *Gentleman's Quarterly* magazine, so let's go down to Soho in New York and go into all the small shops and find his clothing there. You wind up going around and buying lots of clothes. It's fun, but it can also be very exhausting.

Also, sometimes a garment will trigger a whole new concept of who the character is.

INTERVIEWER: While the picture is being shot, what is your role?

ZEA: It depends entirely on the scope of the movie, but I try to get all the changes of the principal characters decided before they begin shooting. You want to avoid the situation where you arrive on the set in the morning not having figured out what a certain person is going to wear in that scene. It detracts from the whole momentum of the production.

When I was working with Franco Zeffirelli on *Endless Love,* we had pretty much decided on everything that Brooke Shields was going to wear, but there were one or two scenes that were undecided. At one point he turned to me and said, "Darling, we have to leave something to chance." So we would then have to figure it out on the day of shooting. That can be a little scary, because he could suddenly say to me, "Well, she should be in blue," and if I didn't have anything blue on the truck, it could be a scramble to find it. You don't want to do that if you can avoid it.

INTERVIEWER: How do you maintain the continuity of a character's appearance throughout the shooting?

ZEA: Well, there are costumers whom I hire. They are on the set all the time, and their job is to make sure that, if an actor is filmed in a certain outfit and then has to continue in another location, when he puts that outfit back on, all of the elements are there exactly as they left him. They take Polaroids so they know if the tie was less than centered or there was a button undone. The costumers are very talented at their craft. They also know how to salvage disasters. If somebody spills something on the clothing or tears something, they are in charge of the maintenance of all the garments.

And the scriptperson takes continuity notes, which is also helpful in a case like that.

INTERVIEWER: How many people are in your costume crew?

ZEA: Each film's requirements are different. On *Silverado* I had a costume supervisor for men and a costume supervisor for women. The women's supervisor in turn had two other women helping her, plus a seamstress. The men's supervisor had two assistants and a tailor and a person who distressed and aged the costumes.

INTERVIEWER: Do you have a certain daily routine during the shooting?

ZEA: I get to the set early to make sure nothing is amiss. Once I feel that everything is under control, if I have other fittings, or if I have to go out shopping, then I leave. But if I knew there was going to be another piece of clothing established that day, I would be on the set when that piece was established. If there were any questions or problems about it, I would be there to sort them out. And the same holds true when you're the production designer. You go there in the morning to make sure everything's OK on the set, to make sure all the props are in place. If you need to go off and do other things, which is usual, then you tell the prop, set dressing, and camera people that you'll be gone and that when they move to the next location, to please tell you so you can be there. You only have one crack at it. Once it's established on the film, it's over.

Shirley MacLaine and Kristi Zea on location during the filming of Terms of Endearment.

INTERVIEWER: *Your days must be quite long, then.*

ZEA: Yes, the days are very long. Once you've finished shooting for the day, then there are dailies. You go to see everything you've done—that there are no gigantic errors, or to check on how something looked that you weren't sure about. Normally, I don't actually come home from work until 10:00 at night if I've started at 6:00 or 7:00 in the morning.

INTERVIEWER: *Does your social life revolve around the film business?*

ZEA: Fifty-fifty. A certain number of my friends are not in the business at all. Sometimes the business can be very claustrophobic. There is a necessity to spend time with film people if only to find out what's going on. And it's nice to talk shop from time to time, and people who aren't in the business just don't understand it. A lot of what goes on in the movie world is oftentimes pretty ridiculous, and people in the business can understand it.

> *"I feel that I am contributing to a larger work in the same way that a performer does."*

INTERVIEWER: *Do you have a family that you are away from for long stretches?*

ZEA: Not really. I have an apartment full of cats and a boyfriend who wonders sometimes why I do what I do. My family and friends have figured out that Kristi is sometimes around but most often not. It's hard to keep friendships going and keep relationships going when you are on the road as much as I am. If I decide to have a family, I'm going to have to change my approach to this business. I will either take jobs closer to home or not work as much.

INTERVIEWER: *Can you recall any embarrassing moments in your career as a costume designer?*

ZEA: Well, I did a TV movie for Viacom called *For Ladies Only*, with Gregory Harrison and Marc Singer. It was about male strippers. I had entrusted the manufacture of the G-strings to a lady in California. When we got down to Atlanta, where they were shooting, the G-strings hadn't been completed yet. They showed up on the first day of shooting, which was already a disaster. When I looked at them, I thought, "Gee, I wonder if she really fit these things." I thought, "Something's wrong here. They look like hats! I'd better get Greg and Marc in to try these on before tonight." There was no resemblance to anything like a G-string! They looked terrible. They were gigantic.

And they'd be worn in very active scenes with the dancers gyrating all over. G-strings are supposed to hold everything that is dear to you close to your body, and, well, these were not going to do that at all! They weren't going to work, and we only had about two hours to get them to work.

So first we had to fit them. Greg and Marc came in and I was terribly embarrassed. I was literally so mortified that I could barely deal with it. I said to my two female costumers, "Why don't you just fit those and I'll be back later," and left the room! They were all squealing and giggling, of course. The next time I saw the boys, they were out on the set with 500 screaming women and they were swinging from trapezes and I was praying to God that nothing fell out! Well, it worked and everybody had a good time!

INTERVIEWER: *Have any of your films been more enjoyable than others?*

ZEA: *Silverado* was fantastic. I thoroughly enjoyed myself on that show for a variety of reasons. These days, they don't make too many westerns. To be a part of that tradition of Hollywood westerns was a wonderful opportunity.

Fame was a wonderful show to work on as well because it was big and it was filled with dancing. That was a tremendous experience.

Shoot the Moon was excellent for other reasons. I was thrilled to work with the people who were in that show.

If you're lucky, every film you do has an experience you'd like to remember. It has to do with the director; it all starts at the top. If the director is kind and also good at his work, you can't help but have a good experience working on the film.

Hopefully, you aren't going to be surrounded by unpleasant crew members or actors.

Filmmaking is a very, very hard process, and you have a tremendous amount of pressure surrounding you most of the time. And people crack under pressure. You have to be able to understand that and allow it to happen if it's going to happen, and be able to rebound and keep going. The circumstances under which you have to shoot can sometimes be extremely difficult. You have to be able to go with the flow, to try and maintain some sense of decency and decorum and humor.

INTERVIEWER: *What project have you just now finished?*

ZEA: I'm recovering from *Angel Heart*, a film directed by Alan Parker. Mickey Rourke and Robert DeNiro starred. I was the art director, not the costume designer, actually.

INTERVIEWER: *How do you recuperate from a project?*

ZEA: I find I have a need to go someplace where I don't have to think about anything. If I come back here to New York, it's to find a pile of mail and all kinds of things I need to take care of. In terms of relaxing, I will take a week or two weeks directly after a show and go off and do something, to completely thaw out.

INTERVIEWER: *Where are your favorite places?*

ZEA: I'm very fortunate to have wonderful places to visit. I have a dear friend who has a house in the mountains of Colorado and another friend who has a great place on the coast of Nova Scotia and another friend who has a farm up in Massachusetts. If those people are interested in having me, I'll go there. But if not, I'll go to an island somewhere or in this case, I'm going to Italy for three weeks.

INTERVIEWER: *How did you get involved in costume design? Did you have a background in fashion design?*

ZEA: No. As a matter of fact, the only way I had any experience is that from a very early age, I sewed clothes. I made clothes for my dolls and I made clothes for myself. But I have not had any formal training. When people hear that, they raise their eyebrows, and say, "Really?"

I started in the commercial field. I was a stylist for commercial photographers for many years. Essentially, the role of the stylist is kind of a concentrated version of what happens in film. You're responsible for the clothes the people wear, the sets or locations they are sitting in—you even help choose the actors. The whole purpose of a print ad is usually to sell somebody something. So you wind up picking things that you think are what America wants to see. Your whole aesthetic is different from film, where people's collars can be dirty.

Commercials usually have people working on them who also do movies. At one point a producer asked me if I would be interested in being the art director on a televised children's film for NBC during the bicentennial. Off I went, and after that it was just one film after another.

INTERVIEWER: *So you didn't start out as a costume designer.*

ZEA: No. Originally, when I first started getting involved with film work, after I had been doing commercials for a while, I was assisting production designers. One of them was Mel Bourne who did Woody Allen's *Interiors,* which I worked on as a design consultant. When Alan Parker came to New York to do

Fame, he hired me as the costume designer. At that point I had to join the union. I became a costume designer officially. However, I had been doing both costume design and production design.

INTERVIEWER: *And recently you've been moving back into the realm of production design?*

ZEA: Yes. I did the clothes on *Silverado,* and after that I received a script from a director named David Seltzer, a wonderful script about adolescence called *Lucas.* He wanted me to do the clothes, so I read the script and called him up. I told him that I really couldn't do the film. He said, "Oh, that's a shame; why not?" And I said, "Basically, for two reasons. The first is, it's out of town yet again, and I really think I'd better go home. The second reason is that if I did any work on it at all, I'd like to production-design it." He said, "Then don't say no so quickly."

> *"Filmmaking is a very, very hard process."*

And so I was hired as the production designer. In the last two films I've done, I've been associated with the art department.

INTERVIEWER: *Does the production designer ever get involved with costume design?*

ZEA: I think they should. Some production designers are more inclined to than others. If they are comfortable with the idea of clothes, they do. And if they are more technically oriented, they don't.

I've been on films where the production designer hasn't really worried about the costumes. He has left all of the designing to me, the director, and the actors. But there are other production designers who are very much involved with the clothes. As a production designer, I like to be involved with the clothes. I've spent so much time in costume design that it's in my blood.

INTERVIEWER: *How do you decide whether or not to become involved with a certain project?*

ZEA: Usually, it has to do with the subject matter, who's in it, or where or when it takes place. I also decide based on whether I want to work with the director.

I was asked to work on a film that may finally surface this year, called *Dead End Kids.* It was based on a play of the same name directed by JoAnne Akalaitis in New York. The play was very well received. The theatrical company that put it on, Mabou Mines, is well known in New York for very good, avant-garde, off-Broadway theater. And it was the subject matter that brought me to the film: It had to do with the history of nuclear power. It was an anti-nuclear piece.

Even though they had absolutely no money, I wanted to be involved with the project. And it was a very wonderful experience. David Byrne and Philip Glass are doing some music for it. It may appear at the New York Film Festival this year. They called me up about a week ago, jumping up and down for joy because they had just gotten another hundred thousand dollars to complete it. Unlike some of the other films I work on, where a hundred thousand is blown in a day! It's so sweet to hear that they are finally going to be able to put it all together. It's been going on for four years.

INTERVIEWER: *The money in the film business doesn't tend to gravitate toward worthy projects, does it?*

ZEA: Oh, it's the biggest gambling game going—how a film actually gets into production, who finances it, why it's financed, what happens to it when it's done. It's just astonishing to me that films can ever get done and that once they're done, they're distributed and people actually go out and pay money to see them.

INTERVIEWER: *Have you ever worked in the theater?*

ZEA: Yes. Recently I was asked to do a play called *The Balcony*, produced up in Boston by the American Repertory Theater and directed by JoAnne Akalaitis. It was a remarkable experience. The action centers around a "house of illusions," otherwise known as a bordello. All the clientele got dressed up in perfectly unbelievable outfits.

It's an altogether different experience than film, from a visual point of view as well as the money. There's very, very little money to spend on theater pieces unless you're in the big leagues on Broadway. From a creative point of view, you're dealing with much broader strokes. You have to remember that there are going to be people sitting seventy or a hundred feet back from the stage and they've got to be able to see what you've done as well as the person in the front row.

INTERVIEWER: *Does your work in the theater tend to be more abstract?*

ZEA: That's a hard question. There is a tendency for it to be more abstract, but I think that film has the capacity for abstraction. I think there's more abstraction in theater because the audience needs to create its own sense of reality in a much more specific way than in film. You can watch a

An unusual suit for Matthew Modine in Birdy.

film and be told that you are watching reality. You are supposed to believe everything you see on the screen, even if it's *Star Wars*. It's done with verisimilitude to the point of absurdity.

In the theater, you know that you are going to be witnessing something that's an abstraction. A whole other set of criteria is utilized in theater. You can just have a black stage with nothing on it and a person wearing a very strange outfit lit in an incredible fashion, and suddenly he could be out on a moor and it's Hamlet. Whereas the movie version of that could be filmed up in Scotland with a hundred crew members waiting for the sun to hit the clouds at just the right moment and then shooting it.

"The only influence I can have is to work on films that I think are saying something worth saying."

INTERVIEWER: *How do you see yourself as a filmmaker, as a contributor to culture?*

ZEA: I feel that I'm contributing to a larger work in the same way that a performer does. I hope I'm subtly influencing the way a person sees something, that my work is going to affect the way people see life—their lives. I would rather it be a subtle influence than an obvious one. It's more effective in the long run.

INTERVIEWER: *Do you think your costume work should be anonymous?*

ZEA: Yes, I think it should be anonymous. It should work very subtly to help the story. There are times when it can be more than that. In *Terms of Endearment* there was quite a reaction to the dress that Shirley MacLaine wore in the scene where she had lunch with Jack Nicholson. People would come to me and say, "Oh, that dress!" It even got as far as a Vincent Canby review in the *New York Times*. But that's very, very unusual. I would prefer my work to be less obvious.

INTERVIEWER: *How important do you think movies are?*

ZEA: I think they are very important. People are not reading as much as they used to. Television and movies are where people are getting most of their information these days. In the future, messages are going to be conveyed more and more in a visual way, particularly in light of what video is doing to the whole movie market. People who might not find the time or the money to go down to their neighborhood theater can see movies in their homes. Hopefully, they will get more out of these films than they would out of films like *Rambo*. Movies can broaden people's sensibilities and influence them.

I was very, very influenced by films when I was growing up. I thought *Billy Liar* was one of the most fantastic films I had ever seen. And Julie Christie was my heroine. I thought if I could just be like Julie Christie, then my life would be complete! Kids do that. Kids are going to look at Tom Cruise and ask, "Gee, do I want to be a top gun?"

INTERVIEWER: So you feel that movies have strong social, even political, implications?

ZEA: Absolutely. Without question.

INTERVIEWER: In those terms, what do you think movies are doing to people these days?

ZEA: I hope they are doing people some good. I tend to get a little dismayed when I see the films listed on the marquees around the country outside the urban centers. I get a little worried because I feel that the substance of these films is very escapist and there is a kind of overriding violence that seems to permeate most of the films seen on a large scale. That scares me. There's more to life than that.

I hope we are just going through a phase. I think we are. I think there is an enormous amount of frustration in this country. Americans feel they are no longer viewed as heroes by the rest of the world. We are definitely the "ugly Americans." Our foreign policy doesn't help that much. Films like *Rambo* and the other one-man-against-the-world type of films are satisfying that frustration. It's because of where we are globally.

I also think that kids are turned on by films like *The Breakfast Club* and *Risky Business* because they are fairly discouraged with the whole adult world and material world. They are angered by it, too. They like the idea of being able to trash someone's father's Ferrari or smoke dope in school, even though most of them wouldn't ever do it in reality.

INTERVIEWER: What films would you like to see made?

ZEA: It's hard to say. I would like to see films that are different from those in the mainstream market, but most people wouldn't want to go see them. The films that exist are there because people pay money to see them.

The distributors are always trying to satisfy the needs of the audience. If the distributor puts a thoughtful film like *A Room with a View* in the theater instead of an action picture like *Top Gun*, he's going to get a different kind of audience, and it may be a smaller one. It becomes a question of dollars and cents. Pornography has an influence there, too. There are definitely people who want to see pornographic movies, and you can almost guarantee a certain income based on that kind of fare. Many top-quality films don't have that kind of automatic market.

The only influence I can have is to work on films that I think are saying something worth saying. I feel very strongly about that. I do not want to work on a film that is in any way exploitative.

INTERVIEWER: *Do you play the saxophone or have other creative outlets?*

ZEA: The saxophone! I've found that working on films is so demanding, creatively and otherwise, that it's very hard for me to maintain any other activities. I've been working so much that I haven't really allowed anything else to grow. I do like to write and paint and, if I were to have more time, I would do more of that. I write stories and impressions of things. If I've been in a city and I've seen something about that city that affected me, I'll write it down or I'll do a drawing.

INTERVIEWER: *What would you like to do in the future?*

ZEA: I seem to be heading in the direction of becoming more involved with production design. I'm very fortunate that the directors I've worked with as a costume designer are allowing me the opportunity to come back to them as art director or as production designer. It's a broadening of my visual contribution to the film. I like that.

Michael Westmore

MAKEUP

Michael Westmore, a Hollywood native, was born into a dynasty. His grandfather started the family tradition of motion picture makeup artistry in 1917. Westmore's five uncles all became makeup artists at five different studios. His father, Monty, was at Selznick studios and was responsible for the makeup on Gone With the Wind *and* Mutiny on the Bounty.

As a university student, Westmore almost ended the line of succession. He intended to become an art historian with a special interest in archaeology. However, upon his graduation from the University of California at Santa Barbara, his uncle Bud at Universal Studios prevailed upon him to give the apprenticeship program there a try.

He completed his apprenticeship and went on to become assistant department head of makeup at Universal and then served as the director of a special makeup lab at the studio until 1970. In 1971, Westmore founded M.G. Westmore, Ltd., a lab for special makeup and makeup effects, and began working as a makeup artist on a free-lance basis. Westmore has been responsible for the makeup on thirty-three films, including

Mask, Raging Bull, 2010, Clan of the Cave Bear, *the original* Rocky, Rocky II *and* Rocky III, New York, New York, Blade Runner, Eleanor and Franklin, *and* The Day After.

He has received numerous awards and nominations, including three Emmys and an Oscar in 1986 for his work on Mask.

Not content with these achievements, Westmore has worked with several plastic surgeons to reconstruct the faces of patients scarred by accidents, burns, cancer, and birth defects. He has written chapters on medical cosmetology for three medical textbooks dealing with plastic surgery, burn patients, and recon- structive dentistry. Westmore lives in Studio City with his wife, Marion, and three children, Michael II, Michele, and McKenzie.

I arrived in Studio City on a typical Southern California morning. In the open, under the white sky, the sun was uncomfortably hot, while in the shade it remained decidedly chilly. Westmore met me at the office of his company, Hol- lywood Magic Cosmetics, just down the street from Universal Studios, where he began his career twenty-five years ago. His suburban good looks belie the fact that he's in his late forties. He has a congenial and casual demeanor despite the impression that he feels there aren't enough hours in the day. I sat on a comfort- able sofa while Westmore talked enthusiastically about the profession of creating beauties and beasts.

INTERVIEWER: How long has your family been producing makeup artists?

WESTMORE: The professional makeup artist literally started with my grandfather and a bunch of actors and wig makers. It's interesting to follow the development of makeup as a craft. My grandfather started it and then he trained his sons, and they all went into different studios in their very early twenties. And from there it started to branch out and grow.

In the theater, actors would do their own makeup because it's a one- night performance and then it's over with. But they found in movies that the variations in the makeup an actor would do on himself were not acceptable as far as the continuity of the picture was concerned. You spend three months shooting a film and maybe the whole story takes place in one day. So what really created the need for the professional makeup artist was the necessity of controlling the continuity of an actor's makeup.

INTERVIEWER: *What got you into this business?*

WESTMORE: I've been painting and drawing my whole life. In college I majored in art education, then I switched to art history when I realized I didn't want to teach. I was interested in archaeology at the same time. I really wanted to go into archaeology from the art historian's point of view, studying the artifacts for their aesthetic value—going on digs and things like that.

Then my uncle called and asked me if I wanted to go into the business as a makeup artist. I was a junior at the time, and nobody in the family had gotten a university degree. So I told him, "No, I don't want to do it." Well, he called me back a while later and said, "If I keep the apprenticeship open for another year until you graduate, would you come and take it then?" So I said, "OK, I'll try it." I thought that I'd give it a try and if I didn't like it, I could still leave the path open to go to Berkeley to do graduate studies.

I got down to Universal, and I was going to try to work on my master's—going to UCLA and being an apprentice at the same time. But the hours were too long at the studio; I didn't have any brain power left at the end of the day, so that didn't work out.

I had the opportunity, at the same time I came in as an apprentice, to work with John Chambers, the man who got the Oscar for *Planet of the Apes.* He had just come to Universal, too. That was part of what made it exciting for me. I was going to be able to study and work with him as well as with my uncles. It was John that made the business interesting for me, because I learned from him how to make teeth and how to sculpt and how to make molds; I worked really closely with John for about three years.

INTERVIEWER: *So you went right out of college into the makeup business?*

WESTMORE: Right out of college into Universal. I had literally one day off. One of my last finals was on Monday, I drove home on Tuesday, and started work on Wednesday.

And for the next three years I studied each phase of makeup. They locked me in a little room where I made beards for six months. I spent six months with my uncle Bud doing nothing but beauty makeups, and at that time I would always work with John in the afternoons. I had an apprenticeship that just isn't offered anymore.

Now with the new people they say, "Here's how you do a beard," and the person will make two or three of them and is told, "Well, it's OK. You're just going to have to learn how to do it as you go along." People today don't have the training I had.

INTERVIEWER: What was your apprenticeship like?

WESTMORE: It was very difficult. As an apprentice, I was forced to do things and learn. "Go up and make beards and let's see what you have at the end of the day." Now there's nobody that pushes you like that. You don't have the learning experience of showing the experts what you've done and getting their corrective criticism. And it wasn't just one person. Whereas now you go to a school or you have maybe one person helping you, I had every makeup artist at Universal. I could walk around and say, "What do you think of this?" For doing a black eye, for example, in my notebook from those days I have sketches of about ten different black eyes—ten different makeup artists showed me how to do a black eye. Then I worked out my own system that I liked and that worked well for me.

> *"The professional makeup artist ...started with my grandfather."*

INTERVIEWER: So you took notes on all this stuff?

WESTMORE: Yes. I kept notes through my whole apprenticeship that I still have today. I still take notes. Somebody will stumble across something that works really well—new products and so forth—and if you don't write it down, you're not going to remember it. That's one of the best pieces of advice I can give to any new person coming into the business: Keep notes. And very few do; they think they can remember. If I'm running a foam rubber formula, or if there's some special kind of mold that I made years ago and I can't quite remember how I did it, I'll stop and take a quick look back in the book just to refresh my memory, to make sure I don't make any mistakes, because mistakes are costly—having to go back and redo them.

INTERVIEWER: What was the first film you worked on?

WESTMORE: Well, I went through my three years there as an apprentice at Universal, took the exams, passed them, and stayed on there. Then the first thing I did was a little movie with Shelley Winters. And then I started doing *McHale's Navy.*

Then John left Universal to go do *Planet of the Apes,* and I took over the laboratory. I did all the special work—the rubber work and mold work and things. When my uncle left Universal, I decided to leave, too. I went independent and began to work for Sid and Marty Krofft. I worked for them for two years. They were doing children's shows, and I was doing the rubber faces and designs for them. I did *Land of the Lost,* which was a very popular children's show; it's still playing on the air today and kids still are familiar with it. After that, I got a break with *Eleanor and Franklin,* the original one. The show was so popular, it really got me recognized outside of Universal, in the independent field. The next one that gave me a shot in the arm was *Rocky.* I can actually pinpoint those events and say, "From here, things really took off." And I would say that even though I've done the *Rockys* and *Raging Bull* and I had the reputation, et cetera—getting the Oscar for *Mask* was another point where I could say, "OK, things change from here." It throws you into another string of work. So now, I'm bridging the gap between doing special makeup—I'm working with Elizabeth Taylor at the moment—and running my cosmetic business.

INTERVIEWER: What can you say about being so accomplished, about having so much recognition, about being so successful?

WESTMORE: Only, that you've got to be able to handle it. I know guys who can't handle it. When they reach a certain level of recognition, their attitudes change, their personalities change. They think they're worth so much more money. I've found in makeup that it's just not so. You get treated differently; you get treated more as a very integral part of the picture, as part of the crew. But you really have to keep your head. Because the makeup business is basically grind-'em-out work. No matter how wonderful you are, it's still twelve-, fourteen-, eighteen-hour days, putting on appliances, standing by the set. You're on salary to the company.

INTERVIEWER: Tell me what kinds of things you are doing now with the cosmetic business.

WESTMORE: They're commercial cosmetics, and the products have turned out to work very well for the screen, too. So they're being used in both places. We have 700 consultants now after just six months. Going into the cosmetic business has been a complete change of roles for me.

INTERVIEWER: What's the outlook for new people coming into the movie makeup business?

WESTMORE: Things are very slow now, really, in this business. I called the union the other day, and there are over a thousand people on the list. We just took six new people into the union and we've got a thousand members unemployed. One of our problems is that we really have more people in the union than there are jobs.

On top of that, a lot of things are going nonunion now, which creates a tremendous amount of competition in the field. On the special work, competition makes wages go up because the more qualified you are, the more you're in demand. But competition between unqualified people doing something straight and simple makes wages plummet because the competition's so strong. This whole situation with the unions is interesting. I thought it was going to happen when the nonunion work became popular and the unions started to break up. Now the unions are starting to renegotiate all kinds of things to try to save themselves, because there is such a problem with all the nonunion shows that are being done.

INTERVIEWER: *Aren't a lot of people running scared in Hollywood now?*

WESTMORE: Yes, studios are leaving. It used to be that there were studios in New York and there were studios in Hollywood. Now De Laurentiis has them in the Carolinas and anouther group is building studios in Florida. There are facilities in Vancouver, B.C.—a gigantic bus repair building. It's cold or it's hot, and it leaks, but they can build gigantic sets in there. And most of these new studios are in right-to-work states. So if they're just doing a straight little picture, they can hire people locally; they can hire a girl who does makeup out of a beauty salon if they don't really care about good quality. They can get the grips there, they can get the electricians there. So the film business is moving out of Hollywood; movies can be made cheaper outside Hollywood.

INTERVIEWER: *Hollywood's going to have to take the lumps with the bumps because in all the arts, in painting and dance and theater, culture is becoming more decentralized.*

WESTMORE: Well, there are more people interested. Maybe a Russian ballet star decides she wants to live in St. Louis. So all of a sudden there's a prima ballerina in St. Louis and that becomes a center because people want to study with her. And you're right, with the growth of our population and the growth of talents, there's more of everything going on. When I travel around now, every city has its own niche that it's famous for.

INTERVIEWER: *Let's talk about the craft a little bit. What sort of things are involved in lab work?*

WESTMORE: Lab work is mainly learning how to sculpt. Taking molds, learning how to work with plaster, working with clay, then working with products such as plastics, urethanes, and latexes to make your final product. And then there's the painting and finishing. There are a lot of people that are really interested in doing this type of work. I have found that it's quite simple to teach somebody how to take a cast and make a mold. It's also very easy to sculpt. But it's the final result of the sculpting that makes the difference between a product that is totally, 100 percent believable and something that looks like it should be in a joke shop or on the stage. That knowledge only comes from having put in a lot of years and knowing what's good and what's bad.

"They locked me in a little room where I made beards for six months."

INTERVIEWER: *It seems to me that's where the art comes in. You either know that it's right or you don't. You have a certain feeling and you can visualize the final result.*

WESTMORE: Or anything, no matter what it is; you've got to visualize it ahead of time. That's what gets a lot of new sculptors into trouble. They don't do that. They just start putting on clay and sometimes it develops and works for them. But when I start something I see the finished product. I know exactly what my final result is going to be.

There are things I know that you just aren't going to pick up on your own. Somebody has to show you and tell you or you're going to keep making mistakes for a billion years until you figure it out. If you're really interested, you might figure it out—the little tricks of turning it into reality. For example, my old-age work in *2010* was, I think, a little bit more mobile than the work with Dustin Hoffman in *Little Big Man*, because Dustin more or less just sat there. In *2010*, I had my man as old except he was more movable, more pliable. Some other aging jobs just look plain bad.

INTERVIEWER: *What makes the difference between everyday lab work and something terrific?*

WESTMORE: It's really the difference in the sculptor. That's where the first big difference is, because if it isn't in the sculpting, you're lost. You can be wonderful in everything beyond that. You can make a wonderful mold, you can apply it wonderfully, you can paint it wonderfully, but if it isn't in the sculpting, it's never in the final product. The sculpting is what separates the men from the boys in the lab.

INTERVIEWER: *In the lab, what kind of materials do you work with?*

WESTMORE: Different types of urethanes and rubber and plastics and epoxies, glues, different types of makeup.

INTERVIEWER: *And some people specialize in just lab work?*

WESTMORE: Yes. When I do a show, I take it from beginning to end. I'm not a specialist and I don't say, "Well, all I do is make molds." Some people just make molds, some people just sculpt. They all like to try putting the makeup on when it's done, though, just to see what it looks like. You don't have people like me anymore. Very few. I will go do Elizabeth Taylor, I will go create a monster, and go do some other show, too. And there just aren't people with that experience anymore. They don't have the time to learn it. People either come out of beauty shops and do beauty makeup, or kids who have been wearing monster masks and have had the feel for ghouls their whole lives go into lab work and learn how to make molds and make monsters.

INTERVIEWER: *That's a shame, don't you think?*

WESTMORE: It is. The apprenticeship system ended about six years after I finished, and so the makeup artists in their early forties are the last of the dual-role people. I'm like a dying breed, one of the lost animals. There are not too many more of them after me.

INTERVIEWER: *What happens when something goes wrong with your makeup out on location?*

WESTMORE: I have techniques now for putting makeup on so that when I go to bed at night before I have to do something, I can sleep. I don't worry about it, because I've done enough of it now that I know I can walk right in, and I can do it and walk away from it. If something goes wrong, I have enough confidence in myself that I know how to adjust for it. In Canada, on *Clan of the Cave Bear*, some of the girls had skin irritations from the glues we were using. So one day I said to one girl, "Let's just stick it down with K-Y jelly." And we put on a thin layer of K-Y jelly, slapped her forehead on, dried the edges of it, put the makeup over it, and it stayed all day long. But some people would tell you, "Well, you can't do that—it won't work, it's not an adhesive. You've got to use Super Glue." It worked and it was fine.

On *Amazing Stories*, there was an episode where, at one point in the story, a young boy made himself up to look just like his grandfather, but the viewer didn't know whether it was the boy or his grandfather. He had to reach up and pull part of his face off and reveal himself—the Alfred Hitchcock type of ending. The director wanted to be able to peel it off and maybe put it back on again.

The director asked me, "Can we do take two?"

I said, "I don't know if we can do take two or not. We can sure try, and I've got some extra pieces here to make up more if we can't." I told him, "We'll put on most of the face—the part we want to stay—with our adhesive. And then this section you want to come off—the nose, the upper lip, a piece of the eye, and the cheek here—we'll put that all down with K-Y jelly." We put it all on, dried it, made him up, blended it all in, and then he did it: All of a sudden he did a take-off right on camera.

The director said, "How long is it going to take to fix him?" I had planned on taking an hour to fix him. Well, I had another guy helping me and we had him done in twenty minutes! We did it five times, and finally I said, "We're going to have to start with a new piece now." Within an hour and a half we were able to get five takes of a scene that somebody new coming into the business could have taken all day with, not knowing how to do it. Everyone was thrilled.

INTERVIEWER: *That's pretty amazing.*

WESTMORE: Yeah, that was an amazing story!

INTERVIEWER: *How do you go about judging good makeup work?*

WESTMORE: John Chambers once told me, "Perfection is all in the eye of the beholder because a lot of people will stop far short of perfection, thinking they have achieved it." And I've found this to be true over and over in the movie business. I look at a television show and I will see not so-so makeup but really horrible makeup, like this stuff that was out in *Dream West* recently. A very bad job, where you say to yourself, "How can this producer—who's paying all that money for beautiful costumes and sets and hauling crews around the country and camera and film—hire someone who's really not that talented to come in and do the makeup?" Because that's his image on the screen; it's not something that can be hidden. This is your product up there. It would be like me putting my cosmetics into cheap bottles. I might have the best product in the world, but all of a sudden, the image that I've put out is horrible; it's what everybody sees first. I really don't understand it.

INTERVIEWER: *When you look back on the films you've worked on, which ones were particularly wonderful experiences?*

WESTMORE: Makeup-wise I've been nominated for Emmys ten times and won three. I think the one I enjoyed the most was *Why Me?* with Glynnis O'Connor. I had nine days to get it ready and twenty days to shoot it, and it was really a makeup picture from beginning to end. It was the story of a girl's rehabilitation through two years of plastic surgery.

Picture-wise it would be hard to say. *Raging Bull* was an awfully popular, cultish type of film, which I spent fourteen months on. It was quite an experience.

> *"Ten different makeup artists showed me how to do a black eye."*

INTERVIEWER: *What work of yours are you most proud of, and what would you change if you could?*

WESTMORE: As far as old-age work goes—and I've been involved in a lot of that—I look back at my old *Eleanor and Franklin* stuff that I won my first Emmy for and I would change everything, because it can't compare to the quality of the work I did in *2010*. And I don't know where I would go from there. I've reached a certain level in my sculpting and so on, and I don't know where I would take it, except to change the character or make the folds in some different places.

And creature-wise, comparing Rocky Dennis in *Mask* to, say, John Merrick in *The Elephant Man*, the elephant man had his head in a sack for the whole movie except for twenty minutes. And it was all in black and white. This is why Frank Price called and asked me if we could do *Mask*. He said, "We're going to have this kid on the screen for two hours and in color; can it be done?" It became a very big challenge for us. They said it took a long time to put the elephant man makeup on and that it was uncomfortable. I don't know why. If you work your systems out and think ahead, it doesn't need to take a long time and be uncomfortable. You should design your things for comfort and wearability. That's part of being a professional.

INTERVIEWER: *How do you control the continuity of the makeup you do? Do you take pictures every day?*

WESTMORE: Almost every day. I take Polaroids. On *Raging Bull*, for example, we would shoot an exterior scene here, and an interior scene there a month later. The makeup—the shape, color, and size of the bruises, the stitches, whatever—all had to match from one shot to the other, so I kept Polaroids as I went along. And the hair stylist kept them, too, of the hair—front, profile, back. It's a necessity. I usually put the pictures in my script where the scene is. I'll say, "OK, this scene goes from here to here." Then I put the pictures in the book and write the scene numbers and whatever on them, so whenever I come back to that scene, I'll know.

And once in a while, I'll miss. In fact, it happened in Canada, on *Iceman* with John Lone. I got him all made up—I mean we did everything; it took three hours to do John. He had false teeth, he had a false beard, mustache, a whole wig headpiece that gave him a Neanderthal-shaped head, forehead, nose, scars on the body; we made fingernails for him—everything. We were doing one scene where he was out on the ice, and most of it had already been shot previously someplace else. There was one little pickup shot that they needed. So they trucked in fourteen or twenty-eight carloads of snow and filled a parking lot with it one day. Then we had to start shooting fast because it was getting hot. The director said, "Quick, let's get John lying down here in the snow and let's finish this thing." So for that scene I checked all the Polaroids, but I totally forgot to put blood on his hand at the last minute. So they shot the scene. Afterwards, I had to go up to the director. I couldn't just keep my mouth shut and not say anything. The picture was too big, too important, to do that. So I went to him, and by that time they had already broken the cameras down and moved. I said, "I forgot to put the blood on John's hand." And he said, "Oh, hell. We better do it again then." So, real quickly, they got the cameras, set the scene back up, got the blood on the hand, and did it. That's our job—to take care of the details. If you goof, admit it quick.

INTERVIEWER: Where do you draw the line between makeup and special effects?

WESTMORE: So many special effects are done now under the name of makeup. Before, the faces were cast, the sculpting was done, and so forth in the makeup lab. When it came down to the mechanics of things, a special-effects person did it. Now, if somebody makes a big rubber figure that is operated by twelve people pulling cables, they call it makeup, and it really isn't. That's still in the realm of special effects. It might be a train or a waterfall or anything else; it just so happens it's an image of a body.

INTERVIEWER: So there's overlap.

WESTMORE: There's tremendous overlap going on now and people don't know where to put themselves. Like a monster—is the body a costume or is it makeup? Or a head that a person just slips on but he's not really an actor. Just because the guy's eight feet tall, they put him into the suit. Now is that an actor? Is that makeup? The Academy is trying to draw rules on it. They would say, for example, that to be considered makeup, it has to be attached to a performer and he has to use it as part of his character. Which means that what you would see in a picture like *Mask* would be considered makeup, but that somebody in a Jolly Green Giant suit that's being run mechanically from offstage would not. All the Giant has to do is walk around and move his arms, and other people are blinking the eyes and wiggling the ears. Definite lines still have not been drawn.

Mechanics and puppetry are slipping into makeup, and makeup has to decide whether it wants to let them in or not. I don't know if they should. Maybe, as more and more things are produced independently, it will all be considered makeup.

INTERVIEWER: Does this overlap ever create problems between people in production?

WESTMORE: No, because that's usually all settled before we get involved.

INTERVIEWER: When does the makeup artist get involved in a picture?

WESTMORE: It depends. I have been hired even before directors have been hired, when makeup was such an integral part of the picture that it had to be started on while they were finding a director. And then I would get together with the director as soon as he was hired and we'd put our thoughts together. Otherwise, on simpler shows, the production could be going for three or four months before they call up everybody and bring them in, because they don't want to put them on salary too soon; there's no reason to. It varies anywhere from months to days.

INTERVIEWER: What about a picture like Mask?

WESTMORE: The director Peter Bogdanovich was hired; he was already involved in the project. And I went in three months before the actual production started and came up with eight different head/face designs. We did different things because it was designed so the actor could put the face on and work it himself without the use of mechanics or robotics. It took the manufacturing of eight different heads to figure out how we could do that. Then the picture took another three months to shoot.

INTERVIEWER: *For* Mask, *how much leeway did you have in the makeup design, as far as the character was involved?*

WESTMORE: For *Mask* there was a real person. All they did was give me pictures of the real person—eleven by fourteens, profiles, closeups, and a couple different ages of him. I took my calipers and worked on the pictures and also worked on the clay, to get the images as close as possible. If it's a fantasy type of thing, I'm usually so busy that I don't like to get involved in drawings unless I really have to. It's much easier if an art director or a sketch artist sits down with the director. Then, once the director says, "Ah, this is what I want," they give it to me and I'll go to work on it. They give me what they want and I make it real for them.

INTERVIEWER: *Is there some overlap between the production designer and the makeup artist?*

WESTMORE: Yes—some of the makeup artists like to sketch and they like to draw, and they'll get involved earlier and do things like that. But I would just as soon have them give me the drawings and let me sit down and figure it out. Because once I get into it, I'll make changes and do things myself. Maybe I think a certain nostril is better, and I'll talk with the director about it—"Maybe we should change it this way." Or perhaps what somebody's designed isn't going to work on a human face, so we'd better change it. I like to work from an art director's sketches.

> *"That's one of the best pieces of advice I can give to any new person coming into the business: Keep notes."*

INTERVIEWER: *Some people say that there is a problem in filmmaking of people not understanding one another's jobs and not keeping the lines of communication open.*

WESTMORE: Yes, there used to be that communication. When there were studios, the lines were drawn. You were a painter, you were a special-effects person, you were a makeup artist, you were a hair stylist, you were a costume designer, you were a director. Everybody had their little niche, but now they're all starting to cross over. The makeup artist designs something and all of a sudden he wants to direct the scene.

INTERVIEWER: *Is the collaborative nature of filmmaking ever a problem for you?*

WESTMORE: I enjoy the collaboration. A lot of times makeup people fight with the production designer. The designer's job is to make sure it all pulls together—whether it be hair, makeup, wardrobe, sets—that there's a certain look to the film. So, there's a big fight when a makeup artist or hair stylist says, "I know what I'm doing and they can't tell me what to do. I know my research. I know what my work is supposed to look like." That's fine, that's wonderful, but right there you've created a wedge. Why get into a fight? Because when push comes to shove, you're going to go and that designer's going to stay, because the designer's making more money than you. They're going to get a one-name credit up front on the screen; that's big bucks.

You have to be flexible. And honest with yourself. Because even work that I've done that I thought was masterful has been chewed up by some directors. But in those situations I've gone back to the drawing board. My original concept would have worked, but what they wanted, what they had in mind, was different. So it's fine. We talk about it, change it around and move it a little bit. Together we come up with something that works. It's a lot easier working together than it is pulling in different directions. When you find people pulling in different directions, it affects the quality somewhere down the road. It seems that the pictures on which people work together do well—*Iceman* or *2010* or *Mask*. When it goes up on the screen, it works.

INTERVIEWER: *You work very closely with stars. Is it ever difficult for you to work with the star personality?*

WESTMORE: I have no problem with star personalities. I've been working with the biggest ones forever. It's a matter of my personality working with them. I'm an employee. I'm hired to work with them. I have never found it objectionable if Elizabeth Taylor said, "Michael, would you please get me a glass of water?" to go get a glass of water. Or if Sly Stallone yelled at me and said, "Quick, over here. I want to get this really fast. Squirt this down." It's part of the job. Other people will think they're more important than the stars, but they're not. We're all expendable except for the stars, and even they're expendable if they push so far that it's financially not going to work.

INTERVIEWER: *Who do you work with most closely on a typical picture— the designer?*

WESTMORE: No, the director. Most of my pictures have been one on one with the director, because his is the last word. I go to him and say, "Do you want to do this? Do you want to do that?" and it's either yes or no and I've got an answer. And sometimes the producer's in there, too. If the director isn't quite sure, then he'll talk to the producer about it. But I would say 80 percent of the time it's just the director I work with. Unless I'm working with a producer like Norman Jewison.* Norman has definite ideas about what he wants. If he's just producing and not directing, he'll throw his two cents in.

INTERVIEWER: *How many people are generally on the makeup crew?*

WESTMORE: I've been on pictures that I do by myself, but there are generally two; two makeup artists and one hair stylist is an average. There's a problem if you have two big stars and each star brings their own makeup artist in; then you need a third one to kind of run the show. So when you get involved in those kinds of shows, you have, on an average, six people: makeup and hair for each star, then another makeup artist and stylist to do the show.

And then the crews can get gigantic. On *Clan of the Cave Bear*, I had nine makeup artists and five hair stylists. On *New York, New York*, I had even more than that. We had big days when we had 1500 people in the audience and they all had to be dressed and made up for the period; the men all needed haircuts and the women all needed their hair styled.

On *The Day After*, I actually didn't have the help I needed and I couldn't get it. Originally, I wanted to just hire students out of a local college. The producers wanted to do it but then they got scared that the unions in L.A. might get upset if we did. So they sent one extra person from L.A. I had three makeup artists and three hair stylists putting together the gymnasium scene in *The Day After*. We had 1500 people there, all with burns, bruises, scars, and dirt. It took us twelve hours to put them all together. We just kept cranking people out, and they were doing close-ups and little sections of things until they could finally get the one big shot. So the big shot was done at the end of the day.

INTERVIEWER: *Your typical workday is a long one anyway, isn't it? You have to start before everyone else.*

WESTMORE: Yes, but the days on that production were exceptionally long because we would have, on an average day, maybe 100 extra people to make up, aside from our regular cast. Those days were really long. Half the picture was shot in Kansas and half in L.A., so once I got back to L.A., I was able to hire more help right out of the union.

INTERVIEWER: *What are your normal hours when you're on a picture?*

---

* Director/producer whose films include *The Russians Are Coming, the Russians Are Coming, In the Heat of the Night, Fiddler on the Roof,* and *And Justice for All.*

WESTMORE: Usually the shooting schedule is about twelve hours. Many times it goes to around fourteen. Sometimes you only get nine hours between calls. From the time they say one day's shooting is a wrap, the next makeup call is scheduled for nine hours later. That minimum is a union rule. On location, the union doesn't have any control at all.

On *Clan of the Cave Bear*, we worked until we wanted to start yelling and screaming. I was able to spell the rest of the crew, so they had more time to rest and take it easy. I couldn't; I had to be there all the time. We had about two weeks where I would get up around 4:00 A.M. to catch the 4:30 boat that went across to the island and I would get back at 10:00 at night. So I would get back, call Marion, go to sleep instantly, get up, get back on the boat, and go to the island again. I might try to catnap a little bit during the daytime, once I realized everything was going all right, but I'd get so hyped up that I couldn't. There was just so much going on. I was a vegetable when it was over with.

> *"It seems that the pictures on which people work together do well...."*

INTERVIEWER: *How did it come out?*

WESTMORE: I haven't seen it myself. It's a shame, because they had a wonderful model there. Originally it was to be a sixteen-hour miniseries, to be shot in Colorado. Then they cut it down to a two-hour film. It's mainly the story of Ayla, played by Daryl Hannah. But there just isn't enough time in two hours to do a book that's 600 pages long.

INTERVIEWER: *Did the production designer come up with the idea for that very striking white makeup?*

WESTMORE: No, we did that. They also supplied us with tons of research about primitive times and we took it from there; I had pages full of drawings. I made sketches of handprints and leaf prints and the possibilities of combining the different patterns. Then I passed out some sheets to different makeup artists on the crew and I told them, "You just do handprints, and you do leaf prints, and you do such and such." That way, when we made up each person, we had a variety of everything, instead of everybody turning out handprints.

We had to do the same thing on *The Day After*. We'd say, "OK, the next twenty-five people in the door we're going to put blisters on, and then for the next twenty-five after that we're going to put radiation burns on." Because if you just bounce around trying to think of what you're going to do to each one, you lose time. For example, if I gave you a makeup kit and said, "I want you to make up twelve clowns," you'd probably do a real good job on the first two, then on the third one you'd start thinking too hard and you'd start repeating yourself. So you really need research behind you. You need to be able to flip open a book and say, "Oh, good, let's see, I'll do this one and this one and this one, and I'll put this eye and this mouth on this one and that will do it." But when it's left up to your mind, you're good only to a certain point. Then you start repeating yourself unless you have fresh material to look at.

INTERVIEWER: What is the most difficult part for you when you are working on a picture?

WESTMORE: I don't think there is a difficult part anymore as far as appliances or beauty makeup or whatever. What is always difficult is the beginning of doing a special makeup—figuring out how you are going to do it, and doing the R and D to make sure that it works. And that's done before you go to the set. That's something I try to tell some of the new people. Don't go to the set and hope it will work. Because you'll find out that in your mind's eye it might work, but according to the laws of physics it isn't going to. I know people who have done this; they've taken things to the set and they haven't worked, and production companies have turned around and actually sued some of these people, saying, "You've just ruined my whole day; my whole crew and everything is wasted. This doesn't work. Why didn't you test this to make sure it worked?" Now, if you can look at them and say, "Yes, I tested it and it worked and I don't know why it doesn't work now"—that's another thing. That can happen too.

INTERVIEWER: Did it ever happen to you?

WESTMORE: It happened to me on *Psycho III.* I had a scene where I had to pump a lot of blood through a particular appliance. It worked wonderfully at home; no problems at all. It was a joint; one tube went into a Y tube to two separate appliances, so I could pump the blood all at the same time. But on the set, for some reason the blood would not flow through the double tube. I don't know why. To this day, I've never figured it out.

INTERVIEWER: What did you do?

WESTMORE: Well, all the tubes were open, but I couldn't get in there under the appliances to see what was happening. So I quickly pulled the Y off and set up two individual tubes. And it worked. But I wanted to run it all off of one tube so that they'd be simultaneous. By putting it on the single tubes and giving one line to somebody else while I worked the other one, I had to count a rhythm while we were doing it, so that we got a regular spurt . . . spurt . . . spurt.

INTERVIEWER: Is there any separation between the craft aspect of your work and the emotional or artistic part?

WESTMORE: No, it's all one for me; it all goes together. It all works and meshes together.

INTERVIEWER: Do you do any other creative things? Do you still paint?

WESTMORE: I used to like painting little miniature soldiers. I would carry my paint set and soldiers with me on locations. On *Rocky III* in Philadelphia, I'd stay in on Sundays. Sometimes it would be raining; I'd turn the ball games on, and I'd just sit and paint. It takes about fifteen hours to paint one. It's all done under a magnifying glass with a little, teeny brush to be able to paint the plaid on the soldiers' kilts and paint the little designs and stuff on the flags. But I've found that I have so much writing and things to do now that all I have time for is sending postcards and catching up on things.

INTERVIEWER: How long is this dynasty going to continue?

WESTMORE: I'm the third generation. There are a few in the fourth generation. I did an interview with channel 13 the day after I got the Oscar. The questions were more involved with the emotional aspects of winning the award as opposed to talking about the lab work and the craft. It made me think about what would have happened if I had gone ahead and become an art historian or gone into archaeology instead of going into makeup.

In this business, I have so many roots that go back so far. And there are the people that I have trained with. I can't really stand there and say, "This is mine. I did it all myself. Aren't I wonderful?" I'm not. I've studied and I've learned from so many students, from so many other professional makeup artists, from people like John Chambers. I'm really a product of all these different people. The only thing I regret is that I didn't thank John Chambers when I got the Oscar. That's the only name that I forgot. If I could go back and do it over again, that's the one thing I would change.

Sally Cruikshank

ANIMATION

*B*orn *and raised in Chatham, New Jersey, Sally Cruikshank graduated from Smith College in 1971. Her first film,* Ducky, *was completed at Smith. Film courses at the San Francisco Art Institute followed, then Cruikshank did much of her animation work of the last fifteen years in the Bay Area.*

Films like Fun on Mars, Quasi at the Quackadero, *and* Make Me Psychic *established her unique talent in the animation renaissance of the 1970s.*

Her extraordinary films manage to evoke a feeling reminiscent of the cartoons from the 1930s while capturing a variety of styles from art deco to sixties psychedelia to postmodern classicism. Cruikshank transforms these influences and treats us to a genuinely new cinematic experience.

It's a tribute to her that while she concocts modern films that have a startling freshness, absurdity, and poignancy, she remains a character animator in the great tradition of Messmer, Iwerks, and Warner Brothers. While many animators pursue realism, computer graphics, geometric abstraction, or sentimental fantasy, Cruikshank has kept the tradition of wacky character animation alive with her wobbly, funny animals.

Sally Cruikshank moved recently to Los Angeles because she has been involved with an increasing number of projects for feature films. She is married to producer Jon Davison, and they have a black chow named Felix.

Their San Fernando Valley home sits in a surprising amount of greenery. With its weathered natural wood and fireplace, the house looks out of place, as if they had brought it with them from the Berkeley hills. Her home has a comfortable, friendly, country feel about it, like Cruikshank herself. The rooms are an eclectic mix of antiques, modern art, hand-me-downs, and personal treasures.

Cruikshank has taken over one of the bedrooms and made it into her studio. Under one window, a layout table was buried under papers, storyboards, background paintings, books, and other debris. By the other window stood her drawing table, with an animation disk and light box. A full-length closet was jammed with boxes of old artwork, and a bookshelf teetered under a load of fresh paper, cels, and paints.

Cruikshank put Felix in the backyard, and we sat in the living room to talk about her work.

INTERVIEWER: *What are you working on now?*

CRUIKSHANK: Right now I'm working on a short called *Face Like a Frog.* It's taken two years so far. It's about five minutes long. I seem to get more elaborate in my production techniques. It's not the wisest thing. It continues to take me two years to make each film. They have just as many cels in them, but the running time gets shorter and shorter.

INTERVIEWER: *What's* Face Like a Frog *about?*

CRUIKSHANK: It's a very surrealistic, humorous film about some frogs in a strange house. There's a hex on the house which makes everything unpredictably weird. Somebody's led into the house to help get rid of the hex and gets into rather frightening situations. All the characters are frogs, but they don't really look like frogs. I think I just liked the title, and I'd been through an endless string of titles. I put away the old characters like Quasi for a while because for one thing, I wanted to experiment with the two-dimensional quality that I'd been getting in my paintings. I wanted characters with more of the design of the background paintings I had been doing. I also wanted to try something a little more surreal; I wanted the freedom of not having to carry those characters' personalities into it.

INTERVIEWER: Speaking of Quasi, how did you develop those characters? Where do your ideas come from?

CRUIKSHANK: That's one of the hardest things to pinpoint. I'd been drawing ducks for a while and wanted some characters that were more specific. I guess I picked up elements from people I'd known in the past, comic strip characters, and so on, but it's really hard to say where they come from. I think these things have more to do with the "gift" part of what I do. It comes to you—you don't really know how and you don't want to look into it too much. You just sit down with a blank paper. Who knows how it happens? It all just sort of starts. It's not as though I can say, "Well, I spin around twenty times, then I throw coins on the floor, and that tells me what's significant."

INTERVIEWER: Is Face Like a Frog *near completion?*

CRUIKSHANK: I actually will be able to celebrate finishing the inking by the end of today or tomorrow. Then I still have a thousand cels left to paint, which stretches out easily through the middle of the summer, even with people helping me. They're very elaborate and huge. The cels are the standard size, but there's something going on all over the cel on all of them. The image is huge in the cel.

INTERVIEWER: Is Face Like a Frog *your own production?*

CRUIKSHANK: Yes, it's my own production. Like other films I've made, there's no clear market. But it was either that or just sit and wait for an animated feature to get launched, which I got sick of doing.

INTERVIEWER: On your own productions, is there any part you don't do?

CRUIKSHANK: The music; I don't do the music. And I don't do any of the camera work.

INTERVIEWER: Do you write scripts for your short films? Do you storyboard everything?

CRUIKSHANK: I always storyboard first. I really write the short films through storyboards. Actually, on the features also, I write in storyboard form first and then write a script. If you just transferred everything that was in the storyboard to script form, it would seem awkward. And if you don't have it storyboarded first, you won't write visually enough for animation.

So I spend a long time working on the storyboards. Then, I usually start in and do the layouts scene by scene because you're sort of chomping at the bit to get going by the time you finish the storyboards. And then I just go straight through.

But if I have the luxury of recording the music or dialogue first, which I did in one section of this film, then of course the first thing I do is transfer all the music and dialogue onto mag film at a sound studio. Then I run it through a synchronizer and read it frame by frame, listen to it, hear the voice slowly speaking, and transcribe it so that it will all be in sync, hopefully, though it never seems to work out that way. Mouths open and close and nothing comes out!

"Things are in the air. Artists have antennae that pick up the same signals."

INTERVIEWER: *Do you transcribe the music and dialogue onto exposure sheets?*

CRUIKSHANK: I've started using bar sheets. They're simpler. And then I transfer those to exposure sheets.

INTERVIEWER: *When you start each scene, do you create layouts for each of them?*

CRUIKSHANK: Yes, but because I don't use an in-betweener, the layout isn't as critical. I'm doing it more straight ahead. I know what I'm trying to do for that scene, but it's much more up to me at the moment, how I'm going to do it. I'll just take that scene on and get started. Sometimes I'll animate straight through, and sometimes I'll carefully lay it out for in-betweens and then do all the in-betweens myself.

INTERVIEWER: *So you work both straight ahead and from key poses, depending on the scene?*

CRUIKSHANK: Not so much from key poses, because my work tends to be always moving, and key poses is a whole other system where they go from one thing to the next, to the next, to the next. I'm trying to get more fluidity. It's just a different way of doing timing, really.

INTERVIEWER: *Do you usually start inking and painting before you've finished animating, just to give yourself a change of pace?*

CRUIKSHANK: I did in the past. On *Quasi at the Quackadero*, as soon as I had animated anything, I painted it. But on this film, I finished all the animation before I started inking and painting. To avoid cleaning up my drawings, I did the inking myself. Also, at the time, I didn't know any other inkers down here that would work for the small amount I could pay them.

INTERVIEWER: What do you use for inking?

CRUIKSHANK: I use a Hunt 102 dip pen and Cel Vinyl ink, for the most part. But I finally mastered brush inking for the lines that are in color. I really felt that was an achievement! One day, all of a sudden, it just clicked in, after I had been trying to do it for years. I use both methods.

INTERVIEWER: Do you generally use black, or do you use colored inks?

CRUIKSHANK: I love the way colored lines look, especially the way I used them in the *Twilight Zone* movie and what I'm doing with them on this new film. The colored line is in great contrast to—a shock to—the color that's inside. In the song part of the film that I'm doing now, there's a lot of colored-line inking, but the rest of it's all black line. It really takes a long time to do in the colored-line inking, especially if it's more than one color. You're going through the cels, time after time after time.

INTERVIEWER: Have you ever used Xerox?

CRUIKSHANK: No, I hate Xerox! I just hate it! I can't stand the way it looks. Even when you use a marker, it looks crummy. Plus, it's awful on the people who have to clean the cels.

INTERVIEWER: How many cel levels do you usually work with?

CRUIKSHANK: Not very many. I like to be able to see it all when I flip it, to see what's going on. Again, that's because I'm doing it myself. I try to have just one level, but sometimes there'll be some amazingly complex scene where I have to use as many as five levels. That's the way I like to do it, with several characters on a single cel. But it isn't the most reasonable way to do it.

INTERVIEWER: When you produce your own feature or short films, how do you finance them?

CRUIKSHANK: I got an NEA [National Endowment for the Arts] grant to do *Quasi's Cabaret Trailer.* I produced a coming-attraction type of thing for a feature I wanted to do, as if the feature really existed. I got a grant to develop the whole project. I made this little film and thought that it would convince people to back the feature. I wrote a feature script and did a full storyboard and created a lot of extra backup materials, so that if I got a go-ahead, it would be all ready to go.

But aside from that, I haven't really gotten any kind of grants. This year I got a really unusual award from the American Film Institute. It's called the Maya Deren award. They flew me to New York and gave me a cocktail party, a prize, and $5000. But that wasn't a grant for a specific film. I've used the money for this film I'm working on now.

INTERVIEWER: *That's the fate of the independent filmmaker; you have to scrounge for money as best you can.*

CRUIKSHANK: It's really hard, yes, for independent animators, because you only get one shot at the AFI grants. They're the only major source of funding and only for one film. My animation doesn't support making another film. I've broken even on a couple, but that's it.

INTERVIEWER: *How do you usually earn money from one of your films? How is it distributed?*

CRUIKSHANK: Well, there are distributors. There was one distributor whose specialty was animated films. She went out of business. Then there's a company called Picture Start in Champaign, Illinois. It's just about the sole distributor of animated films right now. The market has changed so much! Around the mid-seventies, it looked as if all the doors were going to open up. Film libraries had great budgets and were really buying up independent films. Then Proposition 13 and those sorts of cutbacks came along, and libraries lost all their money and were lucky to just keep their doors open.

In addition, VCRs came along and really knocked 16-mm distribution for a loop. The libraries really couldn't spend the little money they had on films like *Fun On Mars* when everybody wanted to borrow a big Hollywood picture on Saturday night. A new form of distribution has yet to come along. It's in a kind of transition period where there's nothing that's filled the gap. So, for Picture Start in Illinois to still be in business is great. They're doing fairly well, I think, with cable sales.

INTERVIEWER: *The animation festivals that make the circuit every year are very popular. Someone could put those on cassette and market animation that way.*

CRUIKSHANK: I think they will. But they don't quite look normal enough to be something everybody's going to buy. It's too bad they can't be like 45-rpm records, where you get just one short. Videocassettes are so big and bulky. To see just one short film on one cassette is sort of a drag; you have to bend over and put it in, rewind, fast-forward, trying to find the one you want. There is something unpleasant about the process of using a VCR. It's not like loading a stack of records on a record player.

INTERVIEWER: *Do you think that perhaps independent films should be distributed on compact discs.*

CRUIKSHANK: Yes, I really do think something like that will make a difference. Because looking at a big bunch of short films can make you very tired. A short animated film is something to be seen before a feature, or you should watch just one or two. By the time you've sat through seventy minutes, it's pretty hard not to feel exhausted.

INTERVIEWER: *Everybody I know, inside and outside the film business, loves to see a cartoon before a feature in the theater. Their disappearance is a tragic mystery to me.*

CRUIKSHANK: I know, it's strange. A lot of things contributed to it. The owners of the theaters wanted to get an extra show in, and the cartoon adds to the running time. People didn't pay more to see the cartoon, yet the theater owner had to pay more to rent it.

> *"It's artistically liberating working with the music as an impetus to the animation."*

Again, in the late seventies, I was really encouraged. When I made *Quasi at the Quackadero* and *Make Me Psychic,* I thought that the market was going to open wide for theatrical shorts because I was getting such a good response. But the way theaters are run now has changed so much; sometimes there's no one in the projection booth. It also depends on knowing individual theater owners who are film enthusiasts. In California, there are a lot of them who will run a short. But in most parts of the country, where it's just a business, I think you have a pretty hard time.

INTERVIEWER: *Well, what are your plans for* Face Like a Frog *when you get it done?*

CRUIKSHANK: I'm hoping to get it distributed theatrically here. I'm talking to somebody about doing that. A distribution company's quite interested in it, in maybe sending it out with a feature, tied into the negative, but that's not definite. My films have been bought recently by cable TV, a lot more than in the past. And I will have one more film for a videocassette. I've held off putting my films into a videocassette package, waiting to complete this one, because then the cassette would be that much longer.

INTERVIEWER: *You've also been doing some work on feature films, too, haven't you?*

CRUIKSHANK: Yes, I'm just finishing up the animated film titles for the movie *Ruthless People*. It's opening in about two weeks, so it had better be all done! It's a Disney film, and this has been a big break for me. I designed and directed the sequence and used another studio, Playhouse Pictures, to do the actual animation and see the production through. I'm really pleased with the way it came out.

INTERVIEWER: *Are there any of your familiar characters in the movie?*

CRUIKSHANK: No. There's a lot of Memphis-style design in the movie— furniture and things—so I used that as a starting point. Memphis design actually looks a lot like my style, so I really didn't have to adapt it too much. I came up with this idea to treat each person's credit ruthlessly. It's a series of gags running through the titles where each person's name and credit are treated ruthlessly and then the next one comes on, and so on. It's pretty funny. And it looks good. Nobody's done animated titles in a long time.

INTERVIEWER: *You also mentioned the* Twilight Zone *movie.*

CRUIKSHANK: That was in 1983, for Joe Dante's episode. I really enjoyed working on that, as I have on *Ruthless People,* because it was one of the few times where I wasn't responsible for doing everything, like inking and painting all the cels. That was a break.

In both cases, I had some great people to work with. In *Twilight Zone,* one of the top animators working today, Mark Kausler, did most of the animation. And there was an excellent ink and paint woman. That was some of my favorite work. The actual artwork was so vivid and intense looking. The colors were just so hot. But you can't tell when you see the movie because the film's been transferred to videotape and then rephotographed. The color was minimized a little by that. I was just looking at it because I wrapped up a bunch of cels to sell to someone. I had it out and I was kind of amazed by how intense the cels were.

INTERVIEWER: *What did you have to do to get the animation to fit in well with the rest of the film?*

CRUIKSHANK: That was a fairly tricky proposition, because we were putting a live-action character into a cartoon hell on a television. When you see live action and animation combined, it tends to be an animated character in a live-action world. But the live-action person in a cartoon world is less often done, though Walt Disney did a series, *Alice In Cartoonland,* I think it was called, in the twenties, where this little girl was in a barnyard world.

Storyboard panels from Sally Cruikshank's proposed animated feature, Love That Makes You Crawl.

It's fairly complicated, and an immense amount of planning was required in figuring out the process. First, I did a lot of conceptual drawings, and we talked about what we wanted to do. Then we shot a pencil test of the animation. This pencil test was run on a video monitor while the live action was being filmed. When the girl was running away from a monster, for example, she was filmed on a treadmill. And we positioned her in the frame, so that she fit right where we wanted her to fit in the animation, by looking at the video monitor where the pencil test was being superimposed over the live action. It was almost impossible to see, because the pencil test is just these fuzzy little pencil lines with everything transparent. You see everything in front of and behind everything else.

INTERVIEWER: *Did that system work?*

CRUIKSHANK: Yes, that part worked very well. Of course, we had to reanimate sections to fit the girl. Then it all had to be rotoscoped, and the mattes were all done at the optical house. The optical house did a very good job of combining them.

INTERVIEWER: *While you were doing the animation, you conceptually had to keep this live-action character in mind?*

CRUIKSHANK: When I did the storyboards I always drew her in. And when we were doing the pencil test, we just assumed that this was where she would be and that she'd be about this size. We sort of guessed that was how she would fit. It was a really tricky job, about the most technical thing I've ever had to do.

INTERVIEWER: *Did you work most closely with the director?*

CRUIKSHANK: I worked with Joe Dante right from the beginning. Joe's really a great cartoon fan. He is very knowledgeable about old cartoons, and his point of view is that of a very obsessive cartoon lover, I think, which I can identify with.

INTERVIEWER: *You usually work alone. What was it like working with so many other people?*

CRUIKSHANK: I did have to adjust a bit because I hadn't worked in Los Angeles before. I was used to doing everybody's job. I had to pull back. Coming from Northern California, where sometimes I'd train my friends to help with production, I found it to be very different. People are so professional down here. I had to learn that you could, in fact, trust people to take on the other jobs! It was great. I loved having other people do the work! Having painted so many cels, I especially appreciated the color end of the production. The woman who did the inking had worked, I believe, at Warner Brothers, starting in the thirties. She inked beautiful lines! Just did a really nice job.

INTERVIEWER: *Did you do another feature after that?*

CRUIKSHANK: I directed the Pac Man sequence in the movie *Top Secret.* It was done non-electronically, but it had to look and move just like a Pac Man game. It was done with gels, backlighting, and many camera passes. That was really tricky. I'm actually better off in productions that involve mainly the pencil, the paper, ink and paint, and the animation camera.

INTERVIEWER: *During your career, have you tried to find work in commercial animation in order to finance your own productions?*

CRUIKSHANK: Well, I had a great job at Snazelle Films in San Francisco. It was really unheard of. I was paid mainly to do my own work, and to do commercials when we got them. They were nice enough to keep me working even through long periods where there would be only a little animation work needed on a commercial—about once every eight months. It's so uncertain, with animation, when advertisers will decide that it is the thing that sells or, instead, that it's anathema.

So during those slow periods, I got to work on my own films. And the money I made from the TV commercials I could also use for my films. Also, I had the use of the facilities. That was an immense help. It's only now beginning to dawn on me what a big help it was, now that I'm trying to do it all myself here in one little room. It was like a fairy godfather sort of scene, you know. I was spoiled. It was really an extraordinary situation.

INTERVIEWER: *Did they have a video pencil test setup?*

CRUIKSHANK: No, I've never used one of those. I think it would be very helpful. When you're going along, you think you know how it's moving. But if you don't have a video pencil test system, you usually are saving up a big load of drawings before you get them shot. So, by the time it comes back, you forget what it was that you were thinking of at the time you were doing it.

INTERVIEWER: *Were you able to work at Snazelle for very long?*

CRUIKSHANK: I was there almost ten years. And I didn't do that many TV commercials at all. My reel is very small, and yet they let me stay on. It's because of Greg Snazelle. He really liked my work from the first time he saw it, and he wanted to encourage me. You don't find that many people willing to help an artist develop.

Since I've moved to Los Angeles, I haven't sought out commercial work. I don't like doing commercials. The restrictions that they put upon them can be pretty deflating. And I don't have commercial art skills the way some people do. To be a good commercial artist, you have to be able to adapt your style to another style and do it wholeheartedly. Some people are that flexible and that talented, but my work tends to look like my work, so an advertiser would really have to be coming to me for my style.

When I first started at Snazelle, I got to do a great commercial, where I designed it all, and it was all animation and real crazy looking. Then—it happened right after *Star Wars*—everything had to have a twinkle on it! All I did was put these miserable twinkles on everything. And it wasn't the fault of the studio. That was what advertisers wanted. It was all very serious and smooth. It was all hand-drawn animation made to look like computer graphics. I mean, that isn't one of the things I do best.

> *"The freedom of animation is astonishing, but the physical process itself is like a truck sitting on your shoulders!"*

INTERVIEWER: *Computer graphics are good enough now, and computers are so widespread, that perhaps they will leave that kind of thing entirely to the computers and free traditional character animators to do what they do best.*

CRUIKSHANK: Yes, I'm hoping that'll come along. "New-wave" graphics degenerated into a sort of new-wave kitsch and into the greeting card world. But it's also helped make the hand-drawn look more acceptable, which I really appreciate. You're beginning to see more hand-drawn things on music videos. People look at those and think, Oh, that's hip, I like that. It helps when people's eyes are educated in those directions and people are encouraged to think that there are other things they can like, things that don't look corporate, TV clean, or machine-perfect.

INTERVIEWER: *In animated film, I've always liked the spontaneous, freely drawn styles. As if they had photographed the animator's original drawings.*

CRUIKSHANK: It's very dynamic.

INTERVIEWER: *I saw a television ad for* Hill Street Blues *recently that was all hand-drawn, rotoscoped, very loose, done in colored pencils, very beautiful.*

CRUIKSHANK: Well, that's great. Ten years ago there wouldn't have been a chance in the world of getting something like that put across. There is a really nice music video for the band A-ha. It is of a girl who falls in love with a cartoon character. It's rotoscoped, it's realistic animation, but still, there's this great interaction of the human and the cartoon character reaching out of the page. I only saw it once. It was very impressive.

INTERVIEWER: *Tell me what you like best about your work.*

CRUIKSHANK: There are two things: the actual animation process and the coloring. I love choosing the colors and seeing the cels when somebody else paints them, when they look really good. And I love animating to music. That's my favorite thing as far as the animation process goes. When I was doing the song for *Face Like a Frog* earlier this year, I would get so excited while I was doing it, I could hardly stand it! I really loved it. You get this intimacy with the characters. You feel like the music opens up possibilities and that the things are coming together in such odd ways. It's artistically liberating working with the music as an impetus to the animation. And when they really work together, there's something so magical to it. The freedom of animation is astonishing, but the physical process itself is like a truck sitting on your shoulders! It takes too long; it's too hard.

INTERVIEWER: *Animation seems like a medieval craft, one of the last vestiges of feudalism, like being a cobbler or carving books on stone tablets. It's so incredibly painstaking.*

CRUIKSHANK: It really is. You just can't believe it! Fortunately, every time you start a film you think, Well, it seems so awful, but I must have been goofing off; it couldn't have been that bad. And then you get in the middle of it and you see the cels stretching out all around you. It's incredible that anybody ever thought that animation was a possibility. It's really the pits.

Computers may ultimately help everybody out, but I'm waiting to see. They are starting to color with computers, but Hanna–Barbera spent all this money to buy a computer to do that, and ultimately they were so discouraged that they sent the work to Korea to be done by hand.

INTERVIEWER: *Have you ever worked with a computer drawing system?*

CRUIKSHANK: I was allowed to try one out or, rather, to see how it worked. And at the time I saw it, it wasn't something I wanted to do. You had to draw a map of each drawing, so that each time you drew it, you drew the drawing the same way as the previous one. Which is inhibiting. I don't want to feel so conscious of the drawing process. And then you couldn't have lines cross in front of lines, and it all looks so smooth that it looks weird anyway. I don't work with in-betweens the way most people do, so it didn't seem very promising to me. And those systems are so expensive it's unbelievable.

I thought, Let other people get involved with it. There are so many other people who know so much about it already, who have the talent and will forge new ground. The people who love it describe computer animation as being a lot more sophisticated, as having a lot more capabilities than it really has. There's a lot of hype. It's often not what people imagine. It's great for those logos with all the twinkles.

INTERVIEWER: *It's also good for changing perspective of geometric forms. Trying to animate stuff like that can be a nightmare.*

CRUIKSHANK: I know; I can remember having to do that! I had to find one of those security devices you look through to see who's at the front door— you know, it distorts everything. I had to hold that up and look at a Styrofoam tube, draw it, turn it, and draw it again so it would look like a computer had turned it.

INTERVIEWER: *Why did you get interested in animation and not other forms of art?*

CRUIKSHANK: I majored in drawing in college. I didn't do very much painting. I took sculpture classes, but mainly because I had a great teacher, not because sculpture was the medium I felt I was meant for. I think I chose animation because it was partly a way to proceed with drawing and to make drawings that do more than sit on a wall. Growing up, I always thought I was going to be a writer.

INTERVIEWER: *Has animation taken over your life; are most of your friends animators?*

CRUIKSHANK: No, not at all. But I'm sort of a solitary person, so that's probably why. I was appalled at how few animators I knew when I had to put this job together. It's a solitary existence, doing your own films. And on my own films, I usually don't hire other people. That was one of the things that was so exciting about *Ruthless People*—there must have been four or five animators. I'd never seen all these different people take on a design of mine. They did such a good job, and often funny things I hadn't thought of came up. It was kind of exhilarating to see that.

INTERVIEWER: *What kind of work day do you usually have? Do you set hours for yourself?*

CRUIKSHANK: I spent ten years at Snazelle, where I had to be there at 8:30 and leave at 5:30, so that's pretty much a built-in routine. I think having a steady job in your twenties sort of locks in the kind of hours you keep. And although I don't get as much done working at home, I don't have the problems that some people do when they work at home. There's just so much work I have to get done, I don't have a reluctance to go in and get started. I don't work at night. I try to avoid going out for lunch in Los Angeles because you go to lunch and then it's 3:30 and it's time to make dinner. I don't think I get as much done as I did at Snazelle, because there, I couldn't leave. I only got an hour for lunch there.

"Computer animation... is great for those logos with all the twinkles."

INTERVIEWER: *Do you set deadlines for yourself?*

CRUIKSHANK: Well, I try to, but the work has been so much bigger on this project than I expected that I keep going beyond them. I don't have a problem with time and deadlines, although it's taken me a long time to finish the film. I'm a hard worker, and I can get pretty obsessive when I'm working.

INTERVIEWER: *Whose work do you like to look at?*

CRUIKSHANK: Well, I love cartoons of the twenties and thirties. That's my favorite period. At the moment, the studio from that period that I enjoy the most is Van Beuren Studios, which was in New York. Their things are very peculiar and kind of creepy. Funny, hand-drawn looking, but always with a sort of sweet sensibility. There's just something about them that I like. They'll often do weird dance steps, and it just delights me.

There are a lot of animators whose work I like, but many of them aren't doing independent films any more because of the marketplace. It's the 1980s! I've heard that George Griffin has a new film, but I haven't seen it. I like his work a lot. Cathy Rose got out of animation; I liked her work a lot. She's doing some kind of performance pieces now, but I haven't seen any of them. Susan Pitt has gotten out of animation; she's a painter and set designer. And there are other people who have come along, but I haven't seen their work as much.

I used to see more in Berkeley because I could walk over to the Pacific Film Archive. And for some odd reason, where we live now we don't get cable TV, so I don't see shorts on Showtime or Home Box Office. Somebody whose work I love, who's working now, is Isabel Jankel. She's working in England, doing music videos for Cucumber Studios. Her work is really great. In fact, the best new animation I've been seeing is coming out of England.

INTERVIEWER: *How would you judge the quality of animated features being produced today?*

CRUIKSHANK: Many of the animated features that are produced now are so bad. It sure doesn't help the other people who are trying to get animated features made. You read reviews in the paper that are so devastating. And unlike some film reviews that you'll read and think, How could it be that bad?, you read a bad animation review and you can just see it in your mind. You can see the characters standing there with nothing moving.

INTERVIEWER: *It just reinforces the view of most producers, which is that animation doesn't make money.*

CRUIKSHANK: Well, yes, because these movies are so rotten, who's going to go see them?

INTERVIEWER: *What do you think has been wrong with animated features in the past?*

CRUIKSHANK: Well, they're written very badly, for one thing. The writing's terrible. The animation's terrible. And they're unappealing. So that's a real winning combination. They're boring. The work speaks for itself. I don't know why they're so awful, why somebody didn't see that early on and say, "This is awful; why are we doing this?" Maybe they make the decisions in a hurry and then nobody bothers to think about it.

INTERVIEWER: *Many people think animation is mainly for kids.*

CRUIKSHANK: That's one of the problems in getting it produced, because that's how it's perceived. I've done a lot of traveling around the country, giving talks, as have so many animators. The crowds come and fill the auditoriums! And they're adults; they aren't children. The enthusiasm is so intense, it's almost depressing. All this enthusiasm and yet those people can't go see the animation they'd like to. The enthusiasm doesn't carry through to the people who can implement production. But of course animation is for adults. It's a medium that has so many possibilities. One problem has been that the films for adults have tended to be films that people might classify as art films. So there's been a distinction between art films and films for children.

Unfortunately, for a lot of animators—the ones who just like to animate and who do that very well—the only work possibilities are in the big factories,

Finished painted cels from Sally Cruikshank's animated short, **Make Me Psychic.**

like Hanna–Barbera. Somebody was just saying to me the other day that she was going to break down and work for one of the big factories because there wasn't any other work. What's bad about it is, they train everybody to make things move the same crummy way. And it's so hard to maintain your own vision while you're doing this. I can remember when I went to high school in the south, I was being taught French with a southern accent. At first I knew it was wrong, and I tried not to pick it up. But eventually, I spoke French with the same crummy southern accent as everyone else.

> ## "It's a solitary existence, doing your own films."

INTERVIEWER: *Have you seen any Japanese animation?*

CRUIKSHANK: Yes. I recently saw a program of it in St. Louis when I was there showing my films. I saw some terrific films. They weren't showing the mainstream Japanese animation, which I think is also interesting. I liked *Phoenix 2072*, or whatever it was that Osamo Tezuka did. I think that is really interesting.

INTERVIEWER: *He also did a film in the old twenties style, with cowboy characters. It played with the concept of the characters having a life of their own on the film itself. The film frame would go up and down in the projector gate and they would climb up from one frame to the next.*

CRUIKSHANK: *Broken Down Film*, I think it is called. That's really good. He has another film called *The Jumping Film*, and it's also terrific in a whole different way. He grew up on Betty Boop cartoons; he's a big Betty Boop enthusiast. I met him one time. I would assume he's about sixty now. Tezuka is sort of the father of animation over there. He's the Walt Disney of Japan. He's done commercial animation; he's been really successful. He's done features like *Astro Boy* that were so much in the mainstream. And now, what's so unusual is that he's doing his own personal films later in life, and he has such an original approach. That doesn't usually happen when you've spent all that time in the mainstream. It would be like Hanna and Barbera suddenly doing personal films.

INTERVIEWER: *Do you have any ideas for your next projects?*

CRUIKSHANK: I don't expect to start another short as soon as I finish this one, I'll tell you that! I have two producers who have been working hard to find backing for a feature called *Love That Makes You Crawl*. It's a combination of live action and animation. And it looks as if it's likely to happen, but that could go on for a long time. There was a flurry of activity last week that seemed very promising. I'm toying with the idea of writing another animated feature. It's obvious that the right animated feature could make a ton of money for somebody. The features I have written have been a little too adult-oriented. So I'm considering writing something that would be more suitable for children, not little children, but something that would cover a wider range. I am longing to do some writing, after having spent two years on this short.

INTERVIEWER: *You'd like to write and direct an animated feature?*

CRUIKSHANK: Yes. I've also written a live-action feature that there's been some interest in.

INTERVIEWER: *What's that about?*

CRUIKSHANK: It's a contemporary ghost story. And I have an idea for another live-action feature. It has a little animation in it, and I would like to start writing that when I finish this. You always think when you're doing animation, I can work on the writing in my head while I'm doing this. But even though the work is so tedious, you really can't think about anything but what you're doing. It's amazing how your mind works. Like when you're coloring something in, you're not thinking about a whole lot other than, Here I go around the corner, along this line, putting the color down.

INTERVIEWER: *What's your feature,* Love That Makes You Crawl, *about?*

CRUIKSHANK: It features my characters Quasi, Anita, and Snozzy. It's actually a love story between Anita, who's the world's meanest stewardess, and Snozzy, who's a secret agent who can't keep a secret. He's on the trail of some stolen robots, and she's just flunked out of stewardess school. She's also hooked on a live-action soap opera called *Love That Makes You Crawl.* I think I'll stop there. It's really unusual, and that's why I'm having trouble getting it made. Some people have found it to be kind of subversive.

INTERVIEWER: *Well, great, sounds like just what we need.*

CRUIKSHANK: It's also all storyboarded. Joe Dante wants to direct the live-action part of it. He loved the script. Lots of people are very enthusiastic about it, but we have yet to find the right money person. People that have the money are scared of it because it's so different.

INTERVIEWER: *There's no shortage of great ideas and talented people, but the greatest challenge in filmmaking seems to be getting them all together at the same time in the same place and making a film actually happen.*

CRUIKSHANK: And often, what actually makes it happen is so unrelated to the material. It's just whether the person with all the money likes to have lunch with the person with the material.

INTERVIEWER: *Are you optimistic about the future of animation?*

CRUIKSHANK: I am optimistic. But I don't know if it will happen soon enough. I think that new forms are coming along that people just can't imagine. I think that the appearance of so many animators in the early seventies may be one of those things that people will look back on as a phenomenon that signaled something new emerging. Things are in the air. Artists have antennae that pick up the same signals. They often don't know why, but smaller rumblings anticipate bigger things to come.

Jimmy Picker

ANIMATION

*B*orn *in Queens thirty-five years ago, Jimmy Picker graduated from the New York University film school in 1972. He then spent two years in Munich, where he discovered the charms of clay animation and learned the craft.*

In 1975, Picker set up his current studio and produced clay animation segments for the Children's Television Workshop programs Sesame Street *and* The Electric Company, *as well as for television commercials, public service spots, and other projects.*

His short film, Jimmy the C, *featuring a clay animation caricature of Jimmy Carter singing "Georgia on My Mind," earned him an Academy Award nomination in 1978. Picker won the Oscar in 1985 for his four-minute masterpiece,* Sundae in New York, *about the urban adventures of Mayor Koch as he's giving a rendition of "New York, New York."*

At the time of the interview, he was bringing to completion My Friend Liberty, *featuring both live action and clay animation, for its on-air debut in conjunction with the celebration of the Statue of Liberty restoration on July 4, 1986.*

It was a beautiful spring morning in Manhattan. The sky was actually blue. I hit the subway, the D train to Brooklyn, and half an hour later I emerged into a devastated, graffiti-encrusted urban landscape. Threading my way through the litter of broken bottles and crumbling concrete, I found Jimmy Picker's combination studio/residence not far from the subway station in a large, old apartment building.

Picker occupied every room of what had to be a six-bedroom apartment. The rooms were all crammed with filmmaking activity. Large tables full of clay figures dominated one room, another room was for editing, two rooms were stuffed with materials and sets under construction, the camera room was all painted flat black, and then there was the kitchen, in which Picker's full-time cook prepared the crew's meals. It wasn't quite clear how many people actually lived there, but there must have been bedrooms somewhere.

Picker has always had a soft spot in his heart for New York City. Asked why he located his MotionPicker Studios in Brooklyn, he replied, "I love the death-defying run from the subway to my apartment."

INTERVIEWER: *How did you get into this business?*

PICKER: I was at NYU film school for two years. I transferred there from another college. And I had always liked animation. I had fooled around with it and gotten some jobs doing animation. It was terrible; at that point I really didn't know what I was doing. There was no animation department at NYU, so I just asked questions and fumbled along, experimented.

INTERVIEWER: *Was that cel animation?*

PICKER: A little cel, a little cutout, a little puppet, a little fingerpaint. I just fooled around. I wanted to see what was going on.

And then I got a break. I got a job with an American firm that had gotten a big contract in Munich, Germany, doing children's stuff. I had met one of the producers in New York. Luckily for me, when I went to see him, his projector didn't work, so I showed him some storyboards. That proved to him I could handle a colored pencil.

This company did all clay animation, and I had just seen a black-and-white clay animation movie that I think was made a long time ago, where one thing eats another. I said, "Oh, that's cute, but how can you animate clay? It's so mushy."

So I went over to Munich and I was really impressed with what I saw. I liked the presence and the look of clay on the screen. I spent two years there.

INTERVIEWER: *Is that where you learned to animate clay?*

PICKER: Yes. At that time, I didn't know how to sculpt or anything. They would put a character in front of me and I would copy it; that's how I learned to sculpt. They copied all the characters by eye.

There was only one animator there, and he was Polish. I would watch him and then go do it. We would laugh at each other because neither of us could understand the other. It was basically an "earn while you learn" situation. I knocked out a lot of stuff and got a lot of experience.

After that, I came back here, looked for a spot, and found this part of town in '75. I've been here since then.

INTERVIEWER: *How did you first get your own studio rolling?*

PICKER: When I got here it took me about a year to get a job. I did some work for the Children's Television Workshop—a little character called Clayton for their *Electric Company* show. And I did some public service spots here and there. I didn't have a heavy-duty commercial rep, so I didn't do many commercials. That's not really the direction I wanted to take.

"Unless you have twenty short films out there that are pretty hot numbers, you're really not going to get any money that'll pay the rent."

INTERVIEWER: *What things did you want to do?*

PICKER: I did *Jimmy the C* in '77. It was a caricature of Jimmy Carter singing "Georgia on My Mind." Have you seen that? It was around a lot in '78 in theaters and such. And then I did *Sundae in New York* in '83 or whenever. I did both of those films to do something I'd like and to get my name around.

INTERVIEWER: *How do you finance your own films?*

PICKER: They were all basically made with my own money. I went broke making them. I did it because I saw there was no work coming in and, well, I had a good idea and plenty of time. It took me four years before I felt there was another idea worth doing in clay after I did *Jimmy the C*. With the Ed Koch thing, I went into debt because I knew I had a good idea, but it took a long time.

Any person in this business should get the best thing on their reel that they can. So I took a gamble, and it's paid off; I can't complain. Those short films have gotten me the work I'm doing now, *My Friend Liberty*.

INTERVIEWER: Will you make some of your money back with these films?

PICKER: Uh...theoretically. There's no market for short films. Unless you have twenty short films out there that are pretty hot numbers, you're really not going to get any money that'll pay the rent. With *My Friend Liberty*, the value is the equity in the whole show. It's nice to actually be making a film there's a market for.

INTERVIEWER: How do you get your films distributed?

PICKER: I think *Sundae in New York* should be playing in at least one New York theater all the time, but you have to beg the theater owners to take it. They give you all sorts of excuses, their first line being, "I love short films, I'm a champion of short films, but at our theater, no! We can't fit it in the schedule." When it's new you can, but when it's been around they don't want it. It depends. It's a gratis type thing. If I wanted to be more aggressive and run around to all the theaters and make my own bookings, I could get my work shown more, but I want to make films, not be a distributor.

You can rent *Sundae in New York* on a videocassette; it's out in two cassette packages. It's in one with a couple of other Academy Award-winning shorts and one with short animated films. And it's going to be out in a package with *My Friend Liberty*. They hope to have a cassette in the marketplace the day it's released. A little aggressive, but that's nice.

INTERVIEWER: Tell me something about My Friend Liberty.

PICKER: It's a half-hour special. This particular job is a foot in the door, hopefully—knock on wood. Because, as I said, it's producing for a real market, not doing commercials. If I were doing lots of commercials, I might be a millionaire, if I could get the accounts. But even though commercials pay so much more, I'd rather tell a story.

INTERVIEWER: Who's paying for it?

PICKER: This is LBS Communications. They are the biggest barter syndicator in the country, I think. And they are very aggressive. They have a lot of shows; they produce *Fame*, for instance. They take a lot of these shows that were on the networks and they redistribute them. They're pioneers in knowing how to make money. We're real happy with them.

INTERVIEWER: *When are they going to release it?*

PICKER: Supposedly it's been sold out because it's the first time CBS-owned and operated stations have bought something of LBS's, which is supposed to give this show some clout. So we are thrilled because, hopefully, this will ensure that the film will be shown next year and the year after as a Fourth-of-July special. That way, the equity would pay off. It would be kind of nice. And we have a Christmas special that we're proposing to them now.

INTERVIEWER: *What do you mean by equity?*

PICKER: We own a piece of the show, a percentage of the profits. After the distributor takes off all his costs—God knows what they are—and distribution fee, then whatever's left over we split according to the percentage. Basically, the bottom line is whatever they decide to pay us, that's in addition to the residuals from future airings and the budget we got to do the show in the first place.

INTERVIEWER: *How does syndication work?*

PICKER: I'm not sure I understand it, but essentially they give the show

Jimmy Picker sets up a scene for his clay animation short film, My Friend Liberty.

to the stations for nothing or a very small fee and the people who syndicate the show retain about half of the advertising time. When they know they've sold the show to more than seventy percent of the country, they can then go to Coke or Pepsi or whatever—big national brands—and sell their share of the commercials.

INTERVIEWER: *When's the deadline for* My Friend Liberty?

PICKER: The film has to be in the can May 29. We hand it in June 13, so we are in a big postproduction scramble. It's really hot and heavy now. We started shooting around the middle of February. We're shooting something like twelve original minutes, or a little more. It's a rush job.

> *"This kind of animation is spontaneous; you're doing it in front of the camera, everything's there."*

I have turned down other jobs in the past because the money is either too ridiculously low or they ask, "Can you do it in two weeks?" Commercials are like that.

But *My Friend Liberty* was a great opportunity. I couldn't afford to say no. I looked at the calendar and said, "We can just about squeeze it out if I don't drop dead."

INTERVIEWER: *Your characters have a distinctive style. Where does that come from?*

PICKER: From our heads or from discussion. Yeah, I like the whole cartoony look. I don't like anything that's realistic. I think you can kind of tell my look.

A guy like Will Vinton,* his stuff is very real. He says, "We can duplicate the real in clay," and I say, "Fine, go duplicate the real." That doesn't turn me on—to me they look like corpses.

I always get letters from Vinton's company [Will Vinton Productions], saying, "We heard that you were interviewed and someone used the word 'claymation' and we have that word copyrighted." So, I have to warn you: You have to say in your book that I do clay animation. I was going to write them a letter back, saying, "You have my permission to say that Jimmy Picker does not do claymation, he does clay animation," but why waste my breath? It's all just hype.

INTERVIEWER: *Where do your story ideas come from?*

PICKER: As far as coming up with ideas and scripts, the Koch idea as

---

* Pioneering clay animator and Oscar winner.

well as the Carter idea just came from sitting around and reflecting.

I'm really a ham. I love musical comedy, and that's what I'd like to keep doing, rather than getting channeled into doing either commercials or children's films. I'd rather knock people over the head with some funny stuff and so, why not?

INTERVIEWER: Do you think that clay animation is only suitable for humorous films?

PICKER: Oh no. You can do something really sad. It's just a matter of getting the money to do it! But I particularly like funny things. Not that I wouldn't do a film that had some things to make people laugh and cry.

INTERVIEWER: Do you write your own scripts?

PICKER: I have two cowriters that I did *My Friend Liberty* with. It's nice finding a collaborator you can work with as a writer, because I'm somewhat of an idea or gag man, probably like most animators.

INTERVIEWER: Does having cowriters allow you to spend more time animating, rather than having to work on the script?

PICKER: Not really. I still have to slave over the scripts. I consider myself a fledgling writer. I have the ideas, and because I have somebody I can sit down with who I feel is a decent comedy writer, we were able to come up with a nice idea for *My Friend Liberty*. We have a lot of other projects we would like to get out.

INTERVIEWER: Have you ever developed stories from other people?

PICKER: No. But I would tell someone else's story if they came to me with a story that I felt was right up my alley. I'm picky.

INTERVIEWER: Do you storyboard everything generally?

PICKER: Sure. I did some crude boards for this project. We didn't have time to do them right; it was just do it, fabricate it, and shoot it. But it would be nice to have the luxury of a storyboard artist to do them.

INTERVIEWER: So everyone does a little bit of everything here.

PICKER: I do all the shooting. I have another person who makes designs and made a lot of the characters for *My Friend Liberty*. Two fellows here are building all the sets and props. I've had various sculptors in, but we've had fewer sculptors toward the end of the project to save some money for postproduction.

INTERVIEWER: In cel animation you can either work straight ahead or from key positions. Do you have that choice in clay animation?

PICKER: No, straight ahead's the only way you can do it. It's basically like live action. When you're setting up the set with the character, or a couple of characters, you simply have to choreograph it beforehand and see how it looks. It's a lot easier without a lot of characters to walk around. You have the same problems as in live action. I don't have the luxury of having key positions to look at.

I like to shoot things in chronological order, at least with the short films. That way you can see how it's building.

> *"I'd like to do unique things in clay, like operas or operettas."*

But a lot of the stuff ends up being ad-libbed. Sometimes some of the best shots in the film are ad-libbed, just from the emotion. This kind of animation is spontaneous; you're doing it in front of the camera—everything's there. So if I have a better idea, which I do a lot of the time, I often just go with it. It's just like live action: Anyone's ideas change as soon as they are on the set. That's kind of neat.

But you have to have the luxury of enough time to do it. When I was working on my own films like *Jimmy the C* it wasn't so bad, but now I have to work faster and faster. I eventually hope to train another animator.

INTERVIEWER: *Do you use exposure sheets?*

PICKER: Yeah, my own brand of exposure sheets. We'll break down the sound track—using the frame numbers—to tell where the sound begins and ends. Then I write my notes in right before the shot. That's my road map. I ad-lib everything else.

INTERVIEWER: *How long does it take to set up the characters for each frame of film you shoot?*

PICKER: Oh, it depends. It depends on whether it's lip sync, on how many characters there are, what kind of characters, and what problems there are. Usually, the average shot is a three-hour shot or so. It's hard to tell.

INTERVIEWER: *As far as the clay itself, it's all Plasticine?*

PICKER: Yeah, all oil-based clay.

INTERVIEWER: *How much does it melt under the lights?*

PICKER: It'll get soft. I have an air conditioner going in the room at all times, plus a fan hooked up to a tube that's a couple of feet away from the characters. That's one of the big secrets; that's probably the secret right there. You need the cool air, and you can stick a toothpick up the character's back or something so it'll sit straight. But I don't use any armatures inside them because I find that they work their way out. So I try to work fast. And keep the characters cool.

INTERVIEWER: *What control do you have over the colors?*

PICKER: We have clay that comes in eighteen colors. This is English clay, and you can mix the clays together.

I also like to use a material called Sculpy, which is a clay you can buy in the art store and bake right in your own oven. It's good for props and things that don't animate. We bake them and paint them with acrylic paints. So you might make your wigs and your shoes and your bow ties like this. If the wig is hard, it's something for the animator to grab on to and it won't mess the hair. You can carve it and paint it. So between Sculpy, the clay, cardboard, and wood, that's about it, as far as materials go.

INTERVIEWER: *Do you shoot in 35 mm?*

PICKER: Yes.

INTERVIEWER: *What kind of camera system do you have?*

PICKER: Just the Mitchell that I had converted to a reflex system. It's just like a big Bolex now; it's great.

INTERVIEWER: *What provision do you have for dollying and panning and so forth?*

PICKER: Well, the particular dolly I have, probably one of the only ones in the world like it, is actually made for stop motion. Using it is almost as easy

Courtesy MOTIONPICKER/Jimmy Picker

A scene from Jimmy Picker's Academy Award-winning film, Sundae in New York.

223

as taking still photos. It's all geared and it's all numbered, so I do it all manually. It's easy once you get used to it; I just animate the camera and animate the characters at the same time.

INTERVIEWER: *How do you handle fairing the camera moves?*

PICKER: You've got to make guides. First you walk it [the camera-move distance] off. There is a pointer on the dolly and I'm able to lay down whatever kind of scale I want. I set my frame counter; I have a remote counter, which is nice to have. Then I'll number the scale, so the numbers will correspond to the numbers on my exposure sheets. That way, I always know where I am. I always know if I shot frame number five, and so forth. And, it's the same thing if I want to go up and down: I've got this scale that I can apply. Then if I want to I can go around, panning or tilting; it's great.

It's just a matter of getting used to the equipment. This is from Germany. I worked with equipment like this over there. The great thing about it is that it's real simple. It's easy enough for one man to take down and move if I wanted to shoot a setup in another room.

I've seen other things that are much more complex and much heavier. A man named Nelson Hordell—British, I think—makes a real cockamamie-looking thing, prehistoric. It probably weighs a trillion pounds.

INTERVIEWER: *What kind of lenses do you have?*

PICKER: I'm using automatic lenses like those in a still camera. I'm using Contax lenses, which I find are really great. I'd like to take advantage of the fact that they are automatic. As it is now, when I look through the camera to compose a scene, I look through the lens at [f-stop] 2.8, and each time I shoot a frame I have to make sure it's stopped down to 16 or whatever.

It's possible to have a microswitch installed. Then I could look through the lens at 2.8 and every time I shot a frame, it would automatically stop down to 16 just like an SLR [single-lens reflex]. That would be nice, like having a great big Nikon. As it is, it's better than having to rack over. Every time I racked over, I had to count to ten before I clicked the shutter, just to make sure it had stopped vibrating.

INTERVIEWER: *Do you have any plans to use computer-assisted motion control for your films?*

PICKER: That would be kind of nice if I could hire someone to program all of that stuff, when there is more money around. But the nice thing about this setup is that with very little money, I can do the job. You know, with this I am able to execute all the moves and not have to have a sophisticated piece of machinery that does things I may not have any use for. People say you need a computer now, but it's a luxury.

INTERVIEWER: It's amazing how much sophisticated stuff up on the screen is made with such unsophisticated equipment.

PICKER: Well, the animation camera has not changed since it was invented. So they are all antique cameras. The Mitchell is the standard of the industry—the high-speed one that I have. You either buy that camera or you buy a real animation camera like an Acme or an Oxberry, which cost a hell of a lot more and you can't even find a used one. I was in L.A. a couple of years ago and the big animation studios had just started using one-inch videotape.

INTERVIEWER: Yes, there has been a lot of experimentation photographing the animator's drawings with a video camera and then coloring them digitally on a monitor instead of painting them.

PICKER: Right. I think that's what the studios will probably be doing because everyone else is going to be doing it. Then they won't need any labor; they won't even need the cheap labor of the Orient. All they'll need is the machinery right here.

It's a shame, its sad, because anyone that's interested in animation ends up being in commercials. Basically, that's the only way to make a living. For myself, I realized from the beginning that I had to create my own market. The market doesn't exist, but if you have a product people like, you make it.

INTERVIEWER: That's success, right?

PICKER: Yeah. You take risks. I consider myself lucky. But, you've got to keep your finger on the pulse of what people like.

INTERVIEWER: So where do you envision yourself going from here?

PICKER: Ha! To a better neighborhood! Seriously, we're looking to get more shows. We have proposals for other half-hour films.

And from LBS, even though they haven't seen any of the footage of *My Friend Liberty* yet, we're hoping to get some more projects like this one. And they are also interested in features. They are a very good company to be hooked up with. They're the biggest, very successful, they've been in business ten years. They started off as little barter syndicators when this idea of barter syndication didn't even exist. So I hope to do more things for them. I'd like to do unique things in clay, like operas or operettas.

And I hope to do some live action too; that would be fun. I did make my live-action debut on this project now, directing kids in a classroom. Now I can officially say, "Directing? Oh yeah, it's a piece of cake." At least you don't have to push the clay around, and the heads won't fall off, and the eyeballs aren't missing, and you can ask them to do another take, if you're polite.

Robert Abel

COMPUTER GRAPHICS

*R*obert Abel grew up in the shadow of the MGM studio in Los Angeles. While a student at UCLA, he worked with John Whitney, Sr., Saul Bass, and Charles Eames. He earned master's degrees from the Bauhaus in Olm, Germany, as well as UCLA. After teaching at UCLA, USC, and the University of Minnesota, Abel turned to directing documentary films. His first effort at David Wolper & Associates was A Nation of Immigrants, *and his documentary* The Making of the President, 1968 *won an Emmy. A series of rock and roll films followed, including* Mad Dogs and Englishmen, Elvis on Tour, *and* Let the Good Times Roll.

In 1971, he formed Robert Abel & Associates with Con Pederson. Pederson had been the special-effects supervisor on 2001: A Space Odyssey, *and he applied some of the optical techniques he had pioneered in* 2001 *to television logos and titles. By 1972, they had developed one of the first digitally controlled motion picture camera systems. In 1979, Abel adapted a flight simulation system designed by Evans & Sutherland for film use. The studio developed its own software for this system and began using vector, or "wire-frame," drawings to create moving storyboards as a way to preview proposed commercials. Robert Abel & Associates was the first studio to receive IRIS, the advanced raster-graphics system from Silicon Graphics. This gave them the ability to animate realistically rendered three-dimensional objects. Twenty-four Clio awards have made Robert Abel & Associates the most honored studio in commercial production. Commercials such as* Brilliance *for the National Food Information Council (featuring "sexy robot," a reclining chrome android, sensuously extolling the virtues of aluminum cans as food packaging of the future) and the* Gold *spots for Benson & Hedges's gold exchange in Kuala Lumpur, broke new ground in portraying human movement with computer graphics. Their innovative imagery has been a part of feature films such as* The Black Hole *and* Tron. *Recently, Abel formed Abel Image Research to market their pioneering software and continue the research and development of computer graphics, especially in industrial, engineering, architectural, and scientific applications.*

This interview was the only one that took place in Hollywood—the place, as opposed to Hollywood—the state of mind. Abel's studio occupies a large, brightly colored stucco building in a featureless commercial district south of Sunset Boulevard. It took over half an hour to track Abel down in the studio's maze of corridors, cubicles, offices, meeting rooms, studios, and graphics labs. The flurry of activity seemed intense rather than frantic.

We talked in Abel's office, a spacious yet cluttered expanse of living room furniture, business fixtures, cabinets, papers, books, magazines, and personal artifacts, such as movie posters and a wooden carousel horse. I sat on a comfortable sofa while Abel alternately stood and sat behind a desk the size of a sleeping water buffalo. Behind him stood an altar of gleaming statuettes—the trophies of numerous awards.

Abel was dressed in jeans and a pullover sweater. With his blond hair and trim beard, he resembled not so much an entertainment industry executive as one of the Beach Boys. His speech was full of expression, and he frequently became quite ebullient. He gave the impression of following several different lines of thought at the same time, yet being in total control of them all.

INTERVIEWER: What got you involved with computer graphics?

ABEL: How did I get into this business? Well, I was born in the Midwest. When I was eleven, our family house burned down. My father said that it was a sign from God, put us in a car, and drove us directly to California, on Route 66. We ended up on Hollywood Boulevard, and we pulled up in front of Grauman's Chinese Theater and I saw all the footprints. This was in the first twenty minutes that I was in Los Angeles. I was starstruck even then, because I had grown up on double-feature movies at the Shorewood Theater in Shorewood, Wisconsin.

The first house that we lived in here was down in an area called Beverlywood South, near Culver City, right next to MGM. I used to go around on my bike and hang out around the MGM studios. Eventually I got in and I met a guy named Buddy Gillespie, who was the head of the special-effects department. He taught me how they had done *Gone With the Wind, The Wizard of Oz,* and what have you. It was and still is probably the greatest studio in terms of combining all this talent under one roof.

INTERVIEWER: Did you study film in school?

ABEL: I went to UCLA as an engineering major. Between my senior year in high school and my freshman year in college, I worked for Saul Bass. I got a job doing pasteup. He was doing film titles. As a result of that job, I met a guy named John Whitney, Sr., who shot these titles on an automated computerized camera based on an old World War II tracking device. So I would be his assistant, meaning I got the night shift from 7:00 at night until 3:00 in the morning. Then I took the film home with me and went to sleep and then went to school the next day. But the idea of a camera, run and programmed by an analog computer that was actually a World War II antiaircraft tracking device, was fascinating.

At that time computers were used only for motion control. The artwork existed as an external physiological event. The end result, of course, was beautiful to look at. Then I met a guy named John Newhart through Whitney, and Newhart worked at Eames. I worked down at the Eames office, and they were doing a lot of World's Fair stuff, so I really got bitten by the bug.

INTERVIEWER: So you became involved with computers and film early on. Your film background is quite diverse, isn't it?

ABEL: Eventually, I got my own business and I did documentary films. I did World's Fair films. I was a designer. I've done all sorts of things—music films, rock and roll, you name it—Elvis Presley, Credence Clearwater, Joe Cocker on tour, et cetera. By the early seventies, I wanted to go back to something very personal and very private. After being on a rock and roll tour for six months it seemed really great! I was fascinated by the kind of intimate, personal, almost sanctimonious solitude of working on Whitney's camera all alone at night. I remembered that experience with great fondness. This was now post-*2001*, and my associate and closest friend, Con Pederson, had been the special-effects supervisor on that movie. I knew that most of the camera equipment involved in *2001* was still around.

"CD...the library of the future. It's the ultimate digital storage device."

So I called Con, who had been in virtual retirement after three years of seven-day weeks on *2001*. He only had his phone hooked up an hour a day. You could only call him between 6:00 and 7:00 at night. Con said he was kind of interested, and we got together, hired a couple of guys—a cameraman and Dick Alexander, a technician who would build camera systems and parts for us. He had worked on *2001*; he was nineteen years old, and had been doing it since he was fourteen. So we started running a slit scan and streak camera system out in the valley behind a CPA's office—no address, no telephone number, no stationery. It was supposed to be six months of R and R after being on the road with Joe Cocker and Leon Russell.

INTERVIEWER: *Did you have any computer equipment out there?*

ABEL: The second year we got a young kid who worked at Bernie's Surplus to build us a six-channel motion-control computer to run the camera, so that we could go home at night and be with our wives for reasonable lengths of time. We were doing all multiple-pass, time-exposure photography; all this stuff took forever to do. So we ran our cameras by computer, and we got hooked on the technology.

INTERVIEWER: *How did you make the transition from doing computer-assisted imagery to computer-generated imagery?*

ABEL: By the late seventies we were doing stuff that was so far out, our clients said, "I can't imagine what it's going to look like. I want a preview of coming attractions. I don't want to wait for the finished product to see what it looks like."

So I said to myself, If an architect can draw a blueprint and sell a fifteen-million-dollar building based on just drawings from three points of view and a cardboard model, why can't we draw a 3-D orthographic projection, so to speak, and make it move in space, or make the camera move in relationship to it and create a moving storyboard for the simple things we do?

We went to Evans & Sutherland and bought a PS-2, an early vector system that had been around for a number of years. They gave us the source code, which was the wonder of wonders, and we just took off from there. We could now create this on a monitor, put it on film, and tell people, "This is a stage 100 by 200 feet, these are real people, these are buildings, these are forced-perspective miniatures. We move like this, the next cut is here, this scene is four and one-third seconds long..." We could lay out their entire film for them in two to three days. They thought that was amazing! So did we, frankly. That really got us hooked, but we never thought of doing anything but preview what we were going to be doing in special effects.

But in September of 1979, along came Disney. They called some friends of ours to make a trailer—a preview of coming attractions, ninety seconds long—for *The Black Hole*. We said, "You guys have been working on this film for a year and a half. You must have some stuff—just cut it all together, get some jazzy music..."

"We don't have anything!"

"No black hole?"

"We don't have a black hole."

I told them, "The best we could do would be to give you something from the point of view of the computer that might be on board the spaceship that's being sucked into the black hole. It could be broken down as vector polygonal information. We could actually do a point-of-view thing—have the ship sucked into the black hole and see it as if we were watching it happen on the spaceship's own computer monitor." "Hey," they said, "that's fantastic!" So we said OK; they gave us fourteen days to do it, and we did it in nine.

INTERVIEWER: *What kind of image quality did you have in those days?*

ABEL: It went into theaters on a 50-foot screen, which was really pushing it because we were still shooting off the little monitor screens at the time. They loved it, and we wound up doing the main title and the advertising and the one-sheet poster.

All of a sudden we began to think, Hmm...maybe instead of just previewing, we can make synthetic images for sale. So we started doing more advanced vectors; we did vector fill-in—we did *Tron* with vector fill-in—and we started developing raster graphics simultaneously. Randy Roberts and I did the first raster featurette ever, which was the first use of raster graphics on the feature film screen, called *High Fidelity*. We were really sucked in; we were really hooked now!

Suddenly, we were in the synthetic imagery business. Since then, things have expanded a lot in the way we do our work, the kind of work we do, et cetera. If we had talked six months ago, I could never have told you how we would be working now or what we would be doing now—how we work will change next week.

INTERVIEWER: What do you aim for in the projects you take on?

ABEL: Moving pictures are what we sell. It doesn't matter if the pictures move for Mercedes-Benz or BMW or General Motors or Martin Marietta or NASA or McDonnell Douglas or any other client. They've got to move. They've got to look real. That's when you begin to tell the story. What's a 1988 car going to look like? Let's show it moving through a forest. Cars reflect their environment as they move through it. Someone watching says, "Oh, now I get it! It's real! I have a feeling; I know."

If Martin Marietta wants to see what something is going to look like in the year 2010, let's see it move. I want to see what it looks like now. What's a new plane going to look like? I want to see the outside; I want to see the inside. I don't want to have to paint a real plane—I want to do it synthetically. This car really looks slick; how is it going to react in a wind tunnel? We'll show you that, too. And you don't have to wait six months to do it and pay a million and a half dollars—you can do it in two weeks for a hundred and fifty thousand. You can see it just as realistically and with results that are just as accurate on our monitor or screen as in real life.

INTERVIEWER: What do you think this will mean to most people? How will it affect our lives?

ABEL: The world's changing. The process goes way back to cave paintings. There is something very significant—and this is basically the philosophy of the way we work—in the fact that man used pictures first. At that time not too many people got to see them, except the leaders of the tribe and the people who were going to go on the hunt. Later, they started drawing things out in hieroglyphics and then writing words. As religion developed, it became more and more words and fewer and fewer pictures.

But written communication was a very slow process. An illuminated manuscript was a one- to forty-year project, and of course it was very exclusive. Less than one percent of the population had access to information or knowledge in the year 1400, because everything was still etched in stone in the great Pyramids, which belonged to kings, or in manuscripts owned by the Church. And that was the only source of knowledge.

Then along came Johannes Gutenberg in 1440. He said, "I have something called movable type. I can put all these letters together and make thousands of printed copies of whatever, and distribute them in something called books ...to the whole world!"

"If we had talked six months ago, I could never have told you how we would be working now or what we would be doing now."

And the Church, of course, being in the proprietary ownership business said, "Well, how about printing a Bible as your first book? We are a little suspicious of these books, but the Bible sounds great." It took him seven years to actually get these Bibles printed and out, but by then the book did exist.

Then things began to move very fast, and in the next century, by the 1500s, the book was a common item. Suddenly, a quarter of the world's population had access to information through something called a book. Well, since then, what with Edison and Henry Ford and Samuel Morse, et cetera, we have modern communications. And we have the computer. So the computer is a major breakthrough—IBM in the sixties, Apple and the PC in the seventies, and so on.

Ironically, we went back to words with computers. But symbols, which are our driving force philosophically, are the most pregnant with meaning. In the lowest form of communication, you have words or alphanumeric information. You can process it and put it on screens, and people say, "Well, let's see what the stock market's doing today," and they type it out. Then you have pictures, which are drawn images. If a picture becomes really pregnant with meaning, if it's really communicating well, then it becomes a symbol. A symbol is one picture that's worth a thousand words, and if the symbol moves, as we say around here, it's worth a million. You go back really to where the cavemen were.

INTERVIEWER: And where does your work come in?

ABEL: We believe that making the invisible visible is the key to the future. And that is what drives us. That is our philosophy; that's the way we work. Our job here is to take ideas and then turn them into moving three-dimensional pictures.

Alan Kay, who's running an artificial intelligence project at MIT, told me a very interesting story that goes something like this: Take three kids of different ages and say, "Draw a circle."

A five-year-old kid will gather himself up, pull his arms in and walk around, with little shuffling steps, and he will draw with his own body, which is something he understands, a virtually perfect circle. The ten-year-old is more sophisticated. He says, "Well, I need a compass and a pencil." If you don't give him one, he'll try to draw a circle with a string and a nail. Because the pencil wiggles at the end of the string, he says, "Well, that's kind of a circle." But he'll be frustrated because it's not perfect. He's already learned perfection at the age of ten.

The fifteen-year-old who has had basic math—at least algebra and geometry—says, "Oh, well, let me see…what was that equation?" He goes to work it out, and somehow or other he gets bogged down in it and it doesn't draw a circle because it can't translate the alphanumeric instructions properly into a picture of a circle. So he walks away and he says, "Well, there's a bug in the system, I can't draw it." And you get nothing. You've got x squared times y squared equals z squared. And you don't have anything! Now, that's not communication! And this is kind of where we come in.

We're interested in basic communication, where you can draw something very easily, either with your own body or with your hand or some tool, and then put that picture into a system that allows you to see it, choreograph it, move it, light it, and tell your story—whether you're BMW trying to tell a story about what happens to the frame of a car when it crashes, or Martin Marietta talking about how you are going to put platforms in space thirty to forty years from now, or General Motors saying, "Three years from now this is

Featuring "sexy robot," scenes from Brilliance, *Robert Abel's commercial that brought a new level of human movement to computer graphics.*

what this car will look like, this is how much it will cost, this is how it will be made, this is what the body parts will look like, here are the potential flaws, this is how the robotics will put it together, this is what it is going to look like in our advertising, and this is what it will look like when you drive in the forest." Everything, from the time it is conceptualized to the time that it is finished being built, is all digital information, which in fact is what General Motors wants to do. They said, "By November of 1986, you can't do business with us unless the information comes to us digitally. You can't subcontract parts like windshield wipers, you can't be suppliers, or do design work for General Motors unless you communicate with us digitally."

Right now the majority of our clients are still Madison Avenue based. But rapidly that is diminishing from 100 percent to maybe 50 percent because more and more industrial clients are either buying our software products or using us as a production house or as design consultants. And that's going to touch everyone, because their products do.

INTERVIEWER: You're saying that the applications of computer graphics are limitless.

ABEL: They are limitless. Say you're an architect, and your client, a Greek shipping magnate, wants to know what his condo development is going to look like. "What will I see from my penthouse—what's my view from the eighty-first floor?"

You can sit him in front of your monitor and give him a guided tour: "Well, you start in your bedroom over here, see, and then you walk over here and you stand, and you are 5 feet 11 inches high, so this is exactly what you are going to see of the East River." That's a lot better than having to look at a cardboard model that's 4 feet high and trying to imagine what it's going to look like down there.

So there are a lot of aspects—architectural, pharmaceutical, medical. What happens to these pills when they are inside the body? What is it that the pills are trying to attack? What do the antibodies look like? What does this amino acid look like? How does the lining of the stomach react to this particular medicine? Let's see it. And you can do that—you can actually make them real.. We just did one in 3-D for Hoffmann–La Roche for a Japanese exhibition. You can sit there and be inside the body in 3-D. It's *Fantastic Voyage* all over again. The applications are limitless. It's making the invisible visible.

INTERVIEWER: What kind of progress are you making with depicting human movement?

ABEL: Of course, this is one of the areas that we are heading into. With "sexy robot," we thought the thing that was missing, as far as computer graphics was concerned, was the fact that it was just graphics—it wasn't computer animation. Animation gives form and life to a human or humanlike character. You not only have motion, you have emotion. The emotion is what tells stories. The "sexy robot" solved the problem of hierarchical motion, and while it gave that robot woman some limited sexual and sensual qualities, the work we did on the *Gold* spots gave many more qualities of life to those fable characters. It gave them power; it gave an animation or a life, or a relationship: The elk turns his head to the flute player, you know, he comes alive. Things come alive; there is something there between *The Magic Flute* (and I thank you, Mozart) and Grimm and Aesop and Brer Rabbit.

We're heading in the right direction. A lot of people who have gone before us have paved the way. All we've got to do now is solve the technical problems, and that's the easy part. The technical concerns must never drive what we do. We've got to be driven by the desire to entertain, to communicate, to educate—and to always do it in a better way. Telling stories with emotion and entertaining people is the key, I believe, to filmmaking in the future, and that's what we do.

INTERVIEWER: The limitation with computer animation has always been the human character—the exaggeration and subtleties of emotion. What kind of progress are you making with this?

ABEL: Human character? Well, it's getting better and better. "Sexy robot" was the beginning. Some of the characters are beginning to look more and more stylized or like a fantasy. We haven't been driven into duplicating a real person, a person who looks like Charlton Heston or Raquel Welch, because you already have Charlton Heston and Raquel Welch. We are not interested in having to duplicate that which already exists. I'd say that duplicating a human being is maybe three to five years away. I could be wrong. A month before we did "sexy robot," I said that being able to do human movement was at least a year away. Then we got the job to do the "sexy robot" spot and it was six weeks, and we had human motion. So you are driven; necessity is the mother of invention.

INTERVIEWER: What are your limitations now? Are they in hardware or software?

ABEL: The limitations have always been hardware limitations, computing power limitations. Our software is probably about as sophisticated as there is. We have to be able to buy hardware cheaply enough to be able to get a price-performance ratio that is reasonable for a noncapitalized company like ours. Although we're getting capitalization now, it still doesn't matter. If we had capitalization today, I wouldn't go out and buy a twelve-million-dollar Cray. It just doesn't make sense for us, especially now that we know that our software ports directly to the X-MP; most of the CRAY X-MPs in the Southern California area are used only four to six hours a day. So why not just port over there and make a barter with them on software, instead of laying out the hard dollars? That will be a big breakthrough for us. Right now our biggest systems are the Gould 9080s. Because of a nice relationship with Gould, we get to use Goulds in Fort Lauderdale, Washington D.C., Utah, and San Diego. So when our needs expand, we just go on to similar sister systems and we just type on terminals directly into their systems.

"The technical concerns must never drive what we do. We've got to be driven by the desire to entertain, to communicate."

INTERVIEWER: Do you know how the Japanese are doing with computer graphics?

ABEL: I just talked to my friend Art Durinski, who's a creative consultant at Toyo Links in Japan. He says they have a Japanese version of the VAX 730 and they're running 490 of them in parallel! With ray-tracing algorithms built into the hardware. And he said it's unbelievable the stuff they do. He said their problem is they don't know how to apply it. So that's the other extreme. We have hundreds of applications, but we don't have the hardware yet to apply it. All of this is going to come to a tremendous convergence within the next year to eighteen months.

INTERVIEWER: What role do you see for laser media like compact discs and video discs?

ABEL: CD...the library of the future. Right now it's got better sound than your tapes or your old LPs. It's the ultimate digital storage device. I was paid $7,500 a day three years ago by one of the top twenty Fortune 500 companies to come back to New York and tell them what the video disc might be. I spent an entire day with them. These people were in the music business, so I said, "Take The Beatles, for example." The way you play an LP record of, let's say, *Sergeant Pepper*, it tracks from the outside in sequentially, and you just listen to it from beginning to end. But with a digital disc, perhaps you're listening to "Strawberry Fields Forever" and you say, "Hmm, this is really interesting. I'd like to branch at this particular point and see the influence of Eastern religions on The Beatles." So, you have stored digitally on that disc an enormous amount of other information—The Beatles go to India, Hindu doctrine, Buddhism, Tibetan Tantric yoga, the spin-offs of Eastern religions, how Eastern religions influence other art forms like writing, Hermann Hesse, *Steppenwolf*—you could do a whole trip. And then when you say, "OK, I've had enough of the maharishi, Eastern religions, Hermann Hesse, *Steppenwolf*, and all the other things related to this. I'd like to get back and just listen to some Beatles music." So you press a button and come right back up and you keep playing "Strawberry Fields Forever." The point is that you can scan it sequentially, in analog fashion, but digitally you can also branch out. It's up to you because you've got 54,000 different choices to make here. You can think of this as being layered; you can go up and down in depth as well as along the surface of this thing.

INTERVIEWER: *So what was their reaction?*

ABEL: They said, "This is fantastic! Far out. Wonderful idea." The next day, I had one last meeting with the same guy at lunch, and I said, "I saw you with so and so from RCA at breakfast today. What were you guys talking about?"

"Oh, you should have come over and joined us. We just bought the MGM library."

I said, "For what?" He said, "Old movies."

"What are you going to do with them?"

"Oh," he said, "we're going to buy up MGM's old movies and put them on the RCA disc." I said, "Well, you won't get any more clarity. You guys missed the boat." This is where I get real passionate and get to be like Martin Luther or Joan of Arc: "This is what you've got to do! Listen to me! Listen to me!" I said to him, "You've kind of caught on to the concept that there is a new technology, but not quite; you've still got it all wrong."

Here's an analogy: You are in the blacksmith business. You are pounding nails, as you have for thirty years, into the feet of horses. Along comes a guy and he's driving this black Model T Ford. Then you see a few guys driving them. You think, There's something to this; people aren't going to be riding this horse, they're going to be driving more things like that. I'd better get into that business. So you make a deal with the Ford Motor Company in Dearborn. And what you do is spend the first hours of every day, when the cars come into your shop, pounding your nails into the tires of the cars! Because it's an old habit that you can't get rid of. You can't imagine getting rid of your blacksmith business. But you missed the point! Your cars won't even go down the street because they've got flat tires! People are only slowly beginning to get the idea about new technology. It is a slow process, but some people catch on very quickly. It's surprising.

INTERVIEWER: *What about the computer business?*

ABEL: Same thing. I was talking to somebody from IBM yesterday about the future of desktop computers, about what they can do and how we only use them now to do basic things, like transfer alphanumeric data, project spreadsheets, et cetera. I said, "Here are some of the possibilities," and I talked about the concept of symbols and pictures and communication through three-dimensional events and this and that, how it could affect automotive technology, industrial applications, engineering, and so on.

He said, "Have you ever told anybody else about this?" I said, "Yes, I've told several other people about this." And he said, "Well, would you like to come to work for us?" I said, "No, I already have a job."

It's surprising to me that people sometimes don't see these things. There are obviously other people at IBM who do.

INTERVIEWER: *Are you involved in anything outside the synthetic imagery business?*

ABEL: We are trying to start a thing at UCLA right now. Through the College of Fine Arts, we are building a whole school of visual communication using computers. We believe that for dancers and choreographers, set designers, filmmakers, artists, sculptors, architects, and industrial designers, this will become their basic tool of communication. We really do believe that people should have access to these tools. Phil Mittleman, an old friend of mine, has sold his company, MAGI, and is going to pull it together. We're going to donate the software, and it looks like we're going toward the IBM RT as the workstation for all this. The possibilities are going to be just fantastic! A whole

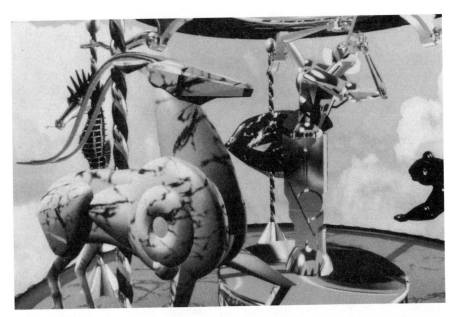

Images courtesy of Robert Abel & Associates, an Omnibus company.

Abel pushed the limits of portraying lifelike movement and emotion with computer graphics in the Gold *series of commercials for Benson & Hedges.*

school right here. And yet now they don't have a single computer in the entire school, as famous as it is.

INTERVIEWER: As far as filmmaking goes, do you think film itself will be eliminated as a medium?

ABEL: I think it is basic to making a film or a visual product to be able to load perforated celluloid into a camera. You know, how could you make a film without film? But also, how can you make it without being able in some way to visualize the possibilities of the film? And your problems—your sets, your costumes, your actors, your blocking—how many camera shots do you need? What are their angles? What lenses will you need to make these shots? This is where computer graphics can play a role.

INTERVIEWER: Do you write your own software here?

ABEL: Yes, most of our software has been written by us. It's UNIX-based, runs on C compilers, but it's all ours. We've always felt that to get where we wanted to go, we would have to write it ourselves, because what existed out there just wasn't appropriate. We were going to make the things we had in our minds, and we had to find the language to do it in.

INTERVIEWER: What's the most difficult part of the work you're doing?

ABEL: Constantly communicating the vision. Because we are always ahead of where other people's thoughts are at any given moment—it's our nature. And then, financially, being able to constantly keep the money flowing in is difficult, because the R and D is so heavy. As the windows of opportunity begin to open up, being able to take advantage of those opportunities by having the money available is very important.

INTERVIEWER: What do you see happening in the near future?

ABEL: If you had interviewed me a couple of years ago—before the *Gold* spots, before "sexy robot," before *The Last Starfighter,* before some of the stuff Digital* has done, before *Tony La Peltre,* done by the French Canadians on a Cyber—we'd have said, "Umm...it's interesting moving geometric shapes around." It's so far beyond that now! We are writing one feature film; we have an offer on another. Certainly, somewhere between *High Fidelity,* which was our little two-minute experiment done three years ago, and the next *Fantasia,* that's where computer graphics is going. And that's only one part of it.

* Digital Productions, Inc.

We tell investors who are coming in here, "Believe it or not, guys, only ten percent of our volume three years from now will have anything to do with the Hollywood film business. The future is in aerospace, automotive, engineering, pharmaceutical, education, architecture, science, geophysics, thermodynamics, military—you name it." Computer graphics is the great tool for the twenty-first century.

I was told by Lásló Moholy-Nagy, one of the founders of the Bauhaus, that the illiterate man of the twenty-first century would be the person who could not communicate by the photographed image. Now to him, a photographed image was the classic definition. We stood in a room or we stood out in nature somewhere, took a camera, light hit an object, bounced back and hit a silver-based emulsion on a piece of celluloid. We took it into a darkroom later on and developed it into film negative, then we printed it and it became a picture. Of course, the concept of synthetic imagery was almost unknown at that point in time.

> *"We believe that making the invisible visible is the key to the future."*

I went to Eastman Kodak three years ago and they asked me, "What kind of future do you see for photography?"

I said, "The future is that fewer and fewer people will be making images based on the fact that a subject really exists, so that particles of light actually hit the subject, bounce back, and are received by Kodak films in a camera." They wanted to throw me out of the room.

When they calmed down and they listened, which took about four more hours, they said, "Could you put that into a report that we could send to the eighteenth floor?" I said, "I normally don't write reports." But they said, "We've got to get it to the eighteenth floor; that's where the decisions are made." I said, "How long will it take to get to the eighteenth floor?" They are on the second floor, and they said, "Two years." So I said, "I don't have that kind of time," and I never wrote the report. We are more interested in doing it than talking about it or reporting on it.

The people here are driven. Everybody here feels that they are driven by what's going on and what they have done in the past. They've got to do better than the past. They've got to do better than the person in front of them. They also know that they have a date with destiny—that somewhere down the line this will become the great art form. We are like Michelangelo, on our backs doing the Sistine Chapel ceiling. We are the Impressionists whose work was continually thrown out of shows. We believe that we are the vanguard. Whether it's the next step of CAD/CAM [computer-aided design/computer-aided manufacturing] in the industrial world, or whether we're the new Disney—it doesn't matter to us. What matters is that we think we're all of those things. You can call us filmmakers, visualizers, visionaries, or what have you. We are driven by the fact that we have a tool here that allows us to see or to visualize anything! Whether an object exists or not, whether it can be photographed or not, whether it is too big to be seen, too far in the future to be seen, too secret to be seen, too small to be seen, or not seen at all because it lurks only in your imagination—it doesn't really matter to us; it is now visible; it can be seen in three dimensions and experienced as a real event.

Gary
Demos

COMPUTER GRAPHICS

Gary Demos is a native Californian. He was born in 1950 and attended the University of Southern Caliornia and Cal Tech in Pasadena.

He became interested in computer graphics while he was a physics major at Cal Tech, and it was there that he met John Whitney, Sr., one of the pioneers in the use of computer graphics in films.

During the early seventies, Demos did computer graphics work at Vector General as an independent contractor. In 1973 he joined Evans and Sutherland Computer Corporation (E&S), where he contributed to several projects, including a simulator for harbor pilots and a flight simulator for Lufthansa Airlines and NASA. While at E&S, he also helped develop the first random-access frame buffer and coauthored two patents for digital signal processing.

Demos and John Whitney, Jr., joined Information International, Inc. (Triple-I), where Demos built innovative hardware and designed and wrote software programs for computer-generated visual effects for motion pictures such as

Futureworld *and* Looker, *as well as for television commercials.*

In 1981, Demos and Whitney, Jr., founded Digital Productions, Inc. They acquired a CRAY-1 supercomputer in 1982, and in 1983 they upgraded to the more powerful CRAY X-MP. Their pioneering work can be seen in several feature films. In The Last Starfighter, *for example, entire scenes, complete with dog-fighting spaceships, star fields, and planets, were generated by computer.*

Demos also has an interest in music and loves to spend time playing his harpsichord and synthesizer. He lives in Los Angeles with his wife, Jill.

I interviewed Demos at Digital Productions, before his recent move to form a new company, Whitney-Demos Productions, with John Whitney, Jr.

One wall of his office was made of glass and looked into Digital Productions' large computer room, a clinical place resembling a hospital more than a film and graphics studio.

From this office Demos tended to the needs of their supercomputer, the CRAY X-MP. And it was here that he designed the hardware systems and software programs that enabled the company's animators and artists to create their dazzling and captivating computer graphics.

Demos met me in the lobby and led me to his office, where we were to talk about his work. Casually dressed and sporting a beard and glasses, Demos, with his relaxed and easy manner, made me feel quite at ease in spite of the dull roar of the X-MP. His office walls were decorated with stills from both recent and old work. Albert Einstein looked down approvingly from a poster.

INTERVIEWER: *Have you always been interested in computers?*

DEMOS: Well, I got interested in computers and filmmaking in the late sixties when I was at Cal Tech. John Whitney, Sr.—John Whitney, Jr.'s father—had a Cal Tech arts program class at that time. And Cal Tech had an IBM 360 model 55 and something they called the 2250, which was really one of the very earliest graphics displays.

There was a project by a professor at Cal Tech named Fred Thompson to do a graphics package—I guess that's what you would call it—that ran under a larger system that he had, called Readily Extensible Language, REL for short. It was a base language that had, on the top of it, several sublanguages. One of them he called English, which was for English database interrogation. You could ask it, "How many of these do you have in your database?" and it would tell you. It also had a graphics system that we played around with. There were quite a few people interested in the project.

Whitney, Sr., showed some of his films, which I found fascinating; all that visual stimulation was very exciting to me. And I heard that he had had some connection to the technology that was used in the original *2001* picture, which I thought was real interesting.

INTERVIEWER: *What was your major there?*

DEMOS: Originally I was in physics, then I changed to engineering and applied science. Basically, electrical engineering and computers were the two main interests I had, which isn't far from what I've been doing ever since.

INTERVIEWER: *What drew you to computer graphics?*

DEMOS: I had a great deal of interest in how the images were made and what it took to make them. I'd always been interested in music, and Whitney, Sr., was essentially doing visually what musicians do musically, so it seemed to me that it potentially could be as aesthetically rewarding and interesting to me as music had always been.

I'd always enjoyed fooling around with musical instruments. Science tends to be kind of dry, especially the way it's taught at Cal Tech. It's nice to get something coming back that's creative—not just a result or a discovery—where you are not solving a problem and there is no right answer. It's just playing on the medium, and in that case, it was playing on computers with graphics displays.

Eventually, the IBM 360 went away and a PDP-10 from Digital Equipment Corporation came in with a Tektronix display. I fooled around with that for a while. There was quite a big group of fifteen or twenty people who were originally interested in Whitney, Sr.'s work. But it became very obvious very soon that it meant staying up all night, baby-sitting the computer, trying to get it to do—and waiting for it to do—its very slow computations. Because even back then, with just line drawings, graphics took a lot of computations—it was major computing on those big machines. We figured out ways to get on these machines and get off without having them bill us. Once, I made a mistake and a bill for $20,000 showed up. I didn't get out without it knowing. Somebody logged me off or did something when I wasn't there.

A lot of interesting things happened during that time. There was an earthquake one night when we were filming. The camera sort of slid over, so the film slid to the right in the middle of the shot. That was an interesting effect. And there were other very odd and unusual events. I sort of learned the computer graphics life during that whole period.

And that original group of fifteen or twenty people dwindled down to two or three of us who actually stayed with it for six months or a year and fooled around with it.

We went out to Whitney, Sr.'s house to use his optical printing system. We optical-printed the black-and-white high-contrast film that we made onto color, Ektachrome, and made Kodachrome prints. We did a couple of short films, basically student films. That launched us into the field. Every once in a while I hear about the other guys that were there. They're still doing artistic types of things. They weren't all scientists. One of the students was an artist that heard about the program and was working at Cal Tech as a staff member.

> *"When I was in school, the visualization and imagining abilities were not at all valued."*

INTERVIEWER: *What did you do after you finished up at Cal Tech?*

DEMOS: I was still very interested in computer graphics, and I got hooked up with a couple of different, interesting projects. One was a consulting project for a series of films that IBM was doing to teach about computers. I worked with them on the storyboards, and we used a color Xerox machine to make a lot of different panels showing the architecture of how a machine computes. You could see how the numbers flowed and how the program counter updated and how an adder works and all those kinds of basic things. We began to experiment with different film stocks and how to get better images off the cathode ray tube and different functions that make interesting line patterns.

INTERVIEWER: *When was that?*

DEMOS: That was in the early seventies.

INTERVIEWER: *I remember those early geometric computer graphics. There were always one or two in the touring animation festivals at that time.*

DEMOS: Yeah, I had some films that went around with those festivals. Then I ran into the work that was being done at the University of Utah by the Evans and Sutherland Computer Corporation. They were shading the surfaces, not just doing line drawings. That was pretty radical, advanced work for 1972. I ended up going to the Evans and Sutherland company in Salt Lake City and working there for a while directly with Ivan Sutherland. He had a similar interest in filmmaking. We both felt that certain technical things had to be developed before you could really do it. He had various projects and grants at his company, so we worked like dogs for about a year, preparing different things. We built a frame buffer and we developed some software: a hidden-surface algorithm, data input, and some other things.

Then we came down to Los Angeles to start a company. It was originally called Picture/Design Group, in Santa Monica. The other principal players in the company, besides Ivan Sutherland, were a designer named Glen Fleck, who had worked with Charles Eames for many years, and also John Whitney, Jr., who was going to be in sales and marketing. I had met John, Jr., over at the Whitney's house when I was working with John, Sr., on optical printing. The printing takes a long time, so we would sit around and I got to know all the kids—the whole Whitney family.

INTERVIEWER: What sorts of things did the company do?

DEMOS: The Picture/Design Group only lasted about nine months. We did some design for a museum exhibit on economics, which is open now as of a year or two ago. It took a long time to actually happen. It's down at the Museum of Science and Industry. We designed some ways to teach economics using pinball machines, with pinballs representing capital and investments and various other things. It was pretty funny. We also did some research on the series that eventually became the PBS *Cosmos* series with Carl Sagan. It was originally going to be a feature film out of Wolper Productions. We did some galaxy models and some planet models and molecular models. We were generally looking for new, interesting projects.

There was a company out of Ohio named Battelle that was interested in funding the Picture/Design Group for what it wanted to do, but the fellow who had been involved in the funding died of a heart attack in the middle of the discussions, so they essentially were stopped cold. Other people were interested in funding, but they moved very slowly. Eventually Ivan Sutherland got frustrated and gave up.

INTERVIEWER: Did you have your own computers then?

DEMOS: We had been using computers at Rand Corporation in the middle of the night. We would go in at 4:00 in the morning and work till 8:00 or so, Sutherland and I. He ended up liking the people at Rand and he stayed on there and eventually went to Cal Tech. Now I guess he's back at Carnegie–Mellon doing other things.

INTERVIEWER: *What was your next move?*

DEMOS: When Picture/Design Group broke up, John Whitney, Jr., and I decided we still wanted to stay with it, and we thought there was probably a way to make it happen. We went to Information International [Triple-I], where Michael Whitney and John Whitney, Jr., had both done some film work. We met their board of directors, and they were interested in proceeding. They had PDP-10s, which we were very familiar with. Those computers were getting a little bit old by this time. The directors were willing to sort of walk their way into it. So we started. We called the new group The Motion Picture Project. We thought that the technology they had with regard to film—exposing color film and scanning color film, which they hadn't done yet—would be very relevant to what we wanted to do. We could bring in the technology for making the simulated images and then work with them on how to get really good recording quality out of the system.

We got our first project, *Futureworld,* in 1976. We simulated Peter Fonda's head for that project. We also did some image processing in a scene of some Samurai warriors in a kind of decompression chamber at NASA. They used NASA Houston for the set. We had the warriors materialize in the chamber as part of the story. That involved scanning color film and re-recording it at fairly high resolutions, 3000 lines.

After that, we started doing some logo spots; little two-second or four-second things for CBS and ABC and whoever. Then we did just a couple of thirty-second commercials, which is a lot more storytelling than a quick logo. A two-second spot is forty-eight frames, and even if it takes a half hour to do a frame, you can do that fairly easily. But a thirty-second spot, that's 720 frames. At twenty minutes a frame or whatever it took in those days, why, it was really pretty hard.

INTERVIEWER: *What sort of computer equipment were you using?*

DEMOS: We were using a custom computer that Triple-I had developed with some consultants. They called it the Foonley. That machine was about ten times as fast as the PDP-10s. It was a one-of-a-kind system, and that made it a lot of trouble. We learned a lot about computer design and hardware reliability and some other odd things. And we also developed a little bit of special-purpose hardware there in the way of computing units to do some of our graphics processing.

We also developed film recording and scanning technology for really good-quality color film recording and scanning. We had some equipment from Triple-I that was pretty good, but we were able to do much better with a custom design. Digital Productions was fortunate enough to be able to acquire all of that equipment, although it wasn't finished. We've had to finish it here. In fact, we're still working on it. I've been working on it for almost ten years now!

INTERVIEWER: *Did you do work on other films besides* Futureworld?

DEMOS: We did a project in 1980, seven or eight minutes for a feature film called *Looker.* It was a big chunk of work for the times. We simulated Susan Dey, who was the actress in that film—measured her face, her head, and did a lot of graphics and overlays and different things for that film, a lot of effects work.

And then we worked on the preparation of the film *Tron.* We were designing it to do ourselves at Triple-I. At that time, we were hoping to have more computing power available, to really make our group take off. Unfortunately, Triple-I was not terribly healthy at the time, so they really didn't want to back that project. John and I actually had a fight with Triple-I over the subject of computing power, because we didn't want to develop all the technology and then just sit on it. We wanted to move on to the next step. So we left and started Digital Productions.

> *"We have some lights that do things that aren't physical, like suck light out of the scene, or turn anything they shine on dark red, or other odd things."*

INTERVIEWER: *Who ended up doing* Tron?

DEMOS: What happened was that the *Tron* film got farmed out to several different companies. We did some tests for it and worked on the story for about two years before we left. The third part of the film was done with the software and technology that we developed there. I'm sure they added to it, but basically we left them with the whole means of producing their part of the film. Triple-I ended up doing the Solar Sailer and the Master Control

Program sequences and some of the scenes near the end of the film. I thought that the Solar Sailer came out very nicely.

INTERVIEWER: *What was the next step then, more computing power?*

DEMOS: That was the original concept at Digital Productions—to increase computing power. The first way we thought of doing that was by building our own special computers. We wanted to capitalize on what we had learned with the machines we had worked with at Information International. There was a supercomputer at Livermore, called an S-1, that was very similar to the Foonley machine we had at Triple-I. Physically, it looked very much the same. We thought that would be a good machine to build on, to update the Foonley design, which by then was a couple of years old. However, when you figure the cost of mounting a project like that—you have to hire a bunch of highly paid engineers and they have to work for two or three years before you even have a machine! And then you start developing the software. It was way too expensive.

It looked like it would be much better if we could find a computer that would give us enough power, something that we could get into operation quickly. We had rejected the Cray and all the other systems because they really didn't have enough power to do what we wanted to do and were pretty expensive. However, about that time, Cray announced the CRAY-2, which was significantly more powerful than the CRAY-1/S. When we started talking to them, they began to tell us about the X-MP, which is the machine we acquired. The cost/performance improvement of the X-MP and the CRAY-2 were both very significant. The CRAY-2 was a ways off; they were still very early in the development of that. But the X-MP was fairly close, so we placed an order for an X-MP and also got a 1/S. We had a 1/S for a year and a half and then replaced it with the X-MP.

INTERVIEWER: *How long do you figure you are going to be able to use this particular system?*

DEMOS: We are looking at different kinds of projects that would involve maybe getting more computing power. Cray has two new products that have come out since the X-MP. We have the two-processor X-MP, and they have a four-processor model that came out about a year and a half ago, which is quite a bit more expensive. They also have the CRAY-2, which has been out for a little over a year now. Both of those machines have about twice the computing power of the two-processor machine, but they are also about twice the current value. If you measure it in comparison with a lot of other machines, it really has a lot of power. We measure this machine at about 350 times the VAX 11/780, which is a machine a lot of people have and know the power of. That's a lot of computing power. This machine is still very much state of the art as far as we're concerned.

INTERVIEWER: *Are all of your programs written in-house?*

DEMOS: For the most part, it's pretty much all written here. Not because we wouldn't like to get it from other people, but we find ourselves making our own path for the most part. Other people really aren't aiming at what we're aiming at.

INTERVIEWER: *What are you aiming at?*

DEMOS: I can tell you very simply what the three criteria are—what we developed our software around and what other people haven't gone toward. One is very high scene complexity—half a million or a million polygons in a scene, which is what we did on *The Last Starfighter*. We finished that project two years ago. That's technology we developed very early at Digital.

Another one is very high resolution. That picture was done at 2000 by 2500 resolution. We went even higher when we did the *2010* project for 70 mm;

Frames from the computer-generated title sequence of Labyrinth.

we went up to 3000. The high resolution in addition to the high scene complexity demands a lot more computing than if you are working for television. And a lot of the software that exists is really oriented toward the low-resolution end of things.

And the last principle is to use one program that is extremely flexible. We really have one program that does all of our work. We call it DP-3D—Digital Productions 3-D software. We think having one program that has all the capabilities in it is a much better way to work than having lots of little programs that each do single things. You have the whole system at your command; every feature there is available to you. That flexibility and generality in the software gives us the ability to respond rapidly to any kind of request that we think we can actually accomplish.

Flexibility is one of the keys to succeeding in both feature films and commercials. Commercials have very short time frames. From the time you start until the time you finish might be only four weeks or six weeks. And it might be a very elaborate project. It's like a mini feature film sometimes. Having that ability to create an environment and make it move fluidly and do everything else you have to do in a very short period of time demands that the software be very stable. You have to be very fluent in it, and it has to have all the capabilities you need.

INTERVIEWER: *Can you tell me about the work you've done with scene complexity?*

DEMOS: If you look at the spaceships in *The Last Starfighter*, the level of detail in those objects is very, very high, and I don't think anyone else has done that level of detail. The first time we did something like that was at Triple-I in 1979 as a test for the Lucas people, to prove to them that we could do a higher detail ship. We simulated an X-wing starfighter, the kind they used a model for in the *Star Wars* film. But at twenty minutes a frame, we weren't able to fly it around very much. We only made a little bit of film of it, but we were at least able to prove the concept.

People have made complex images through techniques like fractals, and they have used graftals and other special-purpose things, but in terms of objects like these spaceships for *The Last Starfighter*, I think we are still the only people that have made any significant amount of very, very complicated imagery, in terms of scene detail.

INTERVIEWER: *What's involved in getting more scene detail? What is it a function of?*

DEMOS: Basically, supercomputing. You have an enormous amount of data that you need to sort, antialias, and shade. You have to process this large amount of data, in high resolution, as a big computing problem. You have to write your software such that it solves that big computing problem efficiently. And that's really how we've designed everything to work.

We've also given the software the full lighting and modeling capabilities, the reflections, the texturing, and all those sorts of things. But the overall structure we're building it on has the inherent capability to do very large things. It really takes the supercomputer to do it. It takes all the power, the memory, the disks, the I/O capabilities, and all the rest of the factors that are inherent in a very large-scale system like this.

And we stretch it to the limit in all those directions. We utilize all the computing power, all the memory, all the disk capacity, and even at that, we have had to build a lot of custom equipment.

"We took film of the real Mick Jagger and scanned him in on the computer and put him into scenes with the simulated character."

We've interfaced the film recording and scanning equipment, we have developed custom displays to improve throughput, and other assorted things. No one yet has developed the equipment that serves our needs, so we really had to go ahead and develop it ourselves. And as far as the hardware is concerned, we developed only what we had to, because we really wanted to concentrate on the software problem.

INTERVIEWER: *When you're doing a scene for a movie or a commercial, do your animators create it frame by frame, like a conventional animator does?*

DEMOS: Well, the computer does. The computer creates it frame by frame like an animator would. We do the basic frames, called key frames, first. Say the action is going to begin here at the start of the scene and end over there. The animator will build those two frames and then the computer will make all the frames of the movement between them. The front-end Vax computer will tell the Cray what it should do, and then the Cray will make all the frames when it actually films the thing.

It is pretty much like having an actor hitting his mark: He starts over here, he goes there and hits that mark, then he goes there and hits that mark.

Animators use the key frame concept, but they are working in two dimensions. These are three-dimensional key frames—more like hitting your mark if you're an actor.

INTERVIEWER: When the animator creates a key frame, does he begin with a blank screen and build up a wire-frame image of the spaceship or the toaster or whatever it is?

DEMOS: The first step in the process we've evolved is very similar to the way any art director would work. We make a storyboard and make it as accurate as possible. It's done with conventional techniques—colored pencils, airbrush, or whatever. That storyboard is where we do all the changes.

Once we've got the storyboard worked out and everybody agrees on what we're making, then the storyboard will tell us what objects we need. I need this rabbit here, and I need this house and the tree and the rock—all the things we are going to need in the system. And at that point, we have done enough projects so that sometimes we have some of those pieces already.

INTERVIEWER: You're developing an image library?

DEMOS: Yes, a little prop library on the computer—simulated props. We certainly have telephones, streets, skies, star fields, planets, and a few other things. So then we'll make all the objects we don't have, which is usually anywhere from half to all of them, depending on the project. But there are always special things. If you're doing a car commercial, you have to make that car; it's new, it's never been made before. Or you're doing a company logo and you haven't done one before, so you have to make that logo, or whatever it may be. That's why a television series is so appealing: It's got the same characters in every show. Maybe it has a few new locations, but you get a lot of benefit from the reuse of those databases, those established characters and locations.

INTERVIEWER: Once you have the wire-frame objects—the basic three-dimensional shapes—in the computer, how do you animate them?

DEMOS: Once you have the objects, you put them into the line-drawing system where they build up the animation action, in the way I described with key frames. There's another technique called interpolation that lets you change the shape of one thing into another. You also put in lip sync if there's dialogue. Those techniques are used to build up the motion, tell the story.

Then we move to the lighting of the scene, and we spend a lot of time doing that, just like on a movie set. We will spend a lot of time lighting the set, getting the lighting and the shading and the color of all the surfaces just the way we want them. Our lamps are very different from the lamps on a stage. Ours have a lot of flexibility, and we can do some very unusual things with them. The lighting can be different for every object. We can have a rock next to a book and there can be completely different light on each of them. That can't be done in a physical scene unless it is composited optically. We have some lights that do things that aren't physical, like suck light out of the scene, or turn anything they shine on dark red, or other odd things. Because of that, people spend a lot of time lighting, and the more time they spend lighting, the more interesting the scene starts looking. So they will put lighting in the scene and they'll describe all the surfaces and colors for the objects. They can be made out of any sort of material we have in our library: marble, wood, glass, plastic, paper.

Then we make a low-resolution film test, where we shoot it every couple of frames and with just enough detail to give an idea of the motion. It isn't a perfect, polished thing, it's just a rough look, like an animator's pencil test. But it is shaded and lit, and it's done with the motions from the line-drawing system. It gives us some idea of what we are getting, so we can then make some adjustments.

When we've got the film test all ready, we put it in what is called the film queue, which contains all the shots that are ready to go. Then, when there's computing time available—say, that evening or on the weekend—it will be computed, put out to film, then we get it back, and we're done.

INTERVIEWER: *So a producer coming here with a concept can leave with the film in the can?*

DEMOS: Yeah. Or we can generate the concept. We have art directors that can come up with ideas. Often, an ad agency will have some kind of a campaign or a theme they are working to. But most of the time we do our own design, which is more fun, because we can design for some of the capabilities we know the system has that have never been explored.

INTERVIEWER: *What kind of human movement and emotion are you capable of generating now?*

DEMOS: A lot of what's been going on here in the past couple of years has been directed toward developing the system so it can animate figures. We've done several very fluidly animated things. We did a project for Hitachi for Expo '85, animating some hypothetical creatures in the atmosphere of

Jupiter. We made them fluid, living things. It was done in 3-D. You put on po-larized glasses and you have a different view for the left and the right eye, so you can really see them in this spatial environment.

Then we did a rock video, "Hard Woman," which was John Whitney, Jr.'s project, for Mick Jagger. We did line-drawing characters, a Mick Jagger surro-gate that John calls Vector Mick, and the girl he calls Vector Girl. The charac-ters are actually tubes, three-dimensional lines, that move in a fluid way. We developed a lot of software to be able to do that. There was also some com-positing. We took film of the real Mick Jagger, scanned him in on the computer, and put him into the scenes with the simulated character.

> *"...computer graphics is not like traditional computing.... It's really using the computer as a creative tool."*

And then we've done some other figures. We did an RC Cola commercial with a little man that runs around, and we've done some cereal commercials with little cereals that hop around, and then we've done Spider-Man for Marvel Productions, where he flies in and lands on the Marvel Productions logo.

The most recent thing we have done along those lines is the titles for Jim Henson's movie called *Labyrinth*. We did a sequence for the movie's titles—about three minutes of an owl flying through a labyrinth with his feathers articula-ted and with reflections on the walls.

INTERVIEWER: *Do you see your work leading you in a certain direction?*

DEMOS: What we've been doing is moving from short segments to com-mercials that bring a simple message, and from there to pieces of feature films. Now we're really in a position to tell entire stories with the computer. We've worked out a lot of the technology necessary to do the storytelling. All the problems we've solved with software and hardware, those were all steps for us in solving the problems of telling stories.

INTERVIEWER: *So you think the fully computer-generated feature is not too far away.*

DEMOS: I think we are ready at this point. It's really a matter of who's going to sign up. But it's not just feature films, it's also television series, spe-cials, and anything that involves storytelling. We're ready to tell stories.

INTERVIEWER: *What's the toughest part of doing a project for film?*

DEMOS: A feature film? Oh, I don't know, I think that depends on the project. In the case of *The Last Starfighter*, it was making all the software and getting it to the right level on such a short time schedule. We also developed special software for the *2010* project, to make the fluids on the planet Jupiter move and swirl. That was also difficult. Whenever a production project requires special software development, it's hard on me—looking at it from my viewpoint in the company, which is software development.

But we've done such a broad range of projects in our software development. We are working on ways of having more flexible video output, using some of the random-access video equipment that's just come on the scene. We'll be interfacing to some of those machines to enable a broadcaster to send out not only precanned routines, but new, unplanned scenarios of precanned images, similar to the concept of video games that use videodiscs.

You can see the application of that. For example, if you are going to have a sports event, you don't know how it's going to come out, but you could have premade versions of the scoreboard or different things. If you've got them all on the random-access disk, it gives you enormous flexibility and elaborate

Not a miniature, this is a computer-generated spaceship from The Last Starfighter.

ways to tell your graphics story. We're doing projects in that area and it's been interesting.

Also, when we've had peak work loads, when we needed more computing power, we've gone out and used other people's Crays. That's been very interesting also. We've even used some of the four-processor Crays as well, to help even out the load. That's been kind of fun, making our software run on other machines.

INTERVIEWER: *How many people did you have working with you on* The Last Starfighter?

DEMOS: I guess the organization was about fifty people at the time. About fifteen or twenty of those were actually doing the production, and the rest were developing the software! They were trying to get the software ready, so that when they needed it, it was there. We still have twenty or so people that do software development. But the organization's got more production people now and we have a new group, the scientific applications group.

INTERVIEWER: *What does that group do?*

DEMOS: Our graphics capability tends to be a good way to visualize complex data that people might not be able to see otherwise. They're providing a service to scientists and engineers to help them work with their visualization problems, whatever they might be. That's been a significant part of our business the last year and a half or so.

INTERVIEWER: *Are you marketing your software?*

DEMOS: Yes. We have a software license that we've sold to an Australian company. They're going to put it on a CRAY-1/M, which is about like a CRAY-1 in terms of power. That's new for us also, to have other people using our software. They will be using it in a way that is very similar to what we're doing. We'll both be doing commercials and also scientific work.

INTERVIEWER: *What do you see in your crystal ball?*

DEMOS: Computer graphics will be very, very popular once more can be done with home computers. They are still pretty limited, but it won't be too terribly long before there is a tremendous amount of capability in everybody's home. There will probably still be central computing engines down at the phone company or the cable company or whatever that can do more than you can do at home, and you'll be able to buy some of that power as a service. A lot of these graphics capabilities will be coming into everybody's house. You'll be able to do a lot of amazing things.

INTERVIEWER: What do you get out of this work personally? What do you enjoy about it?

DEMOS: As I mentioned earlier on, computer graphics is not like traditional computing, where you have a problem to solve or an equation to work out. It's really using the computer as a creative tool. You're creating something. You are expressing something. It's a communication medium. The computer is something that helps you tell a story or visualize an idea.

We are essentially simulating reality, but we're simulating one view of it, as seen through a movie or whatever, not reality itself. In order to do that, to get ideas for the software, you study reality; you study how light interacts with materials, how shadows are cast, how light reflects off materials, how different materials move and how figures move. If you don't think of it or conceive of it and put it in the software, it isn't going to be there on the screen. You see that a particular capability is not modeled and the imagery looks less real or less interesting for that lack. So doing this work makes you more observant of the physical world around you. That's one of the things that's been very interesting to me.

"Doing this work makes you more observant of the physical world around you."

Another thing I enjoy is the very unusual experience of sitting down and working with the system. Since the system can get you pretty close to reality—real images—it gives you a chance to examine your own abilities to visualize. Normally, if you are an art director or if you are involved in the creative process at all, you'll have some idea in your mind of what you are creating. You'll build some objects and maybe you'll have the storyboards. But when it actually gets to putting the scene up there, when the computer is actually giving you, in great detail and with great fidelity, whatever it was you imagined, it's always very different. In some ways it's more real and more rich, and in other ways it doesn't have some of the richness. So it brings you face to face with the capabilities and limitations of your own ability to visualize and imagine things. It puts you in a state of mind where you think about things like dreaming in color, or the way people conceive stories, or what people see in their minds when they are listening to stories being told, listening to fairy tales.

Of course, artists have faced this for a long time. If they were going to make one of those fabulous paintings that painters have made, they had to have some kind of reference in their mind, a mental image from which they worked. And that image was probably different from what actually ended up on the canvas.

And in our experience in working with scientists, they experience the same thing. They've got this data and they have an idea in their mind of what it looks like. But that's all the scientists have. They have no canvas on which to see their ideas. Now we can start visualizing this data with computer graphics. And when scientists actually start seeing the data, they find that the images they are seeing are very different from the ideas they have in their minds. Both are right in some sense, but they are very different.

[Demos points to the Einstein poster on his office wall.] Well, this quote from Einstein—"Imagination is more important than knowledge"—that's a pretty amazing statement. When I was in school, the visualization and imagining abilities were not at all valued. The idea was to teach people to crank through equations, to work through the mechanics of science. And that's not where creative science comes from at all. If you look at the scientists who have excelled—people like Feynman and Wilson and Gell-Mann and others—if you listen to them talk, they say very visual things. They describe things in such a way that you get a mental image of what they are talking about. And it's that fooling around with fitting the mental pictures up against the data they have that's given them the insights and the breakthroughs. A lot of them will describe the time when they came up with their great insight as being a time when they were just fooling around. I would phrase that differently. I would say that they were using their brains for non-problem-solving activities. They were using their brains in the same way we use the computer—not to solve a specific problem, but rather for exploration or creation.

There's been a lot of talk recently about the left brain and the right brain. I don't know if there is a left-brain or a right-brain function, if you can quite isolate it that way. The basic concept is that there is an essentially analytical part of the brain and then there is a visualizing, artistic side, and generally they don't communicate very well.

When I was at Cal Tech, it was pretty clear that the artistic brain was not very much valued. It was valued by some people—or else John Whitney, Sr., would not have been there—but not by everybody and not by many of the scientists. If you look at Leonardo da Vinci and others who worked with both sides of their brains, they were doing artistic and scientific things at the same time throughout their careers. I think there is something very valuable for all of us in this whole line of thinking.

The idea that we are one person, a single entity, is really wrong. We are made up of multiple facets, almost like multiple entities. It's not schizophrenia so much as it is different capacities that don't communicate. Computer graphics is a very, very direct and abrupt bridge between the two capabilities, because you're really faced with making them communicate. You don't succeed in making interesting computer graphics unless you have managed, in your own brain, to get an analytical formulation for an essentially visual idea.

Roy Arbogast

SPECIAL EFFECTS
MECHANICAL EFFECTS

*R*oy Arbogast is tall and sports a tan from working outdoors much of the time. He's direct in his manner but quiet and unassuming. He was born in Montana and, although raised in the Los Angeles area, he still harbors a strong affection for the outdoors and rural life. After high school, Arbogast spent a few years in and out of college, the National Guard, and a couple of different jobs before discovering the charms of special effects as a prop maker for a Hollywood studio. Since then, he has gone on to become one of the most sought-after mechanical-effects specialists in feature film, working his magic on over twenty-five motion pictures to date.

It was July and the rental car didn't have air conditioning. But through a stroke of luck, the desert foothills of the San Gabriel Mountains had been blessed with unseasonably cool weather. I was early for our appointment, so I drove farther up the canyon, taking delight in the rocky stream. Roy Arbogast's special-effects ranch nestles in secluded hills in a pleasant desert canyon. The property adjoins a national forest, and he and his crew enjoy a natural solitude not often found in the *movie business. Across the valley, the Magic Mountain amusement park garishly displays its own kind of mechanical effects.*

The Arbogasts' Spanish-style house is surrounded by giant cacti, agaves, and leafy shade trees. From the open, breezy living room, you can see beyond a lush lawn and swimming pool to the facilities and artifacts of mechanical effects. On that day, large trucks, lumber, scaffolding, hoses, piping, full-size dinosaur feet, and various other paraphernalia lay scattered about outside the barnlike shop.

INTERVIEWER: You have quite a setup here.

ARBOGAST: Well, what we try to do is independent special mechanical effects. To be independent, you need to provide full-service effects. So we've built the shop and tried to make it as complete as possible. We also have mobile shops—two big, 40-foot and 27-foot trailers. We try to do only one picture at a time.

INTERVIEWER: You have a company, then, and the studio hires you as a subcontractor?

ARBOGAST: Yes, we have a company, but we do not hire out as subcontractors. They hire me and they rent my facilities and they pay my crew. I like to just go to work by the hour, from preproduction through principal photography to any postproduction work we have. That way it keeps me out of the business end of it. I like to do the work, the special effects, and let somebody else worry about the bills and business problems.

When the project's over we sweep the floor and look for another project. It's easier for me. I don't have to try and maintain a constant special-effects business. Once one project is over and we decide to take a few weeks off, we can close the door, go and play, and then when another project comes along we go back to work.

INTERVIEWER: How do you usually find projects?

ARBOGAST: People call. It takes a while. You build up a reputation. Once you've done a lot of pictures, you meet a lot of people, and they learn what you can do. It's all word of mouth.

INTERVIEWER: When do you generally start working on a picture?

ARBOGAST: We like to start from the very beginning, in preproduction. I like to build all the props, rig all the gags, rig all the special effects. You noticed the dinosaur feet out behind the shop. We try to do all of that right here. We rig our mobile shops for whatever kind of picture it's going to be, and once we're ready to shoot, we load everything up on tractor-trailers, whether it's a prop or equipment, and head for the location.

INTERVIEWER: *Do you do work on the studio set as well as on location?*

ARBOGAST: Oh, yes. We do it in the studio or on location. It doesn't matter to us. In the past ten years, the majority of our work has been on location. We prefer to build everything here and take it to the set or location, if possible. If not, we like to set up our own shop on the studio lot. We're only concerned with our one picture, not the studio's other productions.

INTERVIEWER: *Do you have a lot of people working with you?*

ARBOGAST: It depends on the project. It goes from myself and four or five people to fifty people. It depends on what that show needs. Manpower-wise, the biggest job was probably *Close Encounters of the Third Kind*. We had a lot of Hollywood people and a lot of local people. We hired some pretty big crews on the road for a few scenes in *Starman*. The *Jaws* pictures and *Return of the Jedi* were jobs that also had pretty big crews.

> *"On Jedi, we worked from an 18-inch model of a landwalker, and we built one 27 feet high."*

We try to keep the crew as small as we can. I would rather get a group of really great people and try to do it mostly ourselves, because when I get too many people, I can't work the way I like to—I'm worried about the payroll and all the problems that go along with a large crew.

You're only as good as your crew. When people ask me what pictures I've done, I say, "I've never done a picture by myself. It's always myself and a crew."

INTERVIEWER: *Do you make estimates of how much all the effects are going to cost?*

ARBOGAST: We try. The more pictures you do, the easier that is. Manpower's the main thing. You figure that out and add a percentage for materials. Every job is a different percentage. You learn that, too—what it costs to burn a building, do a rain job, or build a mechanical effect.

INTERVIEWER: *When you first begin a project, who designs the mechanical effects?*

ARBOGAST: The mechanical parts are designed by us, while the visual look is designed by the production designer. In *Christine*, they wanted to bring in a '57 Plymouth Fury, and they told us they wanted it to rebuild itself. In that case, the '57 Plymouth was in the story, but we took it from there. On *Jedi*, we worked from an 18-inch model of a landwalker, and we built one 27 feet high. We work from photographs, models, and research.

That's the mechanical effects. On the effects like fires and explosions, you read the script, sit down with the director, and figure out how much time they want to spend on it: How big a part of the film is it? Is it worth making a big control rig, or should we just go in and do a quick job?

INTERVIEWER: *It must be interesting to have to figure out how a mechanical prop is going to work and then build it. What are some of the more interesting ones you've created?*

ARBOGAST: We've created every kind of prop you could think of—every kind of breakaway, hand prop, and large mechanical prop. We built all the oversized props for *The Incredible Shrinking Woman*. On a picture in England with Frank Langella, *Dracula*, we built a lot of nice props, like the folding bat wings for Dracula. They were all spring-loaded like an umbrella. And we built a mechanical wolf that jumped up and bit the guy in the throat right at the end. When they put the wooden stake through the girl, we made it so you could stick it in one side and it would come right out the other side, all in one shot. Prop shows are very fun projects. We built a lot of props for *Caveman*— all the full-size dinosaur parts, the mechanical lizard that Ringo Starr rode, the big fried dinosaur egg 20 feet in diameter that actually smoked and bubbled and the yolk broke. Those were challenging.

INTERVIEWER: *Where did you learn how to do these effects?*

ARBOGAST: Just by being in the industry. I started in the construction end twenty-two years ago, working as a prop maker and set builder. When I got into the business it wasn't something I knew much about. And it wasn't as if I always wanted to work in the movies. A friend of mine was working on a summer job and I went in and they hired me. I was like a kid in a candy store; I really liked it. Once I was working, I learned a lot. Then I went back to school again, and I learned a little more about things that would help— mechanical classes. I did have a construction background, so that helped.

INTERVIEWER: *How do you account for your success?*

ARBOGAST: I don't know. I guess I always liked what I did. Once I got out of the construction end and they let me get involved in the effects part, I would have gone to work for free—that's how much I liked it. To me, the money was like a bonus. I'm sure that's probably why.

I was accepted by some of the people who were involved in the production—the writers, designers, and directors. I think they were happy to see someone who was as interested as they were in seeing that a scene worked.

They dream up something and say, "Boy, if we could only do this." I'm sure that when they walk in and find somebody who is as excited about it as they are, it makes them happy. I know that when I hire somebody here to work on a project of mine, I can tell by the tone of their voice. If they say, "Oh boy, all right, I'm ready," that's a load off my back right there.

You have to be willing to put in a lot of hours. And you have to put up with defeat. Your gags don't work all the time. You have to be able to figure out a quick alternative, knowing that there is only so much money.

If you're interested enough and you want to see a good product from your end of it, you will take the money that's available, if it's a realistic amount, and create a lot of nice stuff without wasting money.

I put myself in the producer's shoes. If I got a million or half a million dollars for special effects and I turned it over to the effects guy, I'd be pretty worried. You just try to do your best, that's all.

INTERVIEWER: *Do you prefer any particular kind of picture?*

ARBOGAST: We like to take on bigger projects that require no fewer than myself and four or five people. Between us, there's nothing that we can't do. Nobody knows how to do it all. When we're out on location, there's enough work for us all to do plus we have enough brains between us that we can solve any problem that comes up. If you're a one-man show out there, it's pretty tough. You're always scrambling, looking for outside help.

Some shows, they just want you to come out and blow up a couple buildings and that's the end of it. I'm not real crazy about that. We like to become as involved in a project as we can.

The bigger shows make for a better credit for us and make it more fun. The bigger the project, the better. It's a bigger challenge. We like that. It's nice to know they want you to do the hard ones. It's also easier to get jobs if you turn out a few good projects like that. We're looking for the challenge, nice people, and the credit. The people are very important. There are a lot of great companies to work for.

INTERVIEWER: *Is there a dream project you'd like to work on?*

ARBOGAST: Not any more. When you're younger, you always want to do the biggest and the most, but now it doesn't matter. I like working on the water. I'd love to do a picture like *Pirates;* I think that would be great. I like working outside. We've done a lot of water work—all the *Jaws* pictures were done out at sea. It's always very hard—physically hard, mechanically hard— but it's so rewarding, it's so nice to be out there. If we could do a swashbuckler, we'd be doing a lot of rigging, a lot of flying, and all the boat work is a real challenge. There'd also be a lot of great props to build, which I like to do.

> *"Some shows, they just want you to come out and blow up a couple buildings and that's the end of it."*

My favorite kind of picture to work on is one that has lots of props, lots of effects, and is a good-quality movie besides. Something that everybody can enjoy. *Silverado* was a film like that.

Personally, I'd rather not work on something right in a city. *Escape from New York* was tough for me because we lived in a hotel right in the city and worked there as well. We never actually got out of the city. I didn't care for that. I'm not a city person.

I'd like to be able to spend two or three months in the shop here building all the props and all the gags and then spend two or three months out on location. That would be the perfect formula. We like to have enough time. When it's well planned, with a good production designer, we can start far in advance and build these things. It's nice to have everything ready, built and rigged, so that when you start shooting, everything is all set to go.

INTERVIEWER: *What are your main problems on the set?*

ARBOGAST: It can be something breaking down, changes in the script, changes in the shooting schedule, added scenes, anything. When the director comes to you and asks, "Can we do this instead of that?" it's great when you can say, "Sure." They're happy, everybody's relaxed, it takes the pressure off. That's nice. And when you do that, everybody thinks, Boy, that's really great. Everybody's looking for a little reward out there. And it's easy to do when you have the people to do it.

I try to put myself in the director's shoes. I know how nervous I get and how much sleep I lose just doing the little part of the film that we do. The poor director, he's out there with this whole thing on his mind. I like to have a group big enough to really serve his needs.

On the set, whenever anything goes wrong, somebody is always hollering for the special-effects man. And you're always horrified because you don't know what broke this time. Whether the sound man's wheel fell off his cart or the wagon wheel fell off the buggy or the wing fell off the airplane, it's a job for special effects.

Another thing is that, when you're in the preproduction meetings, first they start out grandly with big ideas—"Boy, we're going to do the best picture in the world." Then in come the money people and they start cutting and chopping. There's a squeeze here and a squeeze there, and you get out on the set and there are some things you can't do the way you wanted to do them. We can usually sneak them in there somehow, and solving those kinds of problems gives you a nice feeling.

INTERVIEWER: *A lot of techniques, such as making snow or rain, are pretty routine, aren't they?*

ARBOGAST: They're routine with the materials and equipment, to a certain extent, but every time you get to a location, you have new problems. Finding the source of water for a rain job is usually a problem, as are the wind and the weather, the neighborhood, the light, the dark, trying to light the rain. Whatever it might be, every time you go out on the set to do rain, dust—those things—you're going to be in trouble because it will never work routinely. Whenever you do something like that, you know you're going to be the bottom man on the totem pole. Everybody's mad at you because you got dust in the equipment, you got them all wet, you got snow in their eyes, or they hate the smoke because it stinks. You're never a hero when you do any of those jobs.

INTERVIEWER: *What kind of exotic locations have you been to?*

ARBOGAST: We've worked in England, Hawaii, Mexico, Canada, the East Coast, the South Coast. When we worked on *The Thing* with John Carpenter, I thought it was great when we flew by helicopter into the big ice fields out of Juneau, Alaska, a couple of hundred miles back in. We stayed right in a scientific ice station. We slept in sleeping bags in Quonset huts. We shot all of the opening scenes out there. That was pretty exotic; we had a great time. When the sun was shining we'd film, and when it got dark or there were whiteouts we'd go and eat.

The ice station set was built near Stewart, British Columbia. We were actually right on the edge of a big glacier there. We were way out. It took two hours every morning to get from the hotel up to the location in old buses. We drove up on a mining road, and the drivers of the buses would have to be in constant radio contact with the big ore trucks: The trucks would be coming down this solid-ice road lickety-split, and we'd have to get out of the road. So every eighth of a mile or so the bus drivers would have to call in. It was a constant white-knuckler every day, two hours up and two back. Unbelievable.

INTERVIEWER: *Did you bring your trucks up there?*

ARBOGAST: Yes. I have a picture of my truck, and you can only see it through a little hole in all this snow; it was completely covered in snow. Oh, boy, what a mess that was. We brought up our wind machines, all of our explosives, all of our mortars. We blew up the whole village—a tremendous, tremendous explosion—all in twenty-below-zero weather. We certainly earned our money on that one!

As far as the nicest places to work, I like the Gulf Coast, Alabama, the Florida Panhandle. I like the South—the people, the mood, the weather.

INTERVIEWER: *So you're away from home quite a lot.*

ARBOGAST: We've been away on location as long as ten months. Sometimes we'll be just finishing one picture and starting another one. We try not to do that; we try to space them out.

INTERVIEWER: *When you're away for so long, do you fly back for visits?*

ARBOGAST: The family usually goes with us. My kids have gone to school in quite a few places—Hawaii, England—pretty much all over. Some of them liked it and some of them didn't. Whenever I said we were taking off again they'd get a bit upset, but when we were there it was OK. Now that they're older, when we get together we remember those times, and I think they had a pretty good time. At least they're a little more broad-minded. They know there are other kinds of people in the world.

INTERVIEWER: *What is the most exciting part of this work to you?*

ARBOGAST: Well, in most lines of work, if you build something, you very seldom get to see it, even when it's finished. The plumbers, electricians, and other subcontractors who work on a hotel, for example, can drive by the hotel and say, "I worked on that," and it's great, but that's it. With film, we get to see our work on film and everybody in the world gets to see it. That's nice.

And it's easier to build a prop than it is to build a house. You don't have to worry about all the building codes and all the plumbing. You just have to build it so it looks good. Nobody has to know what's behind it. It's a really quick way to get rewards. Once the word is go, you build like crazy. Nine months may sound like a long time, but it isn't. In nine months or a year you've done your thing and you can go to the movies to see what you've done.

And it helps if people like it. The greatest thing is to work on a film that is a success.

INTERVIEWER: So you think film's main role is to provide an audience with good entertainment?

ARBOGAST: Good entertainment, I think that's what everybody's looking for. I don't know how I could ever be a producer, because about the time I start thinking that I know what the public wants, something totally different comes out and they just go crazy for it. It's like going to the race track—it's anybody's guess. If you did know the answer you'd be the richest guy in the world. It's tough. I've worked on some movies I've thought were going to be the greatest movies of all time and yet they were received as mediocre.

"On the set, whenever anything goes wrong, somebody is always hollering for the special-effects man."

We have been really lucky. I can honestly say we've never worked on any really bad films. And I've never worked with any bad people. I think that's what has enabled me to keep my enthusiasm. I've known some people in the movie business who have gotten slapped down a few times, had raw deals, and lost interest.

INTERVIEWER: What sort of things do you like to do when you're not making films?

ARBOGAST: We've got our small ranch here. And we like to travel and camp. We like to pack with the horses. We do about whatever we have time for. We have dune buggies. We have boats. We have more toys than we could ever play with. We like to ride the horses right out of here. We can spend two days on the trail from our house. We're right on the national forest, so we'll never be totally encroached on, as long as I live anyway.

What I look forward to now is to have more free time. And I'd like to spend it outdoors. The house is just a place to sleep and eat as far as I'm concerned. From early morning, I'm outside.

I used to like to spend a lot of time working in the shop. But I get enough of that working on the pictures. Now, after a project, I lock the door so I can't go in there.

We do a lot of entertaining here. It's fun for us when we have a lot of people come and stay for the weekend. We can barbecue and swim, and some of our friends like to ride.

INTERVIEWER: *Are most of your friends film people?*

ARBOGAST: No, I'd say fifty-fifty.

INTERVIEWER: *Is there anything that you really don't like about the film business?*

ARBOGAST: The hardest part about this business is the pressure. Nobody likes it, but we all work with it. You're always pressed for time. And what is happening nowadays is that they keep cutting down on preparation time. That's very hard.

Every day on a busy picture you never go to bed without thinking, Is it going to work tomorrow? or What can go wrong tomorrow? You never think about how great it can be; you're always worried about what's going to go wrong. Either something will go wrong with the gag itself or they will change the location or the angle of the shot. Something will always change when it's a pressure situation. Very seldom does it ever just work.

And I used to thrive on the pressure; I used to be able to work sixteen hours a day and love it. I still do it sometimes, but the pressure's not so much fun anymore. I think that's just the way it goes getting older; we're all in the same boat.

One bad thing that's happening now is the liability. It's incredible—all the lawsuits and everybody suing each other. For a special-effects man to be liable for everything is insane. You are in the most vulnerable spot of any job in the world. Every fire, every explosion, every car crash we rig is a gag, and a gag is a trick, and a trick is dangerous. There's always room for a mistake. Now, everyone is so anxious to point a finger at someone; that's taken a lot of the fun out of it. It's terrible. These days you have to go in with a whole legal system in front of you before you can take a project.

INTERVIEWER: *What would you like to see happen in the future?*

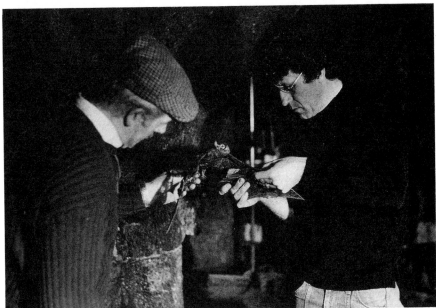

Roy Arbogast at work: (above top) "burning down a house;" (above) adjusting a vampire bat puppet for Dracula.

ARBOGAST: I would just like to see it stay busy. There are some studios that make a lot of fast, schlock movies, often with unqualified crews. They are creating a lot of bad material and a lot of bad feelings among filmmakers. It used to be, if not prestigious, a nice business to be in—a lot of good, talented people, and it was fun to make a good movie. Now some of these companies are trying to make movies like they're on a production line. They don't allow you to get involved in a good way. You're fighting for your money, you're fighting for your time, fighting for your crews, and you're fighting not to be sued. That's awful.

> *"Basic special effects are pretty old. . . . I hate to say it, but we're no great pioneers."*

INTERVIEWER: *What do you suggest to young people who want to do mechanical effects?*

ARBOGAST: That's a tough one. You just have to force your way in, I guess. It's a lot different now. When I started as a prop maker, the union was very strong in those days. The prop maker didn't even pick up a rain stand, for example. It took me twelve years to get my special-effects card. You need perseverance. It's a lot easier nowadays to get in than it was when I started.

INTERVIEWER: *Is there anything they can study?*

ARBOGAST: For mechanical special effects, get a good mechanical background. You should have an idea of what looks good artistically. You need to be able to watch a movie and understand what a mechanical-effects person does and understand, from the ground up, what it takes. One person does not do it. You need artists, sculptors, mold makers, and the people who do the mechanics, the plastics. You need to have a broad knowledge of the mechanical end of it.

The special effects—wind, rain, fire, and smoke—that can come later. To learn how to do those things, you have to be there and learn by doing it.

The way most people get in is by being pretty much qualified in one field or another, by being a good machinist, good with electronics, sculpting, or model making. Once you get in, you learn what can be done and what has to be done, and you go from there.

INTERVIEWER: *Are there any new technological developments that help your work?*

ARBOGAST: There are, but mostly in materials, and some of the electronics. They make your life a little easier, but basic special effects are pretty old. We saw an old Chaplin movie the other night, *The Gold Rush*, and it had fantastic special effects. That film was from the twenties, a long time ago. They had the set on a gimbal. They had wind machines and snow-making equipment. It was good. So I don't think we've come up with a lot that's new. I hate to say it, but we're no great pioneers. I think it's just the execution of it that's evolved.

The real advanced technology is in the opticals, the visual-effects end. On our end, our methods are still pretty basic—nuts and bolts and water hoses. There's not a lot you can do about that. I like it that way. I'm not really a high-tech person.

I appreciate all of these new developments, and if you could live to be 2,000 years old, you could do it all. But you can't, and for me this end of the business lets me work in the shop, go on locations, and work with the production companies, and that's about as big a bite as I can handle.

There will always be a mechanical-effects shop. They can use electronics and video or whatever, but they will always need what we do. And it's always fun to do it.

Dennis Muren

Dennis Muren was born in California in 1946. He attended Pasadena City College and California State University at Los Angeles, majoring in business and advertising.

Muren has made films since childhood, including an $8,000 feature, The Equinox, *completed when he was twenty. Between 1970 and 1975, he did effects work and was a stop-motion animator and cameraman for commercials, promotional films, and low-budget features.*

Since 1976, he has worked at Lucasfilm's special-effects facility, Industrial Light & Magic (ILM), and his work has appeared in Star Wars, Close Encounters of the Third Kind, Battlestar Galactica, The Empire Strikes Back, Dragonslayer, E.T., Return of the Jedi, Indiana Jones and the Temple of Doom, The Ewok Adventure, *and* Young Sherlock Holmes. *He also supervised the special effects on two films for Disneyland:* Star Tours *and* Captain Eo.

Muren is a four-time Oscar winner for visual effects, for the films The Empire Strikes Back, E.T., Return of the Jedi, *and* Indiana Jones and the Temple of Doom. *His Oscar nominations include* Dragonslayer *and* Young Sherlock Holmes. *He collected an Emmy award for his work on* The Ewok Adventure.

Muren lives in the San Francisco Bay area with his wife, Zara, a landscape architect, and their son, Gregory.

There's not much that tells you you've arrived at one of the most advanced motion picture special-effects studios in the world, just a street address. In fact, the company name on the door is a fictitious one, another illusion from these masters of sleight of hand.

Although it's quite tempting to think of ILM in terms of gleeful elves merrily toiling away on their flights of fantasy and deception, it really is an industrial facility, a film factory. In many respects, it's similar to the major studios of Hollywood's golden age. ILM carries on a broad range of activities under one roof, from creating stories and scripts, through producing special effects, to printing the film.

I talked with Dennis Muren in a conference room at ILM. He's a tall, gentle man with thinning blond hair. His features remind you of the Pillsbury dough boy he animated before coming to ILM.

INTERVIEWER: Tell me what happens when a project comes in the door.

MUREN: The way we have set up ILM, an effects supervisor like myself doesn't deal with the political side of the business. The scripts and directors come to our general manager, Warren Franklin. He weeds through a tremendous number of scripts. Occasionally something comes through that they actually have the money for, there's a director tied to it, and it looks like it's going to be a project worth doing. Then the individual supervisors will read the script to see if there is anyone who wants to work on the show. If there is, we'll take the job.

With some films, only one department may be involved, ten shots or less. On *The Money Pit*, for example, there was only one shot. On *Out of Africa*, there were only four shots of the train during the titles. It goes all the way up to a film like *Jedi*, which had nearly 400 effects shots. We have to make sure we can fit a show into our schedule. We have to turn down a lot of work just because everybody's busy.

INTERVIEWER: How many supervisors do you have?

MUREN: It varies. We have five at the moment. We started out with two, but as we did more and more shows, we felt that it was much better to have one person deal with one show, as opposed to one creative person trying to do three shows until something gives. Inevitably, he has two or three people under him who are doing the work anyway. This way, the person who does the work gets the credit for it or takes the blame for it. He gets the energy from the creative control that he has because it's really his show.

INTERVIEWER: *That arrangement probably frees you from a lot of the politics that can go on, or do you like to get involved in that?*

MUREN: I'm not at all interested in the politics of the business. I'm interested in creating images on film. I've been interested in this since I was a kid. I never wanted to be an agent or producer. It's always been the images.

INTERVIEWER: *What do you do after you've decided to take on a particular project?*

> *"The art is predicting what will work best for a particular shot and then imposing your style onto the shot and sequence."*

MUREN: There will be a meeting with the director, the producer, maybe a couple of other people who have been hired at that point—the cameraman, for example. I'll try to get the director's idea of what the film is. The effects supervisor has to figure out how the work is going to be done, work up a budget, try to get the job done on that budget or less, but he's really here to fulfill the job of the director. The director can't be here all the time and doesn't want to be. He just wants his work done and done on time. He wants all our shots to cut in smoothly with the rest of his film.

So it's important to understand what the director thinks and sees. I've worked on practically all of Steven Spielberg's effects films, and I have a good idea of the way he sees things. Now I'm starting a film with someone else, and I'm trying to get into his mind to see the way he sees things. That's what the meetings are for, as well as laying out how many shots we have and the technical questions: Are we traveling left to right in this? What sort of look should this environment be? How fast are these objects going? And so on.

From there we do the storyboards. Then the storyboards go back to the director for revision and then there will be a bigger meeting for more of the crew. We had a meeting a couple of days ago with twelve people.

INTERVIEWER: Do you ever change the script based on what you are able to do with the effects?

MUREN: Yes, but I try not to do that. We have so many resources available to us here; there are dozens of techniques for doing things. The trick is finding the best technique or the best combination. Or we may come up with something new. If I can't figure it out right away, it doesn't mean that with another three weeks of thinking, I won't be able to figure it out. So I try to delay, as much as possible, the process of deciding how we are specifically going to do it if I've got a gut instinct that there is a way.

INTERVIEWER: How important is it for you to use new techniques?

MUREN: If you fall back on the same old approaches, it shows up in the film. The movie comes out and the audience says, "Oh, I've seen that. I recognize that part from such and such a show." It wasn't the same part, but the same technique.

INTERVIEWER: How do you proceed from the storyboard phase?

MUREN: Well, after I have some rough idea of how we're going to do it, we'll work up a budget. From then, I'm kind of stuck on getting the job in for that amount of money, even though this department, later on, may not work on it at all and another one will. Those numbers then will go back to the executive producer, and they'll decide if they can afford that much for the effects in the show. Sometimes they say, "Great, go ahead." Other times they say they can't afford that much and they'll cut shots out.

Then there will be a contract drawn up for it and we'll start the show. And they'll start the live-action work at about the same time.

It's pretty dangerous to jump the gun too far on shooting our work. If we do, it shows up; something doesn't look quite right. And the effects work can often change even with the best intentions of the director, based on changes that occur with the live-action work. For example, we'll say, "We can do this sequence if the background is pretty dark." When they get on the set, spending $80,000 a day, they may find there is no way to make it dark back there. We have to adjust for those kinds of variables.

I try to delay shooting the special effects until the live action's in the can and we know what it looks like. Even better is to wait until there's a rough cut of the film. Then we can intercut our storyboards with the live action. Then we can really start our shooting. Up until that time, we'll be building models and sets, and so on.

INTERVIEWER: Are there any times that you go on the set while they are shooting the live action?

MUREN: Oh yes, always, whenever we will need to add something to the scene later on at ILM, like a giant creature or whatever. I'll make sure that I'm on the set when they're shooting because I need to see everything. I need to see what the movie looks like, how the director is directing, what the cameraman's lighting is like. It's stuff that you can't do over the phone and you can't really tell from the dailies.

Once we have agreed on how we are going to do a scene, I need to make sure that the live-action part is followed through as much as possible. If it isn't—like I said, when you get on the set and things change—that's when quick decisions need to be made. The director doesn't want to have to call somebody on the phone; he needs to know right then and there: Hey, what do we do now? What can we do to save it? That goes on all the time.

It can also be tough for cameramen and directors who haven't done many effects films to know how to shoot backgrounds for effects. If we're doing a shot with a matte painting and the actors are going to be in only a small part of the frame, we won't necessarily shoot the live action with the actors very small in the corner and the rest blacked out. For the best quality image, we shoot the actors full frame and then rear-project that into a small clear part of a matte painting done on glass. Sometimes people on the set wonder, Why is he doing it like that? Then they see the film and they see how it all comes together in the end.

INTERVIEWER: After you've got a certain scene designed and you know that it will be made up of, say, a miniature, a matte painting, and some live action, how do you decide the best way to combine those elements?

MUREN: I look at the style that the rest of the film is shot in. Many times it's a battle between the easy way to do something and the right way. As soon as you add movement to an effects shot, it makes it five or ten times harder. At that point a gutsy supervisor will say, "I don't want my shots to be these formally composed, painting-like shots. I want them to blend in with the film." When you decide you're going to move the camera as much as you can, right away that eliminates 90 percent of the available techniques.

Then I think it through and say, What's the equipment we have available? Maybe something doesn't exist and we'll have to build it. On *Indiana*

Jones, we needed to go through the mine tunnel miniature with lots of camera movement over long distances. If we had used the smallest camera we had here at ILM at the time, which was 9 inches wide, our models would have been 100 feet long. That's getting very expensive—stage space, lights, and a great chance of error. My thinking is, I don't want the money spent unless it shows up on the screen. I don't want it to be spent on bad takes. I don't want it to be spent on making something out of steel instead of wood. You don't see that stuff. Often, the minimum is the best. Then everybody's energy goes into the image that you see on the screen. For *Indiana Jones*, the prospect of making those 100-foot-long sets was just frightening. We could have actually done it, but we found there was a better way.

> *"If you look at a videotape of Star Wars... you can see these garbage mattes following the ships around."*

I came up with the idea for a little camera that was only 5 inches wide. That cut the sets down to 50 feet and allowed them to be made out of aluminum foil and paper. It was small enough and light enough to allow us to mold and shape the aluminum foil for the best-looking image. If it had been bigger and built out of heavier material, we couldn't have done that. We are always looking for new combinations of techniques to make shots look more realistic or to save money.

We came up with the Go-Motion system that we used on *Dragonslayer* about five years ago. In a nutshell, Go-Motion allowed Phil Tippett* to animate a dragon with motion control, but each frame of film had all the blurs a real animal would have, as if it were photographed in live action. We were using motion control applied to a puppet. We spent a week on just one shot in *Dragonslayer* to get what the director wanted. And now we are experimenting with rod puppets. We shoot the rod puppets against a blue screen with the guys right next to the puppets moving the rods by hand. As long as the rods don't have to cross over each other, you don't see them moving the puppets around. That allows us a lot of takes, whereas with Go-Motion, it takes longer to program.

We used this new technique on *Young Sherlock Holmes*, where the food comes to life—all the pastries. I had the pastry characters appear to walk,

---

* Stop-motion animator, formerly of ILM, now heads his own company.

seemingly on the ground. We did thirty takes a day. We could then go through all the takes and pick the best performance for each character. It's like shooting live action.

INTERVIEWER: *Was that the first time you used the rod-puppet technique?*

MUREN: Yes, but actually, we experimented with it on the speeder bike sequence on *Jedi*. That was when Phil first flirted with the idea of shooting in continuous time and grabbing the puppet with a rod and moving it around. Those puppets were on speeder bikes, so their hips were locked and their hands were locked. We just needed to be able to rock their heads and shoulders. And we could do that with a rod coming out of the puppet's head and a rod coming out of its back. The rods were matted out later on. We shot that sequence one frame per second.

I think the next step that someone takes—and I hope we're the ones to do it—will be a much more elaborate creature, something with the puppeteer's hand inside the head to do facial expressions, and lots of rods and mechanics to get an elaborate and realistic performance.

INTERVIEWER: *Human movement is incredibly subtle and complex.*

MUREN: It's real hard stuff to do. And you've got to have the right puppeteers who understand all of those complexities.

INTERVIEWER: *When do you show the director the results of your work?*

MUREN: We generally do sequences of shots. And we'll do some tests of one shot in a sequence and then show it to the director and his crew and start getting feedback from them—and from ourselves—as to what the stuff is looking like. This first shot establishes the look and feel of the sequence. If it's working, we'll begin the sequence. With a sequence, it usually involves the same technique used for each shot.

As we shoot, each shot goes to the editor. Hopefully, the editor has had experience with special effects. We have trouble with this, because it's difficult for editors who are used to dealing with tens of thousands of feet of film. We come along and give them a particular shot with only ten extra frames to work with on either end.

INTERVIEWER: *What's involved in getting your effects shots to cut in smoothly with the live action?*

MUREN: We must carefully duplicate the visual style of the film. The designs for models must match the full-sized sets. Camera moves should match, as should the lighting and the directorial style.

We generally ask for some reference clips of the live action preceding and following the effects shot. Just a single frame, so we can see things like the contrast and graininess of the image, the general colors, the sharpness of the image—not so much the motion but just the technical, Kodak quality of that image that we can then match our stuff to. Some editors will say, "Why do you need that? We're busy cutting the film. We don't have the time to give it to you." Others will say, "Sure, whatever you want."

INTERVIEWER: Is the collaborative nature of filmmaking something that you really enjoy?

MUREN: Yes, it's nice working with a lot of talented people who really care about what they are doing and are here because they want to be. Usually, the decisions come down to one or two people. There are times when someone wants to do something one way and I'll say, "No, I don't think that's the right technique for this." That person may be a specialist in their department, but I need to keep an overview. I need to know as much as I can about everyone and every department, which is difficult in a company of this size.

When I set up a crew, I take into account each individual's skill level, all their strengths and weaknesses. It's sort of like casting. I need the right person in a department for the particular project. The crew needs to have the same vision about a project because a lot of the decisions are based on gut instinct, and I can't be there all the time making decisions in every department.

INTERVIEWER: How do you keep track of everything?

MUREN: ILM could be working on four shows with a total of 250 shots at any one time. That requires an awful lot of good coordination and communication among all the different departments. That's really tough. We have troubles with that all the time. You know—priorities. Right now, a guy wants his show to get through the optical department, but optical wants to do a different show, because they're set up for it. Even with the best of intentions, it's real tough.

INTERVIEWER: You need a traffic cop here.

MUREN: Yeah, a number of them.

INTERVIEWER: OK. You've got your matte paintings done; you've shot your live-action plates; you've shot your miniatures against blue-screen. When do you bring everything together?

MUREN: As everything is being shot, it's being reviewed in dailies all the time. It may be a month or six months before all the elements of a shot are done. Those are approved, one at a time. If something was shot against blue-screen, we have to make sure it was the right exposure, that the lighting was right on all the elements of the shot, and that the lens angle at least seems correct, so that when it all goes together it will look like one shot, not a combination of separate shots. These special effects also have to go into a real-world situation, so we are always reminded that there are certain laws of nature we have to follow.

After a take is picked as a good one, if an element has extraneous material around it, like puppet rods, it goes to the animation department. They make a garbage matte and get rid of that stuff. Then the shot will go into optical. They will do a black-and-white composite that will go to the editor and be cut into the film.

"I got a still camera and shot stills of little spaceships and little plastic dinosaurs."

So very early on, the director and his crew are seeing the actual elements, at least in black and white. When that's OK, we'll go on and do an actual color comp of it. By that time, we can see if it's going to work. But at that point there usually aren't very many surprises. We've been doing this for so long, we can usually catch things earlier on.

INTERVIEWER: If there's an art to this business, it must be in that knack of knowing when something is right.

MUREN: Yes, the art is predicting what techniques will work best for a particular shot and then imposing your particular style onto the shot and sequence. I don't know if you can learn that from studying techniques or studying filmmaking and directing. If you want your effects shot to work and not stand out as an effects shot, you'll worry about it enough and you'll figure out a way to do it.

If I'm trying for an image or motion I've never seen before, I'll need to make sure the crew is working at their best and understands what I'm going for. This can mean they may have to do something in an unorthodox way. Some people don't like that, because they can't visualize the end result as being worth it. But after seeing the first shot or two, they understand.

And I'm not only talking about a shot that is going to work in the screening room; I'm talking about one that will work in the movie. Those are two different things. A shot can look great in the screening room, out of context. But when you plug it into a movie and the contrast is off a little bit, or it's grainy, or the movement changes, it's going to stand right out. I'm always thinking about that end product, putting myself in the audience's place. That's a whole different mind-set than the technical one that has to figure out how to do the effects. There are really two different sides of the brain that I am using all the time.

INTERVIEWER: *How do you keep up with what's going on in the business?*

MUREN: We see stuff. We're always seeing the effects films when they come out. We try and keep track of who's doing the good work. We haven't seen much coming out of other countries, except England. England does some real good effects work.

Some people who work here also work at the effects places in L.A., so everyone usually knows the techniques that everyone else is using.

INTERVIEWER: *When does your involvement with a film usually end?*

MUREN: It goes through the release printing. We've got to be there when the release prints are made, to make sure the color timing on our sequences cuts in and really matches.

All our opticals are done to a certain printing light. So it's important for our stuff that the lab doesn't get too creative in the release printing of the film. That happens; stuff can fall totally apart if there isn't someone there watching it. That's going on right now in video transfers of the Star Wars films. If you look at a videotape of *Star Wars* and the broadcast that was done on TV, you can see these garbage mattes following the ships around. That's because somebody was not watching the transfer. Our film stocks were never designed to be printed that bright. If they need to make these films brighter to show on TV—and I'm not sure that they do—do we need to comp our stuff brighter? And then print down a little for theatrical? We're figuring this out now. It may be something we have to start doing.

INTERVIEWER: *Where does your interest in special effects come from?*

MUREN: I don't know, but I've been interested in it since I was about seven. I think I saw *The Thief of Baghdad* and *The War of the Worlds,* and they just really knocked me out. I got a still camera and shot stills of little spaceships and little plastic dinosaurs. I shot 8-mm movies of special-effects stuff all the time. Eventually, I got a better 8-mm, then a 16-mm camera.

I don't know what it is. I've just been fascinated by seeing something that I can't see in the real world. Seeing it on a big screen in the dark has a lot to do with it. That doesn't happen on TV.

Working at Lucasfilm has been wonderful. We get the pick of the best shows, with the best directors, the best editors, the best actors in them, the best scores, and the best sound effects. Our work is boosted by the incredible craftsmanship that surrounds it.

INTERVIEWER: Where did you get your training?

MUREN: I just learned as I went along. There was a group of us in L.A. and we all got to know each other—Dave Allen, Jim Danforth, and others. We exchanged ideas on special effects while we were shooting our own little films. Some people worked at a place called Cascade doing effects for commercials. They did the most amazing commercial stuff with no money.

I wasn't interested in the film schools. They didn't teach special effects, and I didn't like the idea of somebody judging my work. I resented it then, even though it goes on all the time here now. I didn't think the professors were qualified to do that. I'd rather have my friends do it, have experienced people judge it. Instead, I majored in business and advertising through college. And that's been very useful.

Dennis Muren at work with a speeder-bike miniature from Return of the Jedi.

INTERVIEWER: *What ambitions do you have?*

MUREN: I've got a place in my heart for low-budget, independent films. I did one when I was eighteen, a feature, and there's something I really like about those projects. At some point I would like to do one or two of those again. Maybe I will say, "Hey guys, I'm going to take a few years off and try doing one of these little films." But it's one thing being a good effects man and another thing being a mediocre director, which could be the case!

But I enjoy effects so much, and these films are all so interesting, I don't want to stop doing these projects until they stop coming in. It doesn't look like it's going to happen, but my experience tells me it's got to. It's probably going to go on like this for another ten years. If you look at the ten top-grossing films, nine of them are effects films. But if I can't find something challenging in a project, I'm not going to want to do it. And, hopefully, the challenge will not be a little technical trick, but will involve something the audience can see.

> *"I've got a place in my heart for low-budget, independent films. I did one when I was eighteen."*

INTERVIEWER: *Do you have any ideas for making an independent film?*

MUREN: A few of us here have been kicking around the idea of doing a Vietnam film. But it's tough to raise the money when you're working all the time. And my wife and I just had our first baby a few weeks ago. That's a whole other part of my life that's just wonderful. I'm learning an awful lot that I think is going to be really applicable to storytelling and filmmaking later on.

Here at ILM, we are riding the crest of a cultural wave. Things change so much with what we're doing that it's hard to actually say, "A year from now, I want to be doing this." Because all of a sudden, some other project can come in from a Stanley Kubrick or someone, with a vision nobody ever even imagined! Something so challenging that you'd do anything to work on the show. That's where *Star Wars* came from. Those things can just pop up.

INTERVIEWER: *What do you think of synthetic imagery coming into film?*

MUREN: I've got a lot of faith in that. We did it with the stained glass man in *Young Sherlock Holmes*. It was a horror doing it! Hours and hours every day with guys who didn't understand film, and I didn't understand computers. But it allows you to make images you've never seen before.

INTERVIEWER: *Does your work tend to take over your life?*

MUREN: It used to be a problem before I was married. I was living in L.A., and this work was everything. L.A. has movie stuff everywhere. You go into any restaurant and somebody has a script in his back pocket and another guy's talking about a deal. But that kind of stuff is really just about making deals, not movies.

Since coming up here, I've been able to calm down and not spend as much time thinking about the work as I had been for the last twenty years. You could make a case that if somebody thinks about work sixteen hours a day, he's going to do twice as good a job as the guy who thinks about it eight hours a day. But you also have to think about it in terms of quality time, and knowing yourself well enough to not go on tangents—to streamline your thinking, make decisions, and move ahead rapidly on them. That comes with experience. Also, an outside life gives you ideas and a perspective that you can bring into your work.

INTERVIEWER: *Does a film's content ever affect your work?*

MUREN: There was a film in here a few years ago that some people here wouldn't work on. They didn't agree with its theme. But that usually doesn't happen. The front office turns down films that we feel ILM shouldn't be involved in for a number of reasons.

But I wish there were some way we could do more adult-oriented projects. It would be great to work on something that was going to have an awful lot of social value, some kind of social stimulation.

Then again, you can be working on something like a *Star Wars* that seems like it's just going to be a lot of fun but ends up being a cultural change. If you get carried away by thinking about what is best for you, you could miss out on something that nobody saw coming.

Chris Evans

SPECIAL EFFECTS
MATTE PAINTING

*C*hris Evans was born in Bremerton, Washington, in 1954. After a childhood in Brightwaters, New York, he attended UCLA as a fine arts major. He received his BFA in 1977, graduating summa cum laude and Phi Beta Kappa, and earned his MFA in 1980.

He pursued landscape and portrait painting after college until he saw The Empire Strikes Back. *What struck him was the artwork in the film. Evans thought it would be wonderful to exchange the solitary life of the artist working in his garret for the collaborative involvement of creating a motion picture.*

Evans is now the head of the matte painting department at Industrial Light & Magic (ILM). Matte painting remains one of the more arcane and misunderstood of the filmmaker's arts, so I was eager to hear Evans's elucidation of his work.

Chris met me in the lobby and led me to the matte painting department, a series of windowless rooms on the second floor. He showed me around the place—the areas where the artists work and a storeroom full of huge paintings.

We settled into a couple of chairs in Evans's work area. A painting in progress of San Francisco Bay stood on his easel; storyboard panels and production sketches lined the walls; a large mirror, slide projector, and small cabinet containing paints, a palette, brushes, and various other art materials stood close at hand.

Since coming to ILM, Evans has completed more than 100 paintings for films including E.T., The Dark Crystal, Star Trek II, Return of the Jedi, Indiana Jones and the Temple of Doom, Starman, The Neverending Story, Star Trek III, Enemy Mine, The Ewok Adventure *and* Ewoks II, Star Trek IV, Cocoon, *and* Golden Child. *He received an Emmy Award for his matte painting work on* The Ewok Adventure.

INTERVIEWER: A lot of people dream about working in the movies. How did you go about making it a reality?

EVANS: I naively assumed that I could simply call up George Lucas on the telephone and offer my services. I found out that not only was he not listed, but his company's number wasn't listed. They were about as easy to get in touch with as the Pentagon. Through a lot of persistence, I finally found out where in Hollywood they were located.

I walked in the door with some slides of my paintings. They sent them to ILM in San Rafael, and I was told that if I wanted to work there, I'd have to move to San Francisco, which sounded all right with me. I walked in the door of ILM for an interview, not even knowing what a matte painting was. All I knew was that I could paint landscapes well enough to be able to work in the business. When I was given a tour of the studio, I realized that I had been fooled by fifty matte paintings in *The Empire Strikes Back*! I was totally flabbergasted.

At that point, I really wanted to work there, after seeing the extent of what was going on technically and artistically. They offered me a job, and the first show I worked on was *Dragonslayer.* I did about twenty background paintings for that film.

INTERVIEWER: What does your work here at ILM entail?

EVANS: In addition to painting, I schedule the workload, read scripts, and, along with the director and the storyboard artist, try to determine what the shots should look like. On a good special-effects production, they'll call us in from the start. We'll read the script and serve as consultants, first of all.

Can it be done, and if so, how can it be done? We help decide whether a painting or a miniature or something else might be needed, and how expensive it would be.

INTERVIEWER: *When you start on a new film project, what process do you go through?*

EVANS: All matte paintings evolve from ideas. The director and producer who are trying to get a film made will come to ILM to see if the effects they have in mind can be done and if they are going to be costly. The filmmaker is trying to tell a story through a series of moving images, and there are certain images that can't be photographed in the real world, images from the imagination that have to be generated in a special way. They must be created by some kind of an illusion. That's what the director comes to us for.

INTERVIEWER: *So the matte paintings help bring imaginary scenes to life?*

EVANS: Yes. The important thing in filmmaking is storytelling. When you're telling a really fantastic story, you have to rely on something extraordinary, like a series of paintings. The one filmmaker who has done that more than anybody else is George Lucas. For instance, in the beginning of *Return of the Jedi*, the setting is established in space—star fields and planets. But since we can't go into space, we paint a planet surface, a big curve; the planet's down there. Off in the distance is the Deathstar. The next shot is flying in toward the Deathstar. That's followed by another effects shot, which is a painting—a close-up of the surface of the Deathstar. It's totally a painting with a miniature spaceship flying in. That cuts to another painting, another matte shot, of the interior of the Deathstar, where the shuttle has landed. Darth Vader is walking out to the troops who are standing there waiting for him. That cuts to an even tighter shot of him walking right down the aisle between the troops. So I think there are something like six or seven matte shots combined with blue-screened miniatures right in a row at the very beginning of *Jedi* to establish this extraordinary setting for the movie.

Most of the time we painted settings, but sometimes, as you can see at

> *"I naively assumed that I could simply call up George Lucas on the telephone and offer my services."*

the beginning of *Jedi*, we painted the ranks of Imperial storm troopers instead of hiring extras. Only a few of them were live actors—the ones in the foreground.

The more mundane tasks of the matte artist include minor modifications of a location, like taking a billboard or telephone pole out of the scene. If the film company can save a lot of money by staying on the back lot, you can paint in mountains in the distance, or the top floor of a building.

So basically our job is to help the director tell his story through painting something that he can't otherwise photograph. To me, it's one of the really fun jobs involved with filmmaking. It's always a challenge to visualize something that hitherto has only been imagined. The exciting part of the matte artist's job is bringing the imagination to "reality."

INTERVIEWER: Of all the scenes in a film, how is it decided which will be matte paintings?

EVANS: There are two considerations. First, a scene may be too fantastic to even exist on the Earth—the science fiction genre. Or it may simply be impractical to build a set or to go to a location. You might not want to go to Ireland for just a few shots in a movie because it costs so many hundreds of thousands of dollars to get a crew to Ireland. So you film it off in the green hills of California, and you hire a matte artist to paint in some scenes of Irish villages and stone walls, or the castle on the hill in the distance, things like that. You could, in fact, create Ireland in California.

While filming *Indiana Jones and the Temple of Doom*, they went to India, and for some cultural reason, they were not allowed to film in the temple that they went there to shoot. They did take still photographs, so we reconstructed it through matte paintings.

INTERVIEWER: So you look at the script and decide which elements are going to be shot live, which are going to be miniatures, and which are going to be paintings.

EVANS: Yes. Basically, we know that things that move cannot be painted. Things that move are going to be miniatures.

And if a change of perspective is required in a given shot—let's say that one shot calls for you to drive down the street in a futuristic city, and the perspective is constantly changing—you can't do that with a painting. Certain parts of a painting can move. We have ways of making painted clouds float in the sky, for example.

We go through the script and analyze it to see how we can do each shot. A lot of the shots are combinations of effects—a painting with live action and a miniature passing in front of that.

INTERVIEWER: *Who is involved in the process of deciding how the shots will be done?*

EVANS: Ideally, the matte artist should be working very closely with the director and the production designer. The matte artist can often help the production designer come up with the look of the film without having to build certain sets, thus solving a lot of problems. In the matte department we have the best idea of what we can do, how far we can push things, what kind of moves we can put into shots. Obviously, if we can give them a better deal by redesigning a shot or canceling a shot, we'll do that.

Concurrent with that, the director is working with a storyboard artist. He's blocking out action that he wants to see and deciding how it will integrate with the live-action part of the story.

We like the opportunity to show off our skills. We're always trying to come up with a glorious shot, but the story comes first.

INTERVIEWER: *Once all of these decisions have been made, what is the next step?*

EVANS: When we know what shots are going to involve matte paintings, we'll do a small color painting for every shot. In this way we can establish the look of the scene: we know what the colors are, what time of day it is, where the light is coming from, the contrast—what we are actually going to see in that scene. This is done even before any live action is shot.

Then, when the director goes out to shoot the live-action parts of these effects scenes, he's got some idea of what the rest of the scene is going to look like, how the effects are going to fit into it. During the principal photography, there are often practical considerations that make the scenes a little different from our sketches.

Before we do the actual painting, we'll look at what it cuts in with—what the lighting is, the angles, and all that information. We use that to help us judge all the specifics of how we're going to match the painting with the live action.

INTERVIEWER: *Do you ever contribute to the design of a film?*

EVANS: Most of the ideas of what the film will look like have been established by the director working with the storyboard artist. Our job is really the nuts and bolts of making it look believable. When we are fortunate, we can help come up with the ideas, too; we share that visualization process with the art director and the storyboard artist.

In *Star Trek IV,* as in the other *Star Trek* films, some of the action takes place in the San Francisco of the future. It's really fun for me, living in the San Francisco of the present, to not only imagine what it is going to look like in the twenty-third century, but to also visualize that scene for the audience, so that people actually feel like they are there in the San Francisco of the future.

> *"...at the beginning of* Jedi, *we painted the ranks of Imperial storm troopers instead of hiring extras."*

The question for us was, What will the city look like in the future? But we also wanted to let the audience know that it is still San Francisco. We decided to keep the Transamerica pyramid as a very distinct landmark, as well as to add some things that are futuristic. My idea was to add a bunch of Space Needle–type buildings, like those in Seattle, Montreal, and Dallas. So the scene of San Francisco is something we invented.

INTERVIEWER: *When you do a painting, how much room do you have for the play of your own creativity and imagination—in* The Empire Strikes Back's *forest sequence of the Ewok village, for instance?*

EVANS: Well, in a real redwood forest there are so many branches that you really can't see very far. George wanted the Ewoks to live in an extensive village going on for perhaps half a mile, with dozens of little huts. Then Ralph McQuarrie did some early illustrations about what things would look like. When they actually built the huts on the set in England, it looked quite a bit different.

So we took all the information, including photos of real forests, and we composed a megaforest of the imagination that would enable you to look off into the distance and see lots of houses. It was up to us to make the ramps and bridges between the trees and the hanging vines and all of that. We had four seconds of film time to work within and one image that had to cut in with the film and tell the story. But within that, there was still room for a lot of imagination.

INTERVIEWER: *What do you do to hide the line between the two elements of the picture, between the live-action image and the painting?*

EVANS: Well, if you're a good matte artist, no one will ever see the line. The images will perfectly match in color and tone, right up to the joint between the painting and the live-action plate. We achieve that in our lineup process. Whatever our live action is, we put a clip of that into the camera that's going to photograph the painting, put a lamphouse on that camera, and then project the image out through the lens of the camera to the easel where the painting is set up. We draw on the painting exactly where the live action fits, and then we do the painting around that area. When the finished painting is put in front of the camera, it's already lined up.

One important thing about the matte department, as with all special-effects departments at ILM, is that visual artists (painters, sculptors, animators) are working hand in hand with cameramen. In the matte department the important thing is not only that we paint these images but that we get them on film. Our painters are Frank Ordaz, Caroleen Green, Sean Joyce, Mike Pangrazio, and I. The cameramen we work with are Craig Barron, Wade Childress, and Randy Johnson.

How we combine the painting with the live action is really dependent on the cameraman's art. Craig Barron, whom I work with very closely, is really brilliant in helping to determine how a shot can be photographed and then combined with the painting. Part of our process is designing how the painting will blend perfectly with the live-action plate. Once we've determined how a shot can be done, the practical application of that in photography is really up to Craig.

INTERVIEWER: *What do you paint on?*

EVANS: Usually we paint on 2½- or 4-by-6-foot sheets of glass or Masonite. We paint on glass so that certain areas of the scene can be scraped away, leaving a clear glass window into which we can project live action. The live action is exposed in the photography to balance with the painting.

Back in the early days of Hollywood, the twenties and thirties, trick photography began to be a practical tool. If you had a scene in an old western town, you could easily get a guy on a horse, put them on the back lot at Fox or MGM, and then paint the western town on a sheet of glass that stood between the camera and the guy on the horse. And you could paint it so that it appeared that the town was behind him, over his head. This was known as the glass shot.

All special effects, including matte painting, started as trick photography. The only practical problem with glass shots is that the sunlight falling on the scene and on the painting is always changing. The time it takes to do a good painting makes it difficult to complete one under these changing conditions. The practical considerations of lighting and timing are too delicate these days.

INTERVIEWER: *Tell me what technique you use to combine the painting with the film of the live action.*

EVANS: We use a whole variety of techniques. We use whatever process it takes to get a shot. Often we use the latent image, or original negative, process. In this process, a set is built on the studio back lot, or there is a location where the live action takes place. We line up the camera and the set so that the set corresponds with our design of the shot. We black out everything except the set area where the live action occurs and then photograph it. The only thing that is exposed on the film is the small area of live action. The rest of the picture is black, no exposure on the film. This is known as a latent image matte shot, because the image we've photographed remains latent on the undeveloped negative until we expose it to the finished painting. Then we develop the film and get the whole composite scene.

We also use rear projection, where you have a projector projecting the live action from behind the painting onto a clear window on the glass with the camera in front of the painting. In that case, the camera films the live action and the painting on separate passes.

We use front projection; this is where you have a front-projection screen and you're projecting an image through mirrors back to the camera. We sometimes give the film of the painting to the optical department and they combine it with the live action through their matting process. We have done foreground glass shots on occasion, in a controlled studio environment.

We also do multiplane shots, where different parts of the painted image are on separate pieces of glass. Sometimes miniatures are used in the multiplane shots, too.

INTERVIEWER: *What sort of paints do you use?*

EVANS: We primarily use acrylics and oils. I had never painted with acrylics until I got the job here. My whole background was oil painting. So I struggled with that for a while. With skies, we often use airbrush. A clear blue sky has to be flawless. But other areas can be much more loosely brushed in.

Also, you'll notice that in some of the paintings some of the greens are extremely intense. That's because green tends to drop out on film. It's what we call a fugitive color.

INTERVIEWER: *What makes a good matte painting?*

EVANS: It has to cut. Sometimes the tendency is to try to establish too much story information with it. Some matte paintings will have 50-mile visibility and incredible detail; you see every single element in the whole scene. You see the house where the guy lives, and off in the distance you see one thing and then in the foreground there's something else. You try to tell too much in one shot. That's a real weakness.

"We are synthesizing dream images...."

A well-designed matte shot will go right by the audience, no matter how awesome it really is. It should be integrated into the other images. You don't want to have a whole bunch of footage shot on the set, all medium shots and closeups, and then POW!—one big master shot of some immense vista, and then back into the studio footage. Everybody knows there's something funny going on, because it's not edited correctly.

I've learned through experience that composition is very important in a matte shot. A shot that comes on for four or five seconds is supposed to say something, give some information to the audience. If you try to throw in too much information, they don't know where to look. Even if you've rendered it in detail to perfection, it still doesn't work. So in the composition we try to focus the viewer's attention on the key elements in the frame. We use a lot of the devices or conventions that artists have used through the centuries: centering, diagonals, putting something in silhouette against the light, or focusing the light on something. For instance, in baroque paintings, if there are a bunch of figures in a room, they would at times put a dark figure in the foreground, in silhouette, to give a sense of depth to the scene, so you get the feeling you're looking past the figure to the light in the background.

Or we'll shift the perspective. I find that if you are looking up or down at something, it gives you a different sense of the thing. A spaceship looming overhead conveys the idea of something large better than if you are looking down on it as if it were a toy.

We realize that not all of our shots look real. If they look fairly credible and the audience enjoys them, that's what we're looking for. In *Star Trek*, if the shots are realistic and semibelievable, people will enjoy the movie. I don't think too many intelligent viewers are going to say, "That looks incredible. They really filmed it on Vulcan." But we're always trying. That's our goal, to make something as believable as possible.

INTERVIEWER: Does a matte painting have to contain a lot of detail in order to be believable?

EVANS: That's an interesting thing about matte painting. The public often assumes that a matte painting is like a giant photograph created by a matte artist. A lot of things in matte paintings are really not that photographically detailed.

The average matte shot is on the screen for three to five seconds. In that amount of time, the person in the audience will tend to look toward the center of the screen and their eyes will catch where the action is. Things off in the periphery don't have to be rendered exactly. A good example is the shot in *Jedi* in the forest. The shot comes on and the audience looks at the action. The artist doesn't have to render every single leaf. With a fairly good-sized brush, you can use it in a certain way to create patterns or textures that only suggest foliage or rocks or clouds or whatever. As long as you are giving the right impression of the forest at a particular time, that's all that really counts.

It's possible to detail something so perfectly, yet in the filming process the contrast changes and a lot of detail drops out and the overall impression is unrealistic. I call the technique of matte painting "calculated impressionism," as opposed to realism. Professionally, a matte artist is more of an illusionist-craftsman than an artist who's interpreting life through his own creative vision.

INTERVIEWER: This is a complete turnaround for you. As a fine artist, the painting is everything. All the attention is focused on it. But here, your object is to be invisible.

EVANS: Yes. Anonymity is the sign of the matte artist's success. What really makes an individual artist an artist is his style. But if you are watching a film and a shot comes up that has the style of a particular artist in it, you know it's not real and all of a sudden the whole illusion is shattered.

The good matte artist puts aside his individual style to create an impersonal illusion. There are probably a dozen good matte artists working in this country today. We have five artists here in this department. If you really look hard, you can see the individual styles, but when the shots come on the screen, they all look like actual scenes, not artists' interpretations. We're working in the film business here. The painting is not the finished artwork; the finished artwork is the image on the screen. That's the only thing we're working toward.

My background was as an illusionistic painter. Everyone looking at a painting realizes that they're not looking at reality. They suspend this disbelief to enjoy the image of the landscape or whatever it is. In film, people are still looking at a series of illusions. Everything in the whole film is an illusion, including the characters. Those characters don't even exist. The conversations they have don't really exist. Nothing in a film is ever real; it's *all* a fiction. Using paintings to fool the eye is just another aspect of that fiction.

INTERVIEWER: *Do you like the collaboration involved in filmmaking?*

EVANS: The great thing about this job, for an artist, is that instead of working in a very solitary way, the artist is working with 100 talented and creative people at ILM. It's a great experience. As a supervisor, I am not only involved with the 100 or so people who are working here on special effects—the miniatures, the camera work, the stage, and all—but also work with

Chris Evans conjures up a distant world with brush and paint.

directors and producers. This is a great experience. You really get a feel for how your work fits in with the whole film industry.

INTERVIEWER: *Does your work ever get you out of the studio here?*

EVANS: We often go out on location to film scenes we know are going to involve our paintings, usually during the principal photography. On *Enemy Mine,* an American–German project, we went to Munich and to the Canary Islands. We filmed the live action taking place around a volcano, but the director did not want a blue sky; it wasn't alien enough. So for a number of shots, we went to the location and matted out the sky and replaced it later with a painting—the result was an orange, more fantastic-looking sky.

> *"In a way, you can compare filmmaking to the cultural role a cathedral had in the Middle Ages."*

We go to any location where we have to shoot a plate, any real scene that one of our paintings will have to match. We're going to Seattle soon to shoot a couple of plates for a film called *Harry and the Hendersons.* When we go to a location, we speak with the director: "Is this the angle you want? The right time of day?" and so forth. We set our matte, the actors come in, the action takes place. We shoot it, put it in the can, bring it back to the studio, line it up, and add the painting. When the painting is nearing completion, we bring the director in and ask, "Is this what you want? Do you want the building on the left bigger? Do you want more clouds in the sky?" and so on. We work that way until the image is what the director wants and it integrates right into the surrounding footage.

INTERVIEWER: *When do you leave a particular film project?*

EVANS: The other special effects and the film-editing process also take place while we do our work. We usually work right up to the deadline prior to the release date for the film. We try to refine paintings. If something doesn't look exactly real, we try to figure out what needs to be changed. So we often paint and repaint things.

INTERVIEWER: *How long does it take to do one of these paintings?*

EVANS: It takes an average of about two weeks to do one of our matte paintings. Depending on the shot, it can take anywhere from two days to a month. I wish I could show you more paintings, but most of the work has recently been archived.

INTERVIEWER: *What do you use mirrors for?*

EVANS: We use them a lot. When you look at a painting in a mirror, it gives you an entirely different perspective on the painting. It flops your tendency to read things left to right, thus giving you more of an objective view of your work.

INTERVIEWER: *What about the slide projector?*

EVANS: For example, the boat in that painting—I could spend weeks trying to make it up out of my head, so I'll just take a picture of a boat and project it onto the painting and paint from that.

INTERVIEWER: *Do you think synthetic imagery, computer-generated imagery, might put you out of business someday?*

EVANS: No. We're already in the business. On *Star Trek II*, I worked on the first computer-generated motion picture image, which was the Genesis effect. They used fractal imagery to create that whole scene. When the camera pulls back to show the whole planet, we see the weather patterns on the planet. And I painted that on the Pixar computer. But it was used as graphic imagery, as seen on a computer monitor on a spaceship in the film. It had that grainy quality.

Young Sherlock Holmes was really the first time that high-resolution computer-generated imagery was used in a film. Here again, collaborating with the computer-graphics division and the effects supervisor, Dennis Muren, and the director and the writer who had conceived of the stained glass man jumping out of the window was a great experience. It was an incredible fusion of our different disciplines.

INTERVIEWER: *How was that sequence done?*

EVANS: The stained glass man was created through the computer, working from the storyboards and production designs. Once that image was set— the lighting on him, et cetera—I designed the entire stained glass window around him.

Two windows were designed. One was the window that the priest first looks at, the "before" window with the priest and the knight standing there. He looks at it and thinks nothing of it. He goes back to lighting candles. Then, he hears a tinkling of glass and he looks up again. This time, we see the "after" window and the priest in the window has fallen and the knight is standing menacingly above him. Then, the knight jumps out of the window.

I had the job of designing the windows. I got a lot of different books on stained glass and created an imaginary stained glass window. It had to be bold enough so that you could see the character in it. Usually, stained glass is too broken up so that, at a distance, it's hard to tell what's going on.

My painting for the stained glass window was digitized, scanned into the computer. With the Pixar computer painting system, I modified the painting electronically to match exactly the stained glass knight that had been created previously, making sure to capture the dirtiness of the glass and other different qualities. That was then tilted in perspective mathematically by the computer to fit the angle that the priest is looking up at.

Once that was done, I did a conventional painting of the part of the church around the window, the arches and stonework. That painting was then combined optically with the computer-generated image of the window.

INTERVIEWER: Do you see yourself working exclusively with a Pixar-like system someday?

EVANS: Definitely, if we had a very high-resolution system. There's a lot we could do with that. It would improve our matting technique. And we would be able to collage things electronically. If we wanted a certain sky, we could pick one and scan it into the picture.

But right now and in the immediate future, the efficiency of just painting something, photographing it, and combining it with our traditional methods is the best way to go.

Another problem is scale. We need a certain amount of detail. If you are working on a large painting, you can walk up, put in your detail, then step back and see the whole thing. If you are working on a small video monitor, you have to have the image blown up on the screen to see the detail, and even then you don't see the detail in relation to the whole. If we could work on 4-by-6-foot high-resolution video screens, that would be a pretty good thing.

Also, you're working with a luminous image, which can sometimes throw you off. So there are some technical and perceptual problems when working on a video monitor. But these things can be worked out. I see that through computers and electronics the matte painting process can really be changed.

INTERVIEWER: Do you still do any landscape painting on your own?

EVANS: The film business can be very consuming as you go from production to production. It seems there's always so much work to do, and it has to be done in a very short amount of time. You're busy all the time.

Yet I have made it a point to keep my own artistic and creative ideas flowing. Over the last six years, I've been working on a number of paintings. I've had shows of my personal paintings in San Francisco, L.A., and New York. Matte painting can be very satisfying work for an artist, but you are always fulfilling a filmmaker's ideas for the telling of a story. You are using your skill and your craft, but you aren't always using your deeper creative vision.

INTERVIEWER: *Filmmaking is a collective art.*

EVANS: The filmmaking process is very social and public—there are so many people involved. It's a communal activity, coordinating many individuals' different ideas and talents. When it's coordinated well, you have an amazing result. It's fascinating when you find out just how many people, all with such different technical skills, come together to make a film. Each person plays a very small role in relation to the large scale of the picture.

"The process of matte painting as a storytelling tool in filmmaking is not used as much as it could be."

In a way, you can compare filmmaking to the cultural role a cathedral had in the Middle Ages. The cathedral in the Middle Ages was the focus of much of the creative thought—the sculpture, the architecture, the stained glass, the painting, the tapestry—and the skills of that time: the masons, the architects, the stained glass men, the guys who melted the lead, the guys who hauled the concrete, the weavers. And the general public would come into this building and they would be told these stories from the Bible. They'd hear these stories spoken by the priest. The values, the ideas, and the thoughts of the time were focused into this aesthetic environment.

Now, think of the movie theaters of today: This is where people come to have stories told to them through the work of all the various artists and through skills that work together to produce a motion picture. If you get into the imagery of the cathedral, you've got the gargoyles and the demons. That relates to the horror films, or to the frightening parts of films. You have Satan, and the damned falling, and then the angels. A lot of that involves the anthropological and cultural myths that are transformed in films like *Star Wars*. That would be a worthy term paper for an art history major.

I definitely see my role in filmmaking not simply as a cog in a big machine but as a participant in something that is very important.

307

INTERVIEWER: Yet it seems like you really enjoy being sequestered up here in your studio, away from all the activity downstairs.

EVANS: Yes, we definitely have to be. As an artist, one needs to concentrate and have a sense of solitude to get the work done.

INTERVIEWER: Is there anything about this business that really gets under your skin?

EVANS: Well, there definitely is always a time pressure involved. We are allocated the funds we need to do a certain shot, but there is a lot of pressure. At ILM, we're often doing effects for four or five movies simultaneously, and there are conflicting schedules for productions. You're trying to shoot plates, trying to design shots, trying to discuss things with directors, and also trying to paint, photograph, and finesse them so that the quality of the work is optimum. It can be like a three-ring circus. You're trying to be the best juggler in the world. At the same time, you're jumping a tiger through a hoop and being the ringmaster, too. As a supervisor, I sometimes have a hard time getting concentration time for more than half an hour at a stretch.

INTERVIEWER: Do you have any kind of daily routine?

EVANS: When we come in in the morning, we look at the film we shot the day before. It's been processed overnight. We look at composite tests between the paintings and the live-action plates to see how close our colors are getting and how the composition is looking. We look at the dailies with the rest of the crew, of their shots and our shots, to see how things are going. Then we paint, and at the end of the day, we again give the painting to the cameraman. That's our routine after the live action's been photographed.

In my position now, I am balancing a lot of the business, planning shots, going on location, talking with directors, and painting. During my first four years at ILM, I'd come in at 8:30 in the morning, stand in front of an easel, and paint until 7:00 at night, sometimes until my eyes would no longer focus.

INTERVIEWER: Do you see yourself moving into production design?

EVANS: No. Working as a matte artist, there's a certain completeness to what I do. I have a great sense of satisfaction in creating and finishing an image as you will see it in the theater. It's something I wouldn't get if my work were preparatory or a stepping-stone in the process. Off the end of my brush comes the final image that everyone is going to be looking at.

INTERVIEWER: What would you like to see happen in this business?

EVANS: The thing I want more and more is good-quality films to work on. You can put in your best efforts and create flawless matte paintings, but if the film is a bomb, you feel it was for naught.

The process of matte painting as a storytelling tool in filmmaking is not used as much as it could be. There are only a handful of directors who are aware of what can be done.

It tends to be a time-consuming, expensive process, but it can also open up many possibilities that are otherwise closed by practical considerations. In *Gone with the Wind*, there were 150 matte paintings. That's three times the amount that were in *Return of the Jedi*. They used the paintings for putting roofs on buildings, putting in a tree where they wanted a tree, adding some fallen soldiers off in the distance, little things like that. The matte painting was really integral to the whole process of making the film. It wasn't just a special, expensive shot.

INTERVIEWER: What do you enjoy most about your work?

EVANS: I enjoy being involved with filmmaking. I think film is *the* aesthetic means of communication in our society, in our world today. *Jedi* was translated into I don't know how many different languages and shown around the world.

Painting, in the fine art tradition, has really become something with a very limited audience—an elite group of collectors and museum goers. It's changing a little now with video and the big, public touring shows, and with books. But still, there's a certain social engagement with issues, a directness, an immediacy of communication, in film. I enjoy being involved with that.

In the history of art, there's a long progression from the earliest rudimentary symbols of objects or ideas, like hieroglyphics. Gradually they became more and more realistic. You go through the Middle Ages to the baroque period and the Renaissance, where you have incredible illusionism. The artists enjoyed fooling the eye with *trompe l'oeil* painting. It's always representing, through illusion, reality. In a way, filmmaking, and, specifically, the matte painting process, is the end of the line in this progression of Western art fooling the eye. With a painting, no matter how much it fools you, you are generally aware that it's a painting. Matte painting in film, because it's a luminous image with motion in it, totally fools the viewer into thinking it's actually reality, a hundred-percent reality. So, in this way, matte painting is the ultimate progression of illusionism in Western art. It's fascinating to think of it like that.

I read somewhere that art is a dream for people who are awake. We are synthesizing dream images through a combination of two-dimensional painted images and three-dimensional photographed images. Films can be thought of as dreams for people who are awake, and special-effects matte artists help make those dreams seem true.

Mike Fulmer

SPECIAL EFFECTS
MINIATURES

*M*ike Fulmer comes from a working-class background. Born during World War II in California's San Joaquin Valley, he grew up all over the country as a child in a military family. Making models has been a lifelong interest of Fulmer's. Before becoming involved in film at Lucasfilm's Industrial Light & Magic (ILM), he made museum-quality models for collectors for many years while working as an oil field welder. In the midsixties he did a stint with the Marines and served in Vietnam. As he talked, he brought to mind Jack Nicholson's character in Five Easy Pieces. But while Nicholson portrayed the drifter, the perpetual outsider at war with society, Fulmer has made a successful career in a competitive, creative profession.

The miniatures seen in motion pictures have probably failed to fool at least as many people as they have succeeded in tricking. It's an enormously difficult and at times a dangerous job, despite the reputation the model shop enjoys as being a kind of Santa's workshop.

Mike Fulmer directs a crew of dedicated model makers at ILM. He has been responsible for creating the miniatures seen *in many of the films to which ILM has contributed, including* Indiana Jones and the Temple of Doom, Return of the Jedi, E.T., Poltergeist, Cocoon, Enemy Mine, *and* Golden Child.

Recently he has turned his hand to screenwriting and is involved with bringing these independent projects to life.

Fulmer drove down from his home in Petaluma to meet me at ILM on a Saturday. His leather jacket and tousled hair made me think he had arrived by motorcycle. He grabbed a cup of coffee, and we retreated to the calm of the conference room. He began the interview by telling me something about his rough-and-tumble background.

FULMER: I suppose I was raised in a macho era. A man was either a blue-collar worker or he was an officer and a gentleman. My father was a fighter pilot—you know, *The Great Santini.* I was raised under that kind of influence. I worked as a welder after the Marine Corps—a pipe welder, ironworker. That was after the Vietnam War, when a lot of people were struggling to find new identities and new values and a lot of things. Of course, welding, that's a real macho profession. Men take their lunches to work, they laugh and joke and have a good time. There's no pressure. It's dangerous work at times, but that's an adrenaline factor that you kind of live off of.

It was a real simple life, nonpolitical. I'd weld maybe eight or nine months out of the year. And I'd go home for the three or four months I had to myself. I had a hand injury at one time that was rather severe, and welding helped me to redevelop the use of my hand.

Along the way, I've always loved models. They've always been considered as toys by most people—you know, store-bought plastic kits, that sort of thing. But the heart of model building is the one-off, the scratch-built, museum type of model.

INTERVIEWER: How did you get started building models?

FULMER: Well, years ago, I was working for an outfit where the fellow in charge could not visualize a product that they were going to manufacture. He could see the blueprints, but no one had even drawn an isometric of the thing. So I suggested, "Why doesn't somebody make a model of it?" Of course, the boss said, "That's a good idea; why don't you do it?" I'd never done it before, but I built a model of that particular machine for him.

It just so happened that the man who was involved in this also was a partner with Bill Harrah up in Reno. I ended up building automobile models for him, about one a year. Through the years I just continued. I built some models for the Aero-Space Museum in San Diego. I built models for private collectors all over the world.

INTERVIEWER: *How did you get mixed up with the movie business?*

FULMER: I was up in Oregon in 1978, working as a welder, and I'd built a model for a guy in San Francisco. It was an air racer. On my two days off, I decided to bring it down to him. I could've shipped it, but I just drove like hell from Portland, Oregon, down here—a twelve-hour drive. The man had worked—years ago, before he retired—for Filmways television productions down in Hollywood. He had a fantastic collection of models—cars, aircraft—beautiful things.

He said, "Mike, I'm not going to accept this model from you until you do me a favor. I want you to go over to Marin County; there's a place starting up over there. George Lucas has moved his operation up from L.A. I don't know anybody who's involved there, but I want you to take this model by there and show it to them."

I said, "You know, Herb, I don't know anything about the movies. I've never worked in the film business. I'm a steelworker."

"Well," he said, "I'm not going to pay you for this model until you show it to them."

"That's blackmail! I don't know... "

He said, "Just do it."

I was a little bit chapped, but I drove over here and I had an interview with them. I felt a little silly. Then I left—took the model back and he paid me—and I went back up to Oregon.

Well, two or three weeks later, I got a call from Lucasfilm. I remember after that I was sitting up on an I-beam, eating lunch with these boys, and I said, "Hey, you guys ever see a film called *Star Wars*?"

"Oh yeah."

"Hell, I saw it two or three times."

"Yeah man, I saw that film."

I said, "Well, they want me to go down there and do some work for them for a while."

These guys all kind of looked around a bit, you know, and said, "Oh, that's a lot of bull. I mean, what are you going to do down there? They don't weld down there."

I said, "Well, I'm not sure, maybe make models."

"Models!"

Of course, I was talking with guys I'd been working with for years. They looked stunned. And I had never seen the movie *Star Wars*.

So I came to work here. I remember there was a real definite security dictum because the *Star Wars* film had such tremendous success. They had to move, under the cover of darkness, to a building here in San Rafael without even a name on the door. They were trying to keep public interest away from it and were doing a pretty good job of it. If there was anyone around the work areas that we didn't recognize, we were to double-check on them.

"They had to move, under the cover of darkness, to a building here in San Rafael without even a name on the door."

I was working in the back there one day and a fellow walked in. I kind of eyed him a bit, but he seemed to know what he was doing. He walked up to the table and looked at what I was doing and said, "Looks great."

And I said, "You must be a new model maker."

"No, I don't do that very well."

I said, "I don't know that I do either."

Then he sort of grinned a little bit, turned around, and walked out. I asked the guy I was working with, "Tommy, who was that guy?"

And he said, "Oh, that was George Lucas." That was my first meeting with George Lucas.

INTERVIEWER: *What did they have you doing when you first came here?*

FULMER: I built a version of the Millenium Falcon. In the original *Star Wars* film, they had built a 4-foot model, a big model. The state of the art at that time was such that the bigger the model, the better the detail they could get. As time went by, its weight and its size limited the type of shot that you could do with the big model.

As an example, if you wanted to do some terrific loops or rolls or long panning shots with it, you'd have to have a camera track that went all the way from here to Francisco Boulevard in order to get that model in frame. So the thing to do was to build a smaller version of it. That was my first job.

I also did a great deal of welding for Richard Edlund, who was the director of photography here at that time. Previously, they sent everything out to a shop somewhere. It often came back looking like hell, and they couldn't control whatever it was they wanted built. I actually started the welding shop in this building. I convinced him that we could do all the work in-house—all the armatures that had to be welded, the optical printers they were building, even the high-speed gears for the cameras. There was a great deal of machinery that had to be built.

INTERVIEWER: *Is there a machine shop here too?*

FULMER: Yes. There's a full-blown machine shop, a welding shop, and a camera maintenance shop. So ILM has evolved from the original purpose of doing *The Empire Strikes Back.* That was the reason the building was leased; that was the reason they brought everybody up here for two years. George is, of course, the preferred customer; this is his business. But anybody with any business sense would ask himself, OK, you've built something, but what are you going to do with it when you don't need it? What this eventually became was a business that took on a lot of work from outside—effects for other studios. It's grown from a 25-man outfit to well over 200 people now.

INTERVIEWER: *What kind of problems did you have when you first started making models in the film business?*

FULMER: Well, I think the biggest problem for everyone when they started was that we were building a complex here as we were trying to get the work done. We had a fairly small crew, and we were trying to build this place and do *Empire* at the same time. That included working with circular saws buzzing overhead when they were putting the floors in. I ended up working in the rest room. I had to take a model in there and do some painting by hand on it. That caused a little bit of consternation for some people waiting to get into the rest room, but there was no other place I could do it.

INTERVIEWER: *Can you define the role of the model maker?*

FULMER: Being a model maker really encompasses a whole lot more than making a three-dimensional model of something. In the film business, special effects are sort of the core of the apple. It is highly competitive. It's a very high-tension job, high pressure. There are a tremendous number of hours involved in it.

Being a model maker is probably one of the hardest jobs in the business. For one thing, it's misunderstood a great deal. It would appear to a stranger, if you were to walk back through the various shops, that the model makers were perhaps having the most fun. It resembles, to some extent, a grand toy shop. And the guys and gals who work in this profession are usually pretty zany. They have to be. They have to have a pretty wild sense of humor. They are crowded into an area that has a limited space—and models don't get smaller, they get bigger. They have to work in a noisy, tight atmosphere, around lots of resins and glues and paints and solvents. They often have to concentrate all their energy on an object that's no bigger than a razor blade for an average of ten hours a day. That's an average workday. As the film production begins to snowball, so do the problems, and the hours often go as high as sixteen a day.

Before any effects can be shot, the model makers have to get the models done. And as the shooting starts, they have to start making changes in the models, they have to service the models, and they have to continue building other models. They never get any respite. They start at the beginning and usually go all the way through the film. I'm not trying to compare us with any of the other departments, because all of our work is difficult, but our work as model makers has been kind of overlooked in some ways.

You can train somebody to load a camera and operate it, but you cannot train somebody to be a model maker or a matte painter. They have to be born with it or they can't do it. To be a model maker you've got be an engineer, a machinist, an electrician, a draftsman, a painter, a mold maker, a woodworker, a pattern maker. You've got to know math; you've got to know plastics; you've got to be able to visualize for people something that they don't know themselves.

INTERVIEWER: *Do model makers ever specialize in any of those areas?*

FULMER: Oh, yes, some people specialize a little more in one area than another. Some are better pattern makers, some are better with mechanics. It's a balancing act, getting all of these people together.

INTERVIEWER: *How do you determine the budget and allocate the model shop's resources?*

FULMER: It's based on previous films, the amount of hours required to accomplish various shots. You've got to go through the storyboards, recall how you did certain things, the type of mechanics and electronics involved in each model, and how many hours it took to do all that. We have to consider all that to come up with a working budget.

It's kind of frustrating, because it's all subject to so much change. The film's director and the director of photography start off with an idea, and by the time you get down to the end of the production, the amount you started with is no longer even practical. So the budget is a strange affair. It's kind of like a rubber band.

INTERVIEWER: What differences do you find among directors in their approaches to special effects?

FULMER: Everybody's different. George Lucas is always sure about the way he wants his films to look. George is real fond of the four-second shot: a lot going on to razzle-dazzle you, sixteen elements in one frame, but don't hold too long on it. Other people show off the special effects. And then others give it away; they pan too long with an effect. They've just spent $50,000 on a set that's 4 [feet] by 4 [feet], and they can't bear to just see it on the screen for two or three seconds. Some directors aren't familiar with effects work and end up getting too involved with it.

INTERVIEWER: What would you like to see changed in this business?

FULMER: Well, I'm a pretty direct person. My life experience has been totally different from that of most of the people involved in the film business. Filmmaking hasn't taken over my life the way it has with some people.

> *"Being a model maker is probably one of the hardest jobs in the business ...the guys and gals who work in this profession are usually pretty zany."*

Say you were to come into this business fresh, walk in the front door, and someone says to you, "You know, there's one thing you've got to remember about this business; it's got to be frantic." You would probably ask, "Why?"

"Well, it just has to be. That's the way it is."

You can't say, "Hey, wait a minute. Can't we enjoy this process a little bit more?" We used to, when we first started. But it's gotten bigger, and as it gets bigger, it gets to be more of what we were trying to get away from.

Also, there's a lot of hype about making films, about being involved with films. It's really not the fun I had anticipated it would be. Everybody you meet in the grocery store or wherever always says, "Gee, that must be a great deal of fun."

But I think working with the people here is great. It's a social business and highly competitive. Somebody once told me, "You're only as good as your last screw-up." Nobody remembers in this business. It's a very myopic business. They don't remember all the achievements, everything you accomplished in the past. The minute you fail, the minute you can't pull something out of your hat, or you get burned out, you can forget it. That's the nature of this business. It's the same way with an actor. He could have made four or five great pictures. The minute he makes a bad picture, it's over.

INTERVIEWER: *Well, I imagine working here is quite different from working in the Hollywood system.*

FULMER: There's a great deal of cooperation between people in the various departments. It's more fluid. We go down and change light bulbs or help move the cameras, or some of the electronics people will come help wire the models. That can't be accomplished with any great ease in the Hollywood system because of the tremendous power of the unions. You could be practically hamstrung down there and nobody would come and help you because they are a light-bulb changer and they don't touch cameras.

INTERVIEWER: *Do you work with a lot of dangerous materials?*

FULMER: There are many. Some of our glues, for example, are dangerous. Those, of course, can be very hairy. You can glue your fingers together; you can get it in your eyes. We don't use some things that are extremely lethal. All of the things that we use—the paints, the lacquers, the resins—all give off toxic fumes, even as they sit there, after they've been poured and have cured. They oxidize. It's just part of the business. If OSHA [Occupational Safety and Health Administration] had their way, we'd all be sticking our hands through a rubber-glove assembly to work in a cubicle with an inert-gas atmosphere. You can't wear an oxygen mask for ten hours a day and do this kind of work. We keep it as safe as we can.

INTERVIEWER: *Who talks to you when a project comes in the door, and how do you get involved?*

FULMER: We have a pretty unique system here, I guess. In our department, we have so many talented model makers. A lot of them are capable of being foot soldiers, if you will. Each of them is capable of carrying a rifle just as well as leading the team. It just depends on the nature of the film.

An idea comes across the board and people talk about it—the general manager, the budget staff, the production coordinator. They usually pick a director of photography. That D.P. will say, "I'd like to have so and so do matte paintings, and I'd like to have another person working with me on this, and I'd like to have another person do that." Doing four or five pictures a year, and having such a large crew, obviously the pie has to be sliced somehow. It's not done on the basis of seniority or any kind of a point system. There is a certain amount of politics, and by that I mean that people are people.

So you sit down with all your counterparts and look at a series of preliminary storyboards of the effects shots. That's really when you start working on it. The ideas start buzzing in your head. You start thinking about the sets that are going to have to be made, what's involved in each shot.

At the same time, you're thinking about the old films that you've done and what sort of techniques could apply from them. A lot of the time, you don't end up doing the things that you think you're going to do. All that experience pays off, but each film has unique problems. Any producer or director who needs special effects doesn't want those effects to look like the effects that were just done in the last film.

INTERVIEWER: *Who designs the miniatures?*

FULMER: Usually the art department. Obviously, when a story is developed, months before it gets to ILM, they usually hire a production designer to at least develop some ideas about how the film will look. When they come here, they link up with our visual-effects art director and talk about the film and work together to match our effects to the live-action part of the film.

For example, in *Poltergeist*, they filmed the live action in a certain house. When they wanted the imploding house scene, where it's literally sucked into the ground, we had to match the house in the live action with a miniature. Then, after we shot that scene at high speed and the miniature house was pulled into the ground, the actors were composited into the scene from separate photography.

INTERVIEWER: *Do you build your models from a designer's drawings?*

FULMER: Most of the model makers who work here never work from blueprints. Starting with a pattern and a shape, it gradually evolves through talking about it with the art department and doing a series of sketches and dimensional views of it. Sometimes we do get a firm drawing. It is usually something that has already been built for live action and we're copying it for use with motion control. The snow speeders in *Empire* that skipped across the top of Toth, the ice planet, and the walkers—those were from drawings. But as a general rule, a lot of the models are created from thin air.

INTERVIEWER: Miniatures encompass so much more than just a scale model that looks like a spaceship or train.

FULMER: The things that the stop-motion animators work with—the dinosaur or the boy or the serpent—you could say that those are models. And inside each of those is an armature that's an incredible piece of work. The miniature of an aircraft, spaceship, automobile, or anything you can recognize as an object in many cases has mechanics involved; some of them are really high tech. Today we can use radio control. And we have stepping motors that can be linked to the camera by computer—you can make eyes blink, gear doors open, things like that, in real time. Previously, we had to animate those things one frame at a time.

INTERVIEWER: You get involved with some very sophisticated hardware.

FULMER: Every time something comes along that gives you a new advantage, a new piece of equipment that will make life easier, it also opens a lot of new problems. It's like splitting the atom. It does open up new avenues for you, but it brings in new areas of concern. It doesn't make life easier, it just solves problems.

The hardware that's put into the models is all built by hand. If the landing gear has to retract, we build the retract mechanism by hand, machine it all by hand. We use motors and radio-control equipment that's been upgraded to be used with our motion-control photography system. They have to work precisely, they have to be repeatable, and they have to work at very slow speeds. Sometimes you can barely see them moving. Nothing that's been invented has made models any easier to build than they've been for the past fifty or sixty years.

INTERVIEWER: Recently, in The Last Starfighter, *the miniatures of the spaceships were not models but were created on a computer. What do you think is in store for model makers?*

FULMER: With computer-generated images, the day may come when they won't even have to have actors. They can say, "I want a Harrison Ford head on an Orson Welles body." They'll be able to program this, and that will be the end of the Actors Guild.

I think in the past fifteen years—since *2001,* with the development of the blue-screen processes, motion-control systems, and the special cameras that have been built—we've lived in the golden age of special effects. It's been a combination of high tech and good old manual labor. Making models, sets, matte paintings, all by hand using materials like wood and plastics and using the same tools that have been used for years: needlenose pliers and X-Acto knives. Yet all these things are put together with this incredible technology.

We're living in an age when things happen so fast. In the next ten years, there's no telling. Someday, what I do will be obsolete, except maybe to make a three-dimensional study model of something.

INTERVIEWER: When a film has a weak script or poor direction, does that ever translate into problems for you?

FULMER: Oh, yeah. When any film has a concept problem, there are going to be problems in all areas: matte paintings, models, the printing and the look of the color. Because they aren't quite sure. I was the model shop supervisor on *Enemy Mine*. The German crew tried to combine the Indiana Jones type of action with a story from the original English producers that wasn't appropriate. It just didn't work. It was a good story. It was very well done; it just didn't have any power.

INTERVIEWER: What kind of films do you like to see?

FULMER: I like to see films about real people. That's my personality. It seems that most of America, and perhaps most of the world, is more interested in fantasy than they are in reality. Perhaps that's because of the world they live in. Today it's every man for himself. It takes a tremendous amount of energy just to get to work anymore. We're living under the constant threat of nuclear war, pollution, AIDS, you name it. Just the tension of living everyday life, the tension's right there. Films express this, even music expresses it.

"They calculated that in one year, we work the equivalent of two years of an average person's hours on the job."

The old films, like the Bogart pictures, were about people. Even a film like *The Wizard of Oz* had a lot of adult things in it. This was because adults went to the theaters, kids didn't. Today, most entertainment is designed around young adults.

And I think this is important: Many of the directors and producers now who make these pictures grew up in the age of television. I could be sticking

321

my neck out saying this, but even Steven Spielberg and to a certain extent George Lucas—I know they were greatly affected by television. If you look at *E.T.* and a lot of these films, you can see the television in them. They're completely different from the films of thirty or forty years ago.

INTERVIEWER: *Do you think there aren't many films for adults to choose from these days?*

FULMER: Every now and then a film comes out that adults might like. And those films are usually not real successful. Look at Robert Redford in the film about the baseball player, *The Natural.* Brilliantly filmed, quiet, moody; it had a lot of symbolism. But it wasn't very successful in terms of box-office receipts. Today films cost so much money that they've got to bring back twice what you put into them before they make a dollar.

INTERVIEWER: *You work an incredible number of hours, don't you?*

FULMER: Generally, the film business has always been rather catch-as-catch-can: You got a gig for six weeks or six months and you worked your tail off and when it was over, who knows when you'd get another job? That's why people in this business are paid pretty good money. At ILM we've been fortunate in working year after year. Which is great on the financial end of the scale, but on the human end...it's like the layers and layers in a French croissant; you've built up years and years of competitive pressure, long, long hours, not much time at home with the family, and you get older! They calculated that in one year, we work the equivalent of two years of an average person's hours on the job.

In the Marines we used to say, "If you think you've got what it takes, it's going to take everything you've got." This is one of the few places I've ever worked that takes everything you've got. All people who work in this world, whether they work as chefs or gas station attendants, or whatever they do, they all want to work in some capacity that uses everything they know, that uses them up. People are interested in money only because it replaces other values, other things that they lack, what they need as a human being to survive— identity, the feeling of accomplishment.

All these people who go to work every day and just sit at a desk, they know that if they croaked tomorrow, somebody could take their place. And yet, they may have hidden talents and capabilities—as an artist, as a singer, as a musician, as a story writer—that no one will ever know about. Most people live with it. They don't spend a lot of time daydreaming about it. But to finally work someplace where everything that I know how to do is used—or discovering a skill I didn't know was there—that's a tremendous experience.

INTERVIEWER: *What's the dark side of that?*

FULMER: Well, I'm very fortunate in that this is the finest special-effects facility in the world. We can create anything here. To be involved in that process is worth more than money. But it has its price. It can, if you're not careful, turn eventually into the cat-chasing-its-tail syndrome. The faster you go, the faster you go. And the more you give, the more they want. The "they" is really yourself. There's no one standing there with a bullwhip in this business.

Also, you go away on vacation for a couple of weeks, and being able to relax is an incredibly difficult process, because you've been locked into this work. You have dreams about how to make things work. You live in another world while you're involved with a film.

INTERVIEWER: *What other creative activities are you involved in?*

FULMER: After the Marine Corps and working all those years in male-oriented blue-collar environments and not having a college education, I was a different person when I started working here. I didn't accept this very easily into my life, socially. I was never able to walk back and get a cup of coffee without feeling guilty. I worked all my life with a ten-minute coffee break and a thirty-minute lunch break. That's the way life was. I'd stick my head out in the hall and look around and people were working, but they had a freedom of mobility. It was hard to get used to being treated like an adult.

I think I learned to communicate all over again. I'd never worked with women; that's one thing I'd never done. That was a little hard for me to do. There are some very talented gals working in this profession. I'd just never worked around them and I'd never had a woman as a supervisor or coordinator. To some people that's a minor thing, but there were a lot of changes I had to make. And all of them were pretty much for the better.

Along the way, I discovered I could write stories. I had as many stories to tell as anyone else. Everyone has a story to tell. You could take the life of any person and make it interesting. It just depends on who tells the story.

I started writing with my brother, initially about the Vietnam War. I went through an incredible ordeal writing that, a lot of emotional stuff that I'd never let out of me. And it never would have happened had I not worked here. We're still working on a novel, a major piece of work, and we've finished three screenplays.

We don't want to make a studio picture; we'd like to make an independent film. I'd like to make the film for the enjoyment of it. The money really doesn't interest me. I'd really like to have some fun with it. It's like making a model or painting a picture or working on your car. It's an extension of who you are. I don't think there's any big deal, really, about actually making a film. I think the big deal is getting people interested in the project and getting the money together to make it happen.

INTERVIEWER: *What would the film be about?*

FULMER: It's about the Vietnam War. We hope it will be more of a true picture than what's been done before. It involves the great cultural shift in this country and at the same time the tactical war in Vietnam. We go back and forth, back and forth—the different generations, the men and women, the battles; they're all intertwined. The story's quite elaborate. This is something that should be done.

> *"There's a lot of hype about making films, about being involved with films. It's really not the fun I had anticipated it would be."*

But it's very hard to do something like that when you're working ten, eleven hours a day. Writing is hard enough when that's all you're doing, all day at a desk or out on the veranda. I was never schooled in writing.

And screenwriting is frustrating often because it's so limiting. You have to simplify, simplify, simplify. I'll write four or five paragraphs for a scene, then I'll scrutinize it and take two or three lines out of there, ones with a lot of power. I'm a detailist, so it's excruciating sometimes.

INTERVIEWER: *What do you see coming down the road?*

FULMER: I don't know where the company's going. I don't have any idea of what the future really is. I've been here eight and a half years. It's hard to believe ten years will have gone by pretty soon. I've done fourteen or fifteen pictures here at ILM.

The next ten years will probably be the hardest. You always think the first ten are the hardest. But I think the next ten will be the hardest because of all the changes: the external changes with the films that come in here and the internal changes as this place gets bigger; the departmentalization and the "This is my job, that's your job" attitude. It's becoming more and more like the studio system.

When this place started, we had a tight group of people working to get one project done, and there was a tremendous amount of camaraderie and good morale. You could've lived in a tent and still have gotten the work done because it was fun, it was exciting. As it grows, more people come into the business, and as you get more films, you lose a lot of the personal feeling. It's a natural process. You can't go back and recapture the past. It's history. And having a sense of history makes you a more complete person. All that's in your memory and you don't have to dust it.

Jonathan Erland

SPECIAL EFFECTS
SCIENTIFIC AND TECHNICAL DEVELOPMENT

*J*onathan Erland, forty-seven, comes from a creative family. His father is a painter, sculptor, and ceramist, while his mother had careers in both dress design and journalism. Erland began his career studying theater in his native England. Recruited to work with John Dykstra on the first **Star Wars** picture, Erland stayed on when Dykstra founded Apogee, Inc. in 1978, and has since contributed his talents to many motion pictures.

His son is a commercial artist working in Toronto. His daughter, who is married to Paul Johnson, Apogee's motion-control software wizard, recently made him a grandfather for the second time. He and Kay Beving, a data systems analyst for Los Angeles County, live in a secluded cottage in an older neighborhood of Los Angeles with six cats, two computers, and eleven eucalyptus trees. The trees live outside the cottage, as do some of the cats.

Apogee, one of the world's leading special-effects studios, lies hidden in a light industrial area littered with aging tract *houses and decaying palm trees, within earshot of the planes taxiing at Van Nuys airport.*

It's a scene tinged with irony: The nondescript, two-story building houses an impressive array of cinematic capabilities, including construction and machine shops, shooting stages, and optical printing facilities.

I found Erland on a darkened stage surrounded by machinery whose purpose and function were totally mysterious to me. He's a tall, affable man with a full beard; his dark hair was tied in a long ponytail. We settled into an upstairs conference room, where Erland talked easily and at length about his sorcerer's craft. His enthusiasm for the magic of film was highly contagious.

Special effects for motion pictures is a process of creating images of things that do not really exist; by its very nature it is a process of solving unique problems. These problems can often be extremely technical, and that is where Jonathan Erland enters the picture.

As director of the research and development department at Apogee, Erland has shared in three Academy technical awards—for the development of the Reverse Bluescreen traveling matte process, the Blue-Max blue flux front projector, and an improved method of fabricating front-projection screens. These and other processes, such as improved methods for making silicone rubber molds and a new method known as Reverse Front Projection, have resulted in two issued patents, with three more pending.

Erland's pioneering work has been responsible for expanding the limits of what is possible to create on film, thus giving audiences a more sophisticated, convincing, and enjoyable experience.

INTERVIEWER: *Have you always been involved with special effects?*

ERLAND: I actually started my working life in the entertainment field, in the theater, as a classical actor. I studied at The Central School of Speech and Drama in London. This is the school that trained such people as Laurence Olivier quite some time ago, as well as Carrie Fisher more recently. In my day, about thirty-odd years ago, we had Vanessa Redgrave.

In England, if you wish to study acting at a school like Central, you don't just study acting—you study total theater. So although Vanessa's an actress, and a very good one, if you were to ask her to build the theater, write the script, and even do the lighting, she could do it. We were quite thoroughly trained in all aspects of the theater.

Following Central, I studied at what was then the London School of Film Technique and which is now the London International Film School. There, of course, I was studying film, pursuing what I hoped would be a comprehensive education in film and theater. For the next twenty years or so, much of my life was taken up with theater—technical direction, stage managing, and lighting design, as well as acting.

INTERVIEWER: *This was all in England?*

ERLAND: The training mostly. Then I went to New York, where union problems made it very difficult to work; then to Chicago for more study at the Goodman Theatre; then Toronto, where I was allowed to work; and eventually to Los Angeles.

INTERVIEWER: *What did you do in Toronto?*

ERLAND: In Toronto I worked in radio and television drama, in the white-knuckle days when the shows were live. I was in a CBC production of *Julius Caesar* with Bill Shatner as Mark Antony, in 1961. I doubt if either of us could have foretold then that we'd both be working on a space opera called *Star Trek* twenty years later! During that time, I also started to become involved in industrial design, product development, and prototyping, as well as exhibit work, partly because acting was not a reliable way to eat.

INTERVIEWER: *Did you get your industrial design training on the job?*

ERLAND: Oh, yes, very much on the job. In the sixties, my brother and I had a small fiberglass business. My brother still runs one nowadays, in the Canary Islands, Spain. That business got us involved in industrial design.

We both wound up working at a place called Scale Design, which was a design, prototype, and exhibit firm. The kind of place where one works on everything from door pulls and telephones to Lear jets and trash cans.

There we became involved with the 1964 New York World's Fair. We worked on Charles Eames's exhibits for the IBM Pavilion. It involved a lot of animatronics, in the days of its infancy. Disney did his first three-dimensional, animated figure of Abraham Lincoln, and Eames had several puppet theaters that were intended to explain how computers worked. I worked on those and generally got caught up in that world from then on, but I didn't have any formal training in industrial design.

INTERVIEWER: *How did you become involved in* Star Wars?

ERLAND: They were looking for people who had a background in a variety of industrial processes—injection molding, vacuum forming—plastics technology, mostly. They needed people with a background in industrial processes to augment the film skills they already had. The *Star Wars* group was actually heavily influenced by people with an industrial design background. John Dykstra, for example, studied industrial design at Long Beach State before he got into filmmaking. Bob Shepherd and a number of others had industrial design in their backgrounds. In addition to them, we had people like Alvah Miller, whose background was nuclear physics!

> *"The* Star Wars *group was actually heavily influenced by people with an industrial design background."*

And that, of course, accounts to a large extent for why this whole genre of filmmaking is so different from the normal motion picture production business. All of the technology involved in robotics and animatronics came from other disciplines. It was very effective—people coming from such diverse backgrounds had a very refreshing impact on the motion picture business.

At that time I had a small business in partnership with Lorne Peterson. We became involved with the *Star Wars* project, largely teaching things like silicone rubber mold making, casting plastics—all of the things associated with industrial model making that were not then particularly associated with movie miniature making.

Lorne has continued on with George Lucas and runs the ILM [Industrial Light & Magic] model shop in Marin County now, and I became intrigued with the techniques and the systems that were being evolved then—motion control and blue-screen and so forth.

INTERVIEWER: *Had you been involved in doing any special effects in your earlier film work?*

ERLAND: In my early film training in London, we made a film called *Brief Armistice*, which was set during World War II and involved a lot of what was then quaintly called "tabletop photography." In those days, it was all done in real time, or overcranked, with models pulled by wires that you hoped would never show but always did!

The cost of any sort of composites back then would have been prohibitive, but here on *Star Wars*, the most amazing visual effects were being produced and it was absolutely fascinating. I found it to be a fruitful place to apply new, inventive ideas, and I seem to have been doing that ever since.

INTERVIEWER: The special-effects business seems to continually demand new ways to solve technical problems.

ERLAND: True. The problems, of course, really prompt the changes. The demands keep getting higher. Now, when we see *Star Wars*, we can look at something and think, Oh, boy, how did we let that shot get past us! But as the level of proficiency in producing effects increases, the audience becomes more sophisticated and jaded and more demanding and discerning, so there's been a tremendous escalation in the level of performance. Seeing films now like *Destination Moon* can be quite amusing to audiences that have become very sophisticated.

INTERVIEWER: But even with the benefit of modern technology, effects films can look miserable.

ERLAND: Actually, if you look back to something like the original *King Kong*, and compare it with the modern version, I'll take the first one. For all its lack of current technology, there's a definite charm about the film that didn't survive in the remake. Perhaps because it had a clearer vision, a better sense of what it was trying to do. It's amazing how well people understand Shakespeare in the theater although they can't comprehend it on the printed page. That's because the actor is projecting the thought and the vision rather than only the words.

You can't depend entirely on sophistication, but one really is under some pressure to stretch the technology. Now we're doing incredible things with lasers, for example—things that never appeared in films before.

INTERVIEWER: And then there are computer-generated special effects.

ERLAND: Computer-generated imagery is rapidly coming on. The marriage of that and real photography is something that's being wrestled with now. It's a very difficult thing to do, because they're two fundamentally different media—film of a real object and a computer-generated image. People tend to believe either one or the other.

If you're watching a cartoon, you'll go into a certain mode that says, OK, this is a cartoon, I'll accept this as reality—there's a suspension of disbelief. But you can't, as they tried to do with *Mary Poppins*, put the cartoon and the real person together. It jars the audience. I'm on slippery ground here because *Mary Poppins* was enormously successful at the box office, but I do believe that it's very difficult to juxtapose real photography with cartoons. Computer-generated imagery has this as its major problem. Muppets work with people, but they're real, three-dimensional extensions of people.

That problem is something that's being worked on right now, one of the most exciting things going on. Can you imagine *The Tempest* set in the kind of world we'll be able to create? It could be marvelous!

INTERVIEWER: *Didn't you do quite a bit of work on the Clint Eastwood film,* Firefox*?*

ERLAND: Oh yes. *Firefox* is a film about the stealing of a Russian fighter plane, based a little bit on a real event in which a Russian pilot defected with a Foxbat, MiG-25, I think it was. It was clearly going to be a special-effects job because the plane in the movie was a figment of an art director's imagination. We weren't going to have a real fighter to film.

When we actually tried to fly a radio-controlled model, it flew about as well as a bench vise! So, it was going to have to be done with models and motion-control photography and by blue-screen compositing.

Eastwood originally wanted the fighter to be the way we're all familiar with them—those silvery, aluminum things. We told him, "Well, that's not technically feasible, because the plane will reflect the blue-screen, and instead of having a clean silhouette of the airplane there, we'll have great chunks missing where the blue was reflected. So how about a nice black plane like the SR-70 spy plane?"

And Clint said, "Oh yes, that's much better! Black, sinister, perfect—a nice, shiny, black plane!"

"No, no, you don't quite understand. We can't do shiny."

"Oh, but it's got to be shiny!" And the famous jaw muscles tighten into the trademark Dirty Harry look.

"Yessir, of course, it has to be shiny—how silly of us. Could only be shiny." So we valiantly set about doing that, and we actually did do a bunch of work with a shiny, black, Russian MiG in front of the blue-screen.

INTERVIEWER: *How did that come out?*

ERLAND: Well, it was torture! It took eons of time, numerous assorted extra passes with the camera, taping black tape and paper to the shiny bits, and just general chaos. It was, quite simply, a rout. We clearly had to produce some other system for doing it. And since the issue of shiny things had been around for quite a while, many varied ideas to deal with the problem had been simmering. I began to work seriously on these vague ideas I'd had that maybe there was another way to do it.

INTERVIEWER: *What was the conventional system at that time?*

ERLAND: Traditionally, a blue-screen shot [see diagram on next page] involves photographing a subject against an illuminated background; think of it as a giant light box with the light filtered blue. Because we're using color film, we can make color separations of the picture we get and, since the blue-screen will appear on only the blue separation, we can use that to make a mask, or matte, in which the subject is rendered as an opaque silhouette.

"Turning a problem inside out, or upside down, is apt to reveal a hidden solution."

Using these mattes—there are usually a pair, male and female, for each different subject we'll be compositing—we can combine the picture of the Firefox, for example, with the sky in which it's supposed to be flying.

In this way we can montage many different images together. The *Star Wars* films are probably the best-known examples of having a great many different elements all in the same image at once.

The problem with this approach, of course, is that what you are really using to make your matte is the "hole" that your subject has made in the blue-screen behind it, rather than an actual image of the silhouette, or shape, of the subject itself. Therefore, if the subject has a shiny surface that reflects blue light from the screen behind it you have effectively removed a portion of the subject from the composite image, since the reflected blue light will be replaced by the background scene, as would anything that is actually colored blue on the subject.

Ideally, you would want the subject itself to be the source of the matte, and not the screen. Indeed, you don't want to use a screen at all, because that also limits the field of view of the camera and prevents you from being able to move freely around the subject.

What you really want is for the subject to literally glow as though it were red-hot. One way to do that is to have a subject that is radioactive and then take X-ray movies of the thing, but of course that approach wouldn't go

Background
scene

Model's phosphor coating
irradiated with ultraviolet
light (matte pass)

Model illuminated by
incandescent light photographed
in front of blue-screen (beauty pass)

Background
negative

Filtered
positive image

Beauty pass
negative

Background color
interpositive

Matte pass
negative

Beauty pass
color interpositive

High contrast B & W
hold-out matte

High contrast B & W
burn-in matte

Background with
hold-out matte

Latent negative with burn-in matte

Color dupe
negative

Composite scene

Jonathan Erland's Reverse Bluescreen process.

Background scene

Model illuminated by incandescent light
photographed in front of blue-screen

Background negative

Original negative
of model

Blue separation

Green separation

Red separation

Background color
interpositive

High contrast B & W
hold-out matte

High contrast B & W
burn-in matte

Background with
hold-out matte

High contrast B & W
burn-in matte

Green separation

Red separation

Color negative

Composite scene

Conventional blue-screen process.

335

over too well with our camera crews! So I came up with the idea of using an invisible phosphor as the source of the "radiation."

INTERVIEWER: *How does that process work?*

ERLAND: The way it works is that we take a model that's been finished and painted to look just the way we want to see it, and then we coat it with invisible phosphor. Under white light it makes no apparent difference to the model, and we can film it just the way we would normally.

Because we have extremely accurate motion control, we have the ability to make multiple passes; we can film the same object over and over again, and it will always be in exactly the same place in the frame.

So now we can go back to the beginning of our shot, using a fresh section of film, run the computer back to the beginning, turn out the white lights and turn on ultraviolet, or black lights, and presto! That invisible phosphor glows like mad. It actually makes the subject look as though it were indeed red-hot, or even radioactive! Now we can film the sequence over again with the subject glowing like a light bulb.

From that image it's very easy to make a matte, and you don't have to make the old black-and-white separations to do it. This means that you can use the original negative of the subject, which, of course, could have blue paint on it or any paint you like, or it could be made of chrome or glass—essentially anything you want.

There are all sorts of other variations we can do, involving phosphor backings in complementary colors (so that we can make mattes that are the same generation to each other) and making permutations of the mattes, called "matte difference mattes" and so forth, but that is basically the gist of how the system works.

INTERVIEWER: *And that's what you call Reverse Bluescreen?*

ERLAND: We called it Reverse Bluescreen [see diagram] because it turned the whole process inside out, which is an important insight into how many of these problems are solved: Turning a problem inside out, or upside down, is apt to reveal a hidden solution. It frees us from having to do the color separations, et cetera, in order to produce the matte.

In a blue-screen shot, you have to take the negative, separate it into its components in order to extract the matte, and then recomposite the whole image back again. With Reverse Bluescreen, we have the full-color original negative of the subject by itself and then, separately, we have a matte. We can composite from that original negative.

INTERVIEWER: *How does that differ from the sodium vapor process?*

ERLAND: That's a dual-film matting process that uses the old Technicolor camera, which is now no longer used for Technicolor. It has two film gates. In the old Technicolor days, they put two pieces of film in one gate and one piece of film in the other gate and made three color separations in the camera, all at once.

With the sodium vapor process, you take that three-strip Technicolor camera and put a conventional color negative in one gate and a black-and-white matte stock in the other gate.

Inside the camera is a prism that separates the image coming through the lens. It directs the various colors to either one gate or the other. The prism has a filter in it that filters a very, very narrow yellow wavelength—sodium yellow—which is at 589 nanometers. You would then have a yellow screen behind the actors. Sodium yellow also happens to be an area where the color negative is inherently partly blind.

As this image comes through the lens into the camera, it passes through that prism, and the full-collor image is deflected toward the color negative film. The yellow component, which is that sodium yellow screen, goes through to the other film gate and the matte stock.

"With Star Trek... there were people who seldom left this building.... They came in and lived here."

So you get a matte in one gate and a full-color negative in the other, and you wind up with the same thing produced with Reverse Bluescreen, except it's been done in one pass. We have to do two passes to accomplish that. But because everything we're working with is under computer control, we can do that easily.

In fact, we normally have to do that anyway in our original photography. Our miniatures—spaceships or whatever—all have little running lights and so forth. The exposure times for the little lights are going to be different than for the rest of the model, so we wind up making several passes to get all the images, and then another pass to get a matte of it.

INTERVIEWER: *Do you use Reverse Bluescreen exclusively now?*

ERLAND: No, we use all kinds of techniques, because every shot has different requirements. If for some reason the camera or the subject is not controllable, then we can't use Reverse Bluescreen. This usually means people: If we have live action going on, then we have to use conventional blue-screen—or unconventional blue-screen, in our case, because we now have several ways of doing blue-screen.

INTERVIEWER: *Can you describe those?*

ERLAND: We have a very, very effective transmission blue-screen that is one of the finest in the industry. We did a lot of work to make the conventional process excel. We had special lamps made with a single phosphor that has a very narrow, highly efficient band emission precisely where the color negative is the most sensitive to blue and has the best blue-green separation. Then the light goes through specially compounded filters and so forth. So we have a very clean blue-screen.

But even as clean as it is, it has the conventional blue-screen problems, such as the reflections one gets from a shiny object—the blue spill problem that everybody talks about. And you're limited in size, because you're dealing basically with a big light box with a lot of fluorescent lights in it and there's a limit to how many of these you want to put in a box, pulling all kinds of power and heat.

When we originally became involved with *Dune,* we realized that for some of the scenes an entire atmosphere was going to have to be replaced by blue-screen, and it would have to be far larger than any conventional transmission screen. You could, of course, paint a blue backdrop, but the quality of that has always been extremely bad, and in this case, it would have meant zillions of watts of lights to accomplish even that. So we had to come up with something new.

In the days of *Star Trek,* we had actually done some work with projecting blue light to a front-projection screen, following in the footsteps of what was done on *Tora! Tora! Tora!* We used a big 8-by-10 projector that Don Trumbull* built many years ago, with a 5,000-watt xenon lamp. We had a hell of a time filtering the light to get it exactly right, but what we had done was very promising—the space walk sequences and so forth.

---

* Special effects engineering expert who contributed to *The Wizard of Oz* early in his career and to recent films such as *Close Encounters of the Third Kind* and *Star Wars.* He is a founding partner of Apogee, Inc.

We made that work, in spite of all the difficulties, and we thought that, clearly, if we put our minds to it, there must be a more efficient, more effective means to do it. So for *Dune*, we set about designing what is now called the Blue-Max—quite a remarkable device [see diagram]. It uses a 5,000-watt lamp, as we used in *Star Trek*, but instead of a xenon lamp, it's a mercury-xenon lamp. As soon as you introduce mercury into a discharge lamp, the mercury essentially dominates, and the mercury emission lines therefore dominate the output of the lamp. And mercury emission lines include a spike at 436 nanometers, which is, fortuitously, the ideal place on Eastman color negative to get the best separation between blue and green. And red, of course, is not an issue here.

So with some quite sophisticated optical systems—filters and so forth—we extract just that one spike from that lamp and deliver it out to the screen. And that produced, oh boy. . .in *Dune*, the screens were something like 50 feet high and 125 feet wide—big, huge screens. They were lit up by a 5,000-watt light, which is a relatively small light, especially when you consider how many watts it would take to light a painted backing that size! But we did them quite effectively with the Blue-Max.

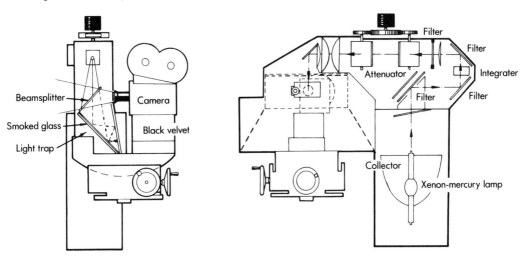

The Blue-Max blue flux front projector.

And you no longer have blue spill, because with Blue-Max you're dealing with a collimated beam of light. A ray of light leaves the projector—and hence the camera because it's been made coincident by a beam splitter—and goes out to that screen and returns along a straight line. So if it's interrupted, it's eliminated because it never makes it to the screen. If it's not interrupted, it goes out to the screen and comes straight back again. You can't run into the situation where a ray of light starts from some point on the screen, bounces off the subject, and is reflected to the camera, because in this approach, the light is a bundle of rays that are all parallel. So not only do we have the huge size, but we also got rid of the blue reflections problem, or blue spill, and it makes very, very clean mattes.

> *"Less than one percent of your time is spent dreaming up new things. Much of the rest is a lot of mundane drudgery."*

After using it on *Dune*, the Blue-Max was used on *2010*. All of that wonderful space-walk sequence was shot with the Blue-Max.

INTERVIEWER: *What kind of material did you use for the reflective screen?*

ERLAND: Scotchlite, which is a quite marvelous material made by 3M. They won an Academy Award for it. It consists of a vinyl film, and on its surface are coated millions of microscopic glass spheres, about 2 mils across—about the thickness of a human hair. These spheres act like condenser lenses, so that a ray of light striking one is returned back along its own axis—it is reflected straight back to the source. This is the same principle you see in highway signs that reflect the light of your headlights back to you at night. In fact, the material we use was developed as a spin-off from highway sign technology.

It's very unlike a mirror surface, in which the light ray will be reflected at the angle of incidence, so that the angle would have to be zero for the light to be sent back to its source. With Scotchlite, the angle of the light to the screen can be quite oblique and the screen will still reflect most of the light to the source.

We've since taken that Scotchlite material and devised a way to make very large screens that don't show any seam lines or nonuniformity, and that has helped with some of the problems associated with front projection [see diagram on next page].

INTERVIEWER: Did the Blue-Max projector bring you up against any new limitations?

ERLAND: Yes, there were still problems, namely those inherent in front projection. For example, whether you're projecting blue or whether you're projecting an image, you can't have somebody light a cigarette in the picture, because that open flame is now a light source as well, and that light will go back to the Scotchlite screen and return to the camera as a bigger glob of light than when it left.

The camera sees the light of the match, but with a tremendous halo around it, which destroys the whole image. Similarly, if somebody's in a white shirt and it's being backlit, the light will bounce off the back of the shirt and go back to the screen, and then a big halo appears around the white shirt.

And then on top of that, actors can't come close to the camera at all. The light emanating from the lens of the camera creates a shadow of the person on the reflective screen. Since the lens of the camera is directly on the other side of the shadow, the camera normally never sees the shadow. That's the whole principle involved. But as a person gets closer to the camera, the shadow they're casting on the screen is getting larger and fuzzier. At some

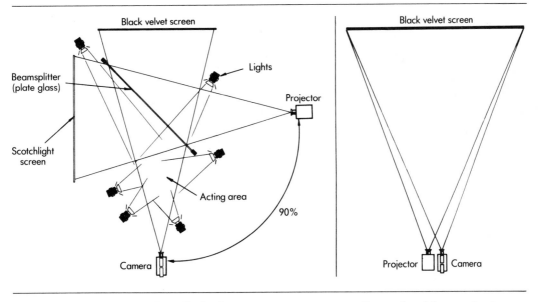

Reverse Front Projection   *Conventional front projection*

point, then, that shadow becomes so fuzzy that even though the shadow is directly on the other side of the subject from the camera, the camera is beginning to see the fuzzy edge of the shadow. Now we've got a fringe effect around the person.

So when you're doing front projection, there are all sorts of rules and tables about which lens to use at any particular distance and how far an actor must be from the screen. To deal with all these restrictions, we have evolved a process, called Reverse Front Projection [see diagram], that takes all of those front-projection elements and rearranges them quite radically.

INTERVIEWER: Can you describe this process?

ERLAND: In the new process, the camera and projector are still at a 90-degree angle to each other, but they are separated by a considerable distance, and the foreground subject is placed between a very large beam splitter—which may be plain glass or a large plastic film—and the camera. The front-projection screen faces the projector instead of the camera, while the camera faces the light trap normally confronted by the projector.

This gives us a system to use for close-ups and/or when there are things that might reflect the projected light from the subject. For example, in conventional front projection, if somebody was wearing a space helmet with a visor, then the visor would reflect an image back to the camera of what was being projected.

Now we have the projector and the camera separated by quite a distance. The projector is aimed at the Scotchlite screen and the camera is aimed 90 degrees to this, looking at a big, black velvet screen. At 45 degrees between this black velvet screen and the front-projection screen is a huge beam splitter. It's actually about a 92/8, which means it's 92 percent transmission and 8 percent reflection. The projector will project the image, and it will go through this huge beam splitter, hit the screen, and come back from the screen trying to go back to the projector that it started from. Ninety-two percent of it will go back to the projector, but eight percent of it will now be deflected at 90 degrees and sent out along this other axis to the camera.

And because the Scotchlite screen is, in essence, a field lens, like a set of condensers, the light coming back off of it is a collimated beam condensing down to a focal point out here in space. In fact, when we're operating it in a dark room, you can find that focal point by sticking your hand up until this

Jonathan Erland works with an Apogee-built model of an astronaut for some special effects footage for the Canadian Pavilion at Vancouver, B.C.'s Expo '86.

spot of light appears on your hand. That glow of light is the reflected nodal point that corresponds to the projector nodal point. So there, of course, is where we put the camera.

The camera lens nodal point is then coincident with the projector nodal point. Now we have the same effect that we had with conventional front projection, except that the light, for all intents and purposes, is originating at the screen and not at the camera. So we're not projecting light onto our subject, although we're getting light back as though we had done so. Hence the name Reverse Front Projection.

With Reverse Front Projection, if the subject lights a match, that light will travel back to the beam splitter, but since it's only a 92/8 beam splitter, 92 percent of that light will go through the beam splitter and go to that black velvet screen behind it. Eight percent of that light will be reflected to the Scotchlite screen and, coming back from the Scotchlite screen, again 92 percent of that light goes through the beam splitter heading in the direction of the projector that's out there, and 8 percent of the original 8 percent, or less than 1 percent, is now coming back to the camera. Same thing for the white shirt with the backlight on it and all the rest.

That gave us a solution to a whole bunch of other front-projection and front-projection blue-screen problems. So you can see that even our "conventional" blue-screen is somewhat unconventional.

INTERVIEWER: *With this variety of techniques available, who looks at the storyboard for a particular project and says, "Well, for this shot, we're going to do it this way?"*

ERLAND: That will depend on the project. For example, if it's a feature film that we're doing, it's the daily work of the director of special effects, in our case, usually John Dykstra. If it's a commercial, it will be the director of the commercial in question. Or, in our facility, it could be a variety of people.

INTERVIEWER: *When do you usually become involved in a project?*

ERLAND: Frequently, far too late! Everybody does that, from the producer on down the line; they invariably seem to consult the people they need to consult way too far down the road. It's just the way it is.

When do I actually become involved? Usually when something's gone wrong. If something hasn't worked the way it was anticipated, and something else is now going to have to be done, that's when I frequently find myself becoming involved.

INTERVIEWER: It seems that because you have a research and development department here, you are able to work fairly independently.

ERLAND: Yes, it's rather unusual to have a research and development department in a facility like this. Lucas has a research and development facility, but not as a part of ILM. They have access to Lucas's completely separate R and D division, which has been mostly involved in doing computer imagery and things like that. It's more efficient, at least in my view, to have an R and D department right on the scene where you're doing the work. This way, you can deal with problems immediately and see your results.

INTERVIEWER: Are you able to pursue your own projects and ideas, or do you have your hands full solving problems for current productions?

ERLAND: I have all sorts of things going on. There are over thirty items on the R and D projects list. I do extensive testing on things like the filmstocks we use, and I work closely with film manufacturers like Eastman Kodak. The development of things like the Blue-Max continues; right now I'm working with people in the electronic compositing field on establishing new criteria for shooting film for electronic compositing.

> *"One can look forward to the stage when we can actually produce a moving hologram, a three-dimensional image."*

There is always a lot of patent office business to attend to, as well as licensing—all of the technology we've been discussing here is made available to the industry via a licensing program. A variety of other new apparatus is being designed—all of which must be patented and licensed.

I spend a fair bit of time on courtesy consultations for our clients, or potential clients, or just plain strangers. I had a call a while back from the Alaska Repertory Theatre asking for ideas on making snowballs that wouldn't melt on stage, and that could be thrown at actors without hurting them.

INTERVIEWER: What did you tell them?

ERLAND: To use grated wax mixed with shredded polyethylene film.

I also think it's very important to maintain links with the industrial design people who I work with from time to time. A recent project was designing a portable kit for an eye doctor to make home calls on elderly patients. All this helps to keep the mind alive and keep one exposed to fresh ideas.

You see, the process that was begun by bringing people in from the outside to work on *Star Wars* has to be guarded, in a sense. If you say, "OK, the rest of the world now ceases to exist," and you're concentrating only on what's in front of you, you'll wind up right where the industry was before—stagnating for lack of fresh ideas.

So, in order to prevent that from happening, one definitely should keep one's mind active in outside projects, solving different types of problems. There's a great deal of cross-pollination that goes on, and that's very helpful, very beneficial.

Apogee is very involved in non-motion-picture kinds of activities—theme parks, the toy business. That helps to revitalize the place and keep everybody interested and learning. And that's the most important thing: to keep learning. It's not easy to say how working on a water fountain for a theme park in Canada would necessarily enhance our abilities as filmmakers, but somehow it all does.

There was an excellent series, on public television a while ago—also a book—called *Connections* by James Burke. It was a superb demonstration of that interweaving of history, technology, and innovation. I hope they keep playing it over and over and over again. In fact, they should run it in every school. That's worth two years of college right there.

INTERVIEWER: As far as your personal life, do you tend to live, eat, and breathe your projects?

ERLAND: Work does rather tend to pervade one's life, and one is forever startling people at the dinner table by stumbling onto some solution or other, or at least thinking one has; it usually takes a number of stumbles before one bumps into a real solution!

INTERVIEWER: Do you generally work long hours every day?

ERLAND: Yes. Of course, it depends on the projects we're working on. At the moment, we don't have a feature in the house. This place gets quite interesting when we do.

For example, with *Star Trek*, there were times when people were working eighty hours a week. We had to produce about two years' worth of work in nine months on that production. There were people who seldom left this building while doing that. They came in and lived here. It was amazing.

Mercifully, it doesn't happen all that often, at least not to me; I'm getting too old for that sort of thing. But even if I'm not doing that, it still winds up taking over. I go home from here, and most of the time I spend a large chunk of the evening sitting in front of the screen doing something for a project.

INTERVIEWER: *Is that a TV screen or a computer screen?*

ERLAND: It's a computer screen. Mostly word processing or database searching. I'm not really a computer programming person, but the word processor is very useful, as is the plotter. It used to take hours to plot film curves; now the plotter does it in a fraction of the time.

INTERVIEWER: *What do you enjoy most about your work? Is there anything you can put your finger on?*

ERLAND: It obviously gives you a kind of high to crack problems, especially basic ones that have gone on and on and defied a lot of previous attempts to solve them.

That actually doesn't turn out to be anything like a major part of the work. Only about a third of the time is actually logged on R and D projects. I spend the rest of my time doing a zillion other things, supporting some of the technologies we already have going.

There are all sorts of things you get involved in with people outside. There are SMPTE [Society of Motion Picture and Television Engineers] papers and various ancillary things that go on.

And of the third that's R and D, the really fun part—the sitting around and dreaming and concocting part—is about one half of one percent of your time. It's minute. That's regrettable, because one likes to think that somebody, in such and such an office, spends all their time dreaming up all these nice things. But no, they don't. Less than one percent of your time is spent dreaming up new things. Much of the rest of it's a lot of mundane drudgery. You should see the filing!

INTERVIEWER: *What do you see happening in the future? What sort of technology is in the works for motion pictures?*

ERLAND: Oh, a great many things: Computers will continue, as they have been doing for several years, marching into the film business in serried ranks, and will be used increasingly as production tools. We've had computers doing payroll and other tasks for years, but I mean their use as image-producing tools.

Everybody thinks that the *Star Wars* motion-control system was a computer system. But it wasn't really a computer system at all. It was a motion-control system. It could record, remember, and replay motion. And that was amazing at the time, but that's not really a computing function. The motion-control system didn't do anything to the information put into it.

We started using computers here in 1979, during *Star Trek*, as a matter of fact. On that project, Paul Johnson actually used an Apple computer, because the Apple was a machine that you could stick boards into and customize. He was then able to interface the Apple to the existing motion-control system, and suddenly we had the capability to not only put the information into the system but work with the information when it was in there and do vastly different things a great deal more effectively. So we've been building like crazy on that. And everybody and their brother jumped onto the bandwagon after that.

The computer will continue to work its way through the system. We now have images being created entirely in the computer. We still have some major hurdles to cross to make those images compatible with live action in the same image, but that's clearly the direction we're going in.

Then we will also eventually switch from photochemical recording to photoelectronic recording. Certainly you can make television images now, but that's still very different from the photographic image. But as time goes on, with the advent of charge-coupled devices and so forth, it'll become feasible to record images electronically.

When you can do that at a level of resolution and image quality that matches photography, we'll be able to work with that image as data and store it and alter it digitally. It is also potentially a great deal more sensitive than silver. Silver's still a phenomenally efficient way of capturing a photon, but electronically we'll be able to improve on that. That will be one of the things that will facilitate the marriage of the totally computer-generated image and the photographed image.

Even when that's in place, the end result will still be pretty much a movie as we know it for the foreseeable future. In other words, it will be delivered as a piece of film. But eventually, film itself will disappear and the show will be delivered as electronic data, or like laser disc, and displayed on a screen that will be internally illuminated. It won't be projected through a piece of film from the back of the theater to a screen. So that will alter the experience of viewing a movie. From there, one can look forward to the stage when we can actually produce a moving hologram, a three-dimensional image. This will take us full circle and have us back, in essence, in a live theater with three-dimensional people up there. Except that then we will have the ability to move around the actors and be anywhere the director thinks the viewer should be. At that point, we're talking years or decades from now before it gets that good.

But that's all out there, all just waiting to happen. No, it's not just waiting to happen, it's out there with people diligently working to make it happen.

GLOSSARY

ADR: Automated Dialogue Replacement. *See* looping.

AIRBRUSH: A kind of atomizer operated by compressed air and used for spraying paint.

ANIMATRONICS: A term applied to the industry and technology of animating, in real time, three-dimensional models and figures for amusement parks and museums, as well as motion pictures.

ANSWER PRINT: A color-corrected print of the original negative film.

ANTIALIAS: To smooth the jagged edges, caused by the nature of display monitors, of diagonal lines in a computer graphics image.

APPLIANCE: A makeup term for devices applied to actors to change their appearance.

ARC SCISSORS: The two electrodes between which electricity discharges to produce the high-intensity light of an arc light.

BARTER SYNDICATION: A system for selling television programming in exchange for advertising time.

BEAM SPLITTER: A piece of optical glass that diverts light in different directions, either by splitting the light into its component colors or letting a certain percentage of the light through while reflecting the rest.

BLACK-AND-WHITE SEPARATION: The process of separating a high-contrast negative into its black and white elements.

BLIMP: A sound-insulating covering for a motion picture camera.

BLUE-SCREEN PROCESS, BLUE-SCREEN COMPOSITING: A technique of photographing objects (or people) in front of a blue screen and using the resulting color negative to create mattes for combining these objects with photography shot elsewhere. *See also* diagram of Reverse Bluescreen process, page 334.

BOOM MAN: The person on the sound crew who holds the microphone boom.

CAMERA OPERATOR: The person who actually operates the camera.

CAMERAMAN: The cinematographer, director of photography.

CEL: A sheet of transparent celluloid or plastic on which props, characters, and parts of characters are painted for use in animated films.

CEL LEVELS: Painted cels that enable the animator to separate the static elements of a scene from the moving elements, eliminating the need to draw the static elements over and over again for each frame. Typically, to create one frame of an animated film, four or five painted cels are laid over the background—each cel carrying a particular character, part of a character, or prop.

COLOR SEPARATION: The process of separating light into its primary colors for photographic printing, or of separating the elements in blue-screen photography.

COMPOSITE: To optically combine elements that were photographed separately. Scenes that combine special effects with live action are composited, for example.

CUTOUT ANIMATION: A technique of animating characters whose body parts are cut out of paper or other materials.

DAILIES: The prints of the day's shooting projected for the crew on a daily basis.

DATABASE: Any group of related information held in an electronic file.

DIRECTIONAL MICROPHONE: A microphone that picks up sound only in a certain directional pattern.

DOLBY SOUND: A process for noise reduction in sound recording.

DOLLY: A wheeled cart for moving the camera.

EXPOSURE SHEET: In animation, a frame-by-frame breakdown of the film, used to synchronize the sound with the frame count for the animator and to record the sequence of the various cels for the photographer.

FAIRING: The smooth acceleration and deceleration of the animation camera's movements, as well as the preparatory mathematical calculations for such movements.

FILL LIGHT: Secondary light source for lighting a scene.

FILM GATE: The bracket holding the film for exposure to the light coming through the lens.

FINE CUT: The final editing of a film (as opposed to a rough cut).

FOCUS PULLER: The crew member responsible for focusing the camera.

FOLEY: Sound effects, such as footsteps and doors closing, recorded in a studio in sync with a projected picture. *See also* looping.

FORCED PERSPECTIVE: A distortion of the size of objects in miniatures or in artwork to make them seem farther from or closer to the camera.

FRACTAL GEOMETRY: In computer graphics, a method for generating irregular natural forms (like mountains) by repeatedly and randomly sub-dividing a basic shape (like a triangle). A *fractal* is the basic image created with this method. This image is then modeled, textured, colored, and lit to produce the final image.

FRAME: The image area on the film. Frames pass through the projector at the rate of twenty-four per second, creating the illusion of movement.

FRENCH NEW WAVE (*NOUVELLE VAGUE*): A term coined by film critics to describe a style of filmmaking that emerged in France during the late fifties to early sixties. As a reaction against the established film industry, the movement was characterized by a more energetic, direct, and personal approach to film. Directors associated with the French new wave included Godard, Rohmer, Malle, Chabrol, and Truffaut.

FRONT PROJECTION: To project an image photographed elsewhere onto a screen behind actors or objects to be photographed.

GAFFER: The chief electrician on a film crew.

GARBAGE MATTE: *See* matte.

GELS: Colored celluloid or plastic placed in front of lights to change their color.

GENERATION: A measure of how many copies removed from the original negative a particular print is.

GIMBAL: A device for isolating the camera (or the set) from its support so that one is capable of moving independently of the other.

GRAFTAL GEOMETRY: In computer graphics, a method for generating irregular natural forms (like trees) by repeatedly branching a basic shape (like a line) according to a specific rule. A *graftal* is the basic image created with this method. This image is then modeled, textured, colored, and lit to produce the final image.

GRIP: A person on a film crew who carries and at times repairs equipment and who pushes the dolly.

GRIP ARM: A device for holding a light or other piece of equipment in place.

GROUND GLASS: The plate of glass within the camera upon which the image is focused.

HIDDEN-SURFACE ALGORITHM: The part of a computer graphics program that determines what parts of an object are hidden from the viewer. An algorithm is a set of rules for the solution of a problem in a finite number of steps. *See also* ray-tracing algorithm.

IN-BETWEENS: The drawings that fill in the movement between the animator's key or extreme poses.

ISOMETRIC DRAWING: A method of drawing an object in three dimensions so that it is shown not in perspective but is foreshortened equally.

K: Symbol for 1000, used in measuring sound frequency, for example 8 K or 8 kHz (8000 hertz).

KEY POSES, KEY FRAMES: An animator's drawings of a character's key or extremes of movement.

LAMPHOUSE: The part of a projector that encloses its light source.

LIP SYNC: To speak dialogue in sync with the actor in a projected film. *See* looping.

LIVE ACTION: Action that involves live actors, as opposed to special effects and animation.

LOOPING: A technique used to replace dialogue in the postproduction phase of a film, as in the case of a bad recording during shooting. The actors read their lines in a studio while watching themselves on projected film. Looping refers specifically to the actual loops of film that are run through the projector over and over while the actor watches and tries to match his original dialogue. A newer technique, ADR (automated dialogue replacement), uses locked picture and sound tracks that can be run forward and in reverse automatically. Looping is used in conjunction with Foley recording of sound effects.

MAG FILM: Movie film coated with a magnetic recording surface, used to record film sound in postproduction.

MASTER SHOT: Of all the shots that make up a particular scene, the shot that best defines that scene in the most general terms. *See also* two shot.

MATTE: Something that blocks out part of the scene being photographed, used to isolate elements in one scene for later compositing with another scene shot elsewhere. A garbage matte eliminates the wires and stands used to manipulate miniatures in special-effects photography.

MEMPHIS DESIGN: Italian post-modern design group known for its dissonant use of bold geometric forms and intense colors.

MIX DOWN: In recording or re-recording sound, to combine various sound tracks onto one track.

MIXER: The person who combines sound tracks, adjusting their volume, tone, and other qualities, usually while watching the projected picture. Also refers to the equipment used in this process.

MOVIOLA: Manufacturer of editing equipment. The term is usually used to refer to the upright editing machine as opposed to the table or flatbed type of editing machine.

NAB: National Association of Broadcasters.

NODAL POINT: The point at which light is focused by a lens.

OPTICAL PRINTER: A machine for compositing images from different strips of film onto one.

OPTICAL SOUND TRACK: A method for carrying sound on film in which a pattern running alongside the picture is read by a light in the projector and converted to sound by a photocell.

OVERCRANK: To run the camera faster than the normal twenty-four frames per second.

PENCIL TEST: A film or video of rough drawings, used to give animators an idea of the movement they've created.

PHOTOGRAPHIC SOUND TRACK: *See* optical sound track.

POSTPRODUCTION: The stage of the filmmaking process that occurs after the principal photography has been completed, normally involving sound and picture editing, looping, special effects, and scoring.

PREDUB: Also called premix. A preliminary sound mix, made to simplify the process when many sound elements are involved in a mix.

RACK OVER: To physically lift the camera body and swing it out of the way to allow the camera operator to view through the lens, necessary in old animation cameras without a reflex (through-the-lens) viewing system.

RADIO MICROPHONE: A wireless microphone.

RANDOM-ACCESS DISK: A magnetic storage device, like a computer's floppy disk, designed so that the information it stores can be retrieved from any point on the disk.

RASTER GRAPHICS: Graphics displayed on a computer monitor on which the grid of dots, or pixels, is formed by an electron beam that scans the screen in a series of horizontal lines.

RAY-TRACING ALGORITHM: Simulates optics and light in computer graphics images by mathematically tracing the path of a ray of light from the viewer to the object and then to the light source.

REFLEX SYSTEM: An optical system that allows the photographer to see through the lens of the camera, as opposed to a *viewfinder,* which is parallel to the camera's lens.

RELEASE PRINT: The print of the film that is released for theatrical distribution.

RE-RECORDING: Postproduction sound recording and mixing.

RESOLUTION: A measure, expressed in horizontal and vertical dots, or pixels, of the sharpness of a monitor's image.

ROTOSCOPE: A film projector designed to project the film, one frame at a time, onto the back of a sheet of glass so that an animator can trace the image.

SCANNING: A process in which an image such as a photograph is converted to digital information that can be displayed and manipulated by a computer.

SCRIPTING: Writing a script.

SECOND UNIT: A film production's secondary crew, led by an assistant director, in charge of shooting parts of the film in which, typically, the major actors do not appear.

SHORT END: The unexposed end of a roll of film, too short to be used unless it is spliced together with other short ends.

DAVID CHELL

A native of Lake Forest, Illinois, David Chell received his bachelor of arts in fine art from the University of New Mexico. He then spent more than ten years in the film business working as an animator, production designer, and scriptwriter for commercial and industrial films and for children's television.

Chell also worked as a free-lance technical writer and copywriter in both the U.S. and Japan before embarking on *Moviemakers at Work*. He now divides his time between Seattle and Tokyo. He is finishing a novel and working on *A Natural History of Games*.

The manuscript for this book was prepared and submitted to Microsoft Press in electronic form. Text files were processed and formatted using Microsoft Word.

Cover design by Becky Geisler-Johnson

Interior text design by Darcie Furlan

Principal typographer: Russell H. Steele

Text composition by Microsoft Press in Aster and Futura Light with display in Aster Italic, using the CCI-400 composition system and the Mergenthaler Linotron 202 digital phototypesetter.

SLIT SCAN PHOTOGRAPHY: A special photographic effect popular in the 1970s, in which, typically, two planes of images in sharp perspective originate on a horizon line and seem to rush toward the camera. Made famous in *2001: A Space Odyssey*.

SMPTE: Society of Motion Picture and Television Engineers.

STOP-MOTION ANIMATION: A technique in which an object is photographed one frame at a time, the object being moved slightly for each exposure.

STORYBOARD: A visual diagram of a film presented as a series of drawings or sketches.

STREAK PHOTOGRAPHY: A special photographic effect, popular in the 1970s, in which multiple exposures create a streak of images behind a moving object, for example, a logo in a commercial.

THIRD MAN: The third member of the production sound crew, responsible for equipment maintenance and general problem solving.

TRANSFER: Moving an image or sound from one medium to another, for example, from film to videotape.

TWO SHOT: A shot, usually with dialogue, that includes two people. A *single* is a shot of only one person. *See also* master shot.

VECTOR GRAPHICS: Computer-generated graphics composed only of lines (vectors). Also called wire-frame images.

WIRE-FRAME IMAGE: *See* vector graphics.